RECORDS

OF

PLYMOUTH COLONY.

COURT ORDERS.

VOL. IV.

1661—1668.

Records
of the
Colony
of
New Plymouth
in
New England

ORIGINALLY PRINTED BY ORDER OF THE LEGISLATURE OF THE
COMMONWEALTH OF MASSACHUSETTS

Edited by
Nathaniel B. Shurtleff, M.D.

MEMBER OF THE MASSACHUSETTS HISTORICAL SOCIETY, FELLOW OF THE AMERICAN ACADEMY OF ARTS
AND SCIENCES, MEMBER OF THE AMERICAN ANTIQUARIAN SOCIETY, FELLOW
OF THE SOCIETY OF ANTIQUARIES OF LONDON, ETC.

Court Orders
Volume IV: 1661–1668

HERITAGE BOOKS
2015

HERITAGE BOOKS
AN IMPRINT OF HERITAGE BOOKS, INC.

Books, CDs, and more—Worldwide

For our listing of thousands of titles see our website
at
www.HeritageBooks.com

A Facsimile Reprint
Published 2015 by
HERITAGE BOOKS, INC.
Publishing Division
5810 Ruatan Street
Berwyn Heights, Md. 20740

Originally published
Boston:
From the Press of William White,
Printer to the Commonwealth
1855

— Publisher's Notice —
In reprints such as this, it is often not possible to remove blemishes from the original. We feel the contents of this book warrant its reissue despite these blemishes and hope you will agree and read it with pleasure.

International Standard Book Numbers
Paperbound: 978-0-7884-0912-7
Clothbound: 978-0-7884-6084-5

REMARKS.

THE manuscript of the fourth volume of Court Orders of the Colony of New Plymouth, from which the following pages are printed, is entirely in the well-known chirography of Mr. Nathaniel Morton, the faithful secretary of the colony. It was intended for the records of the General Court and the Court of Assistants, but, like the other volumes, likewise contains several miscellaneous entries. It embraces a period of seven years, during the whole of which time Mr. Thomas Prence was Governor of the colony.

The first entry is that of the confirmation of a grant of land on the fourth of June, 1661; but the first proceedings recorded were those of the General Court held on the first day of October next following, and the last in the volume bears date the seventh of July, 1668.

N. B. S.

DECEMBER, 1855.

MARKS AND CONTRACTIONS.

A Dash ¯ (or straight line) over a letter indicates the omission of the letter following the one marked.

A Curved Line ~ indicates the omission of one or more letters next to the one marked.

A Superior Letter indicates the omission of contiguous letters, either preceding or following it.

A Caret ∧ indicates an omission in the original record.

A Cross × indicates a lost or unintelligible word.

All doubtful words supplied by the editor are included between brackets, [ ].

Some redundancies in the original record are printed in Italics.

Some interlineations, that occur in the original record, are put between parallels, ‖ ‖.

Some words and paragraphs, which have been cancelled in the original record, are put between ‡ ‡.

Several characters have special significations, namely: —

@, — annum, anno.
ă, — an, am, — curiă, curiam.
ā, — mātrate, magistrate.
ƀ, — ber, — numƀ, number; Roƀt, Robert.
č, — ci, ti, — ačcon, action.
c̃ŏ, — tio, — jurisdic̃ŏn, jurisdiction.
c̣, — cre, cer, — ac̣s, acres.
đ, — đđ, delivered.
ē, — Trēr, Treasurer.
ê, — committê, committee.
g̃, — g̃ñal, general; Georg̃, George.
h̃, — chr, charter.
ī, — begīg, beginīg, beginning.
ƚ, — ƚre, letter.
m̃, — mm, mn, — com̃ittee, committee.
m̃, — recom̃dac̃ŏn, recommendation.
m̃, — mer, — form̃ly, formerly.
m̃, — month.
ñ, — nn, — Peñ, Penn; año, anno.
ñ, — Dñi, Domini.
ñ, — ner, — manñ, manner.
ō, — on, — mentiō, mention.

ŏ, — mŏ, month.
p̃, — par, por, — p̃t, part; p̃tion, portion.
p, — per, — pson, person.
p̃, — pro, — pporc̃ŏn, proportion.
p̃, — pre, — p̃sent, present.
q, — qstion, question.
q̃p̃, — esq̃p̃, esquire.
r̃, — Ap̃r̃, April.
s̃, — s̃, session; s̃d, said.
s̃, — ser, — s̃vants, servants.
ƭ, — ter, — neuƭ, neuter.
ť, — capť, captain.
û, — uer, — seûal, seueral.
ū, — aboū, aboue, above.
v̂, — ver, — sev̂al, several.
w̃, — w̃n, when.
yᵉ, the; yᵐ, them; yⁿ, then; yʳ, their; yˢ, this; yᵗ, that.
ʒ, — us, — vilibʒ, vilibus.
ℓ, — es, et, — statutℓ, statutes.
ℓč, &č, &cᵃ, — et cætera.
viz⸝, — videlicet, namely.
./ — full point.

CONTENTS OF VOLUME IV.

PAGE

COURT ORDERS, 1661—1668, ... 3

GENERAL INDEX, ... 195

PLYMOUTH COURT ORDERS.

1661—1668.

PLYMOUTH RECORDS.

THE RECORDS OF THE COLONY OF NEW PLYMOUTH IN NEW ENGLAND.

[The fourth volume of the Court Orders of the Plymouth Colony commences here, with the record of a confirmation of a grant of land made on the fourth of June, 1661. The original manuscript volume contains the acts of the several General Courts and Courts of Assistants, together with other miscellaneous entries, from the above-mentioned date until the close of the Court held on the seventh of July, 1668. It is in the handwriting of Mr. Nathaniel Morton, secretary of the colony. The original index to this volume, being very imperfect, is, as in the case of the preceding volumes, incorporated with that specially prepared for the printed copy.]

ACTS AND PASSAGES OF COURT AND GRANTS OF LAND FROM THE YEAR 1661 UNTIL THE YEAR 1668.

PRENCE, GOU^R.

ATT the Generall Court held att Plymouth, in New England, the fourth of June, 1661, the said Court graunted vnto Richard Bourne, of Sandwich, a sertaine tract of land lying on the western side of Pampaspised Riuer, where Sandwich man take alewiues; the land is a longe stripp lying by the riuer side, for breadth form the riuer vnto the topp of the hill or ridge that runs alonge the length of it, from a point of rockey land by a swamp called by the name of Pametoopauksett vnto a place called by the English Muddy Hole, but by the Indians Wapoompauksett; the meddow is that which was called Mr Leuerich his meddow, as alsoe the other stipps that are aboue alonge the riuer side vnto a point bounded with two great stones or rockes; alsoe, all the meddow lying on the easterly s[ide] of the said riuer vnto Thomas Burge, Seni^r, his farme; all which tracts and p̃cells of land, both vpland and meddow, with all and singulare the appurtenances belonging thervnto, is graunted [by] the Court vnto the said Richard Bourne, to him and his heires foreuer. Morouer, the Court haue graunted vnto the said Richard Bourne that hee shall haue yearly libertie to take twelue thousand of alewiues att the riuer where Sandwich men vsually take alewiues, him and his heires for euer.

1661.
4 June.
[*1.]
This order & grant is recorded more fully in the next Book of Grants, p. 1.

(3)

1661.
4 June.
Prence,
Govr.
Interlined.

Likewise, the said Court haue graunted vnto Richard Bourne a p̱cell of meddow lying att Mashpe, the one halfe therof to belonge to him and his heires for euer, and the other halfe to [be] made vse of and improued by the said Richard Bourne vntill the Court shall see reason otherwise to order. Morouer, the Court haue graunted vnto the said Richard Bourne a necke of meddow, ‖this meddow lying betwixt two little brookes & the meddow adjoyning to the vpl[and],‖ with a little vpland in it att Mannamuchcoy, called by the Ind[ians] Auntaanta, the said p̱mises, with all and singulare the appurtenances belonging thervnto, excepting the one halfe of the meddow x Mashpe aboue mencioned, to haue and to hold vnto the said Richard Bourne, to him and his heires for euer.

That aboue enterlined was soe done att the Court held att Plymouth the fift of March, 1661, by order and with the consent of the Court.

1 October.
[*2.]

*Att the Generall Court holden att Plymouth the first of October, 1661.

BEFORE Thomas Prence, Goṽ,
Wilłam Collyare,
John Aldin,
Josias Winslow,

Thomas Southworth,
Wilłam Bradford, and
Thomas Hinckley,

Assistants, &c̄.

THE Court haue graunted and confeirmed vnto Mr Josias Standish a tract of vpland lying on that side of Mannomett Riuer next vnto Sandwich, the bounds of which is from the lands of Esra Perr[y] vnto a little creeke alongst the riuer for the length, and for the bredth vnto the topp of the hills which lye in a ridg with twenty acrees of meddow of that which was lately purchased by Mr Aldin, to bee taken together where hee will within the said meddow; the said lands, both vpland and meddow, with all and singulare the appurtenances appertaining therevnto, to belong to him, the said Josias Standish, to him and his heires and assignes for euer.

Mr John Aldin is appointed by the Court to lay out the aboue twenty acrees of meddow to Josias Standish, and to bring report vnto the Court of what remaineth there vndisposed of.

In answare vnto a petition prefered to the Court by Jone, the wife of Obadiah Miller, requesting that shee may haue libertie to make sale of some

COURT ORDERS. 5

of the land that her deceased husband left vndisposed of, the Court, haueing
considered that her request is in the behalfe of her daughter, whoe shee saith
is weake and stands in need therof, do giue libertie that one quarter p̃te of the
said land, and of what is left by her said deceased husband, may bee sold for
the releife of her said daughter; and what it shalbee sold for shalbee carfully
disposed of to the vse of Bathshebah Coggen, att the descretion of Richard
W x and Walter Deane, of Taunton, and the resedue of the said lands, &c̃, bee
reserued by them for the vse of the rest of the children of the deceased Thomas
Coggen, prouided that the said Jone Miller doe put in sufficient cecuritie that
the said estate shalbee soe disposed of.

1661.
1 October.
PRENCE,
Gouʳ.

The Court haue graunted vnto the ancient freemen of Taunton, that
incase any land can bee found on the north side of Taunton bounds, towards
Secounke cartway, which will not fall within any lands alreddy put in for by
the children of the first comers, that they may make report therof to the
Court; and a competency shalbee graunted vnto them, if the Court shall see
reason.

James Walker desireth acom̃odation of lands vpon the west side of
Taunton Riuer, att the southermost bounds, neare about Seketegansett.

Att this Court, Leiftenant Rogers was freed of his milletary office, from
being leiftenant of the milletary companie of Eastham.

Att this Court, adminnestration was graunted vnto Samuell House, Juniʳ,
and Elizabeth House, the sone and daughter of Samuell House, deceased, to
adminnester on the estate of the said Samuell, Seniʳ, deceased.

*Att this Court, John Palmer, Seniʳ, for deludeing one of the ma-
jestrates about the publication of his sons marriage, was fined forty shillings.

[*3.]
Fine.

Zoeth Howland, for breakeing the Sabbath, fined ten shillings.   Fine.
Thomas Lenard, for breaking the peace, fined 00 03ˢ 04ᵈ.   Fine.

The rates to bee leuied by the townshipes of this goũment for the publicke charges of the countrey, as they were ordered by the Court for this
yeare, respecting the officers wages and the charge of the majestrates table, is
as followeth : —

Plymouth, ...	06 : 00 : 00
Duxburrow, ...	03 : 13 : 00
Scittuate, ...	09 : 16 : 08
Sandwich, ...	05 : 09 : 06
Taunton, ...	05 : 09 : 06
Barnstable, ...	06 : 00 : 00

1661.

1 October
PRENCE,
Gour.

Yarmouth,	05 : 09 : 06
Marshfeild,	05 : 09 : 06
Rehoboth,	08 : 04 : 02
Eastham,	03 : 18 : 00
Bridgwater,	01 : 16 : 06
Sowams,	04 : 01 : 03
Cushenag,	01 : 10 : 00
The farmes against Road Iland,	01 : 00 : 00

Wheras very great spoyle hath lately bin made by woulues vpon all sorts of cattle in sundry townshipes within this goûment, to the great detriment therof, this Court, therfore, presumeing on the Generall Court of Deputies fauorable sence heerof in this exegent, doe order and declare, that it shall and may bee lawfull, vntill the next Court of Election, for the seuerall townshipes to pay vnto any Indian or Indians that shall bringe into the constable of any such townshipe any head or heads of woulues halfe a pound of powder and two pound of shott or lead for euery head brought in as aforsaid, besides the coate by Court order in such case prouided.

Att the Generall Court held the 10th of June, 1662, the deputies did vnanimusly consent vnto the abouesaid liberty, that it shall continew vntill the Court shall see reason to order otherwise.

[*4.]   *A proposition ordered to bee recorded, which was sent vnto the four townes, viz§, Sandwich, Yarmouth, Barnstable, and Eastham, by order of the Court held att Plymouth October the first, 1661, as followeth, signed by Constant Southworth, Treasurer : —

Loueing Frinds : Wheras the Generall Court was pleased to make some propositions to you respecting the drift fish or whales ; and incase you should refuse theire proffer, they impowered mee, though vnfitt, to farme out what should belonge vnto them on that account ; and seeing the time is expired, and it fales into my hands to dispose of, I doe therfore, with the advise of the Court, in answare to youer remonstrance, say, that if you will duely and trewly pay to the countrey for euery whale that shall come one hogshead of oyle att Boston, where I shall appoint, and that current and marchantable, without any charge or trouble to the countrey, — I say, for peace and quietnes sake you shall haue it for this present season, leaueing you and the Election Court to settle it soe as it may bee to satisfaction on both sides ; and incase you accept not of this tender, to send it within fourteen dayes after the date heerof; and if I heare not from you, I shall take it for graunted that you will accept of it, and shall expect the accomplishment of the same.

Youers to vse,

CONSTANT SOUTHWORTH, Treasu.

1661.
1 October.
PRENCE, Gou^r.

Thomas Bonny oweth our soû lord the Kinge the sume of . . . . } ˡⁱ ˢ ᵈ 20 : 00 : 00

The condition, that if the said Thomas Bonny shall and doe appeer att the Court to bee holden att Plymouth the first Tusday in March next, to answare the complaint of Christopher Wadsworth about wounding of a mare, and not depart the said Court without lycence; that then, &c̃.   Released.

*Plymouth, × uary the 10th, 1661. Henery Saunders acknowlidgeth to owe vnto our sou^r lord the King the sum of . . . . } ˡⁱ 20 : 00 : 00   [*5.]

The condition, that if Anna Bessey shall and doe appeer att the Court to bee holden att Plymouth the first Tusday in March next, to answare for her vnaturall and crewell carriages towards Gorge Barlow, her father in law, and not depart the said Court without lycence; that then, &c̃.   Released.

Dorcas Bessey oweth our soû lord the Kinge the sume of 10 : 00 : 00.

The condition, that if Mary Bessey shall and doe appeer att the Generall Court to bee holden att Plymouth the first Tusday in March next, to answare for her vnaturall and crewell carriages towards Gorg Barlow, her father in law, and not depart the said Court without lycence; that then, &c̃.   Released.

Mary Bessey oweth our soû lord the Kinge the sume of 20 : 00 : 00

The condition, that if Dorcas Bessey shall and doe appeer att the Generall Court to bee holden att Plymouth the first Tusday in March next, to answare for her vnaturall and crewell carriages towards Gorge Barlow, her father in law, and not depart the said Court without lycence; that then, &c̃.   Released.

An Acknowlidgment appointed to bee recorded.

October the 1, 1661. Wheras I, Abraham Peirce, Junr, haue follishly and vnadvisedly reported to Ruth Sprague and Bethyah Tubbs, att the house of Francis Sprague, that Rebeckah Alden and Hester Delanoy were withchild, and that thervpon wee should haue young troopers within three quarters of a yeare, I doe freely and from my hart owne my fault heerin, and am hartily sorry that I haue so spooken, to theire great reproch and wronge and the defamation of theire relations, which I earnestly desire may bee passed by of them all; and I hope I shall for euer heerafter take heed what I doe speake and report of any att any time.

1661-2.   *Att the Generall Court holden att Plymouth the 4th of March, 1661.

4 March.
PRENCE, GOVR.
[*6.]

BEFOR Thomas Prence, Gour,   Thomas Southworth,
Wiłłam Collyare,   Wiłłam Bradford, and
John Alden,   Thomas Hinckley,
Thõ Willett,

Assistants, &ć.

MR THOMAS PRENCE is authorised by the Court to giue an oath to Hannah, the wife of the late deceased Nathaniell Mayo, att Eastham, for the truth of the inventory of the estate of the said Nathaniell Mayo.

The like to Captaine Thomas Willett, for the truth of the will and inventory of the widdow Martine, of Rehoboth.

Letters of adminnistration is graunted vnto Hannah, the wife of the said Nathaniell Mayo, deceased, to adminnister vpon his estate, &ć.

The like was graunted vnto Faith Clarke, widdow, to adminnester on the estate of Thirston Clarke, deceased.

Major Josias Winslow, Captaine Wiłłam Bradford, and Anthony Snow are deputed by the Court to settle the bounds between the lands graunted to Duxburrow men, bearing date August the last, 1640, and a tract of land graunted to Scittuate men bearing date in Nouember following, and that they doe it with all convenient speed, and make report therof vnto the Court.

Conserning a controuersy betwixt James Leonard and James Bell, both of Taunton, the Court haue ordered and deputed Captaine Willett to heare and determine the same.

Likewise the said Capt Willett is deputed by the Court to take course with such as entrench vpon our lands att Taunton Riuer, and take the wood or timber from of the same, and for that end may imploy one as a constable by warrant or otherwise to act as occation shall require about the same.

Likewise, that incase the squa sachem should bee put of her ground by Talmud, to see that shee bee not wronged in that behalfe.

And likewise to speake to Wamsitta about his estranging land, and not selling it to our collonie.

And likewise to see justice don on Marda his seruant, for fornication the second time.

[*7.]   *Conserning a difference betwixt Quachattasett and Josias, of Nausett, Indian sachems, the Court haue ordeŕ Mr Aldin and Mr Hinckley to heare and determine the same.

Conserning a controversy betwixt Jone Tilson, widdow, and John Barnes, about the prise of a cow by him receiued in p̄te of the pay due for the land att Lakenham, the Court haue ordered, that John Barnes shall repay or discount the sume of twelue shillings vnto the said widdow Tilson; and soe the matter is ended. 1 6 6 1-2.
4 March.
[PRENCE, GOVERNOR.]

Capt Willett is deputed by the Court to take course that a due enquiry bee made conserning the violent death of Robert Allin att Rehoboth.

Att this Court, Wiłłam Bassett, of Sandwich, surrendered vp his libertie, graunted him formerly by the Court, to draw and sell wine, stronge waters, and beer, and of prouiding other nessesaries for the entertaining of strangers.

Wiłłam Randall, for telling of a lye, fined ten shillings. Fine.

Wheras Robert Whetcombe and Mary Cudworth was formerly fined, for disorderly coming together without consent of theire parents and lawful marriage, the sume of ten pounds, and imprisoned during the pleasure of the Court, haueing since bine orderly married, and liueing orderly together, and following theire callinges industriously, and attending the worship of God dilligently, as is testifyed by some of theire naighbours of good report, the Court haue seen good to remitt fiue pounds of the said fine; in respect alsoe of theire pouertie, the Treasurer is ordered likewise to bee slow in demaunding the remainder.

The Court ordered, that wheras Wiłłam Randall trauersed his presentment about the teling of the lye for which hee was afterwards fined as abouesaid, the charge of the jury should bee payed by the said Randall, and that the Treasurer should demaund it when hee demaunds his fine.

*The agents for the towne of Yarmouth appeering att this Court, according to agreement, to debate and determine a difference between them and others about whales, were desired by the Court to giue in thire result conserning that matter vnto the Court, as being that wheruvnto they would stand; who gaue in theire answare as followeth:— [*8.]

The sixt of the first month, $\frac{6}{6}\frac{1}{2}$

Right Wor^{sh}: Wee intreat youer worshipes reddily to accept these few lines for a positiue answare, to which wee promise to stand: that the Treasurer shall haue the two barrells of oyle out of each whale, according to his proposition made vnto vs for the yeare past, soe as there may bee a full end of what troubles hath formerly past about it. Witnes our hands,

ANTHONY THACHER,
ROBERT DENIS,
THOMAS BOARDMAN,
RICHARD TAYLER.

1661-2.

4 March.
PRENCE,
Govr.

The Court, haueing considered of thire returne, haue accepted of the same; and soe the said differenc̃ is ended in refference to things past about the same.

An order directed to Richard Williams and Walter Deane, of Taunton, as followeth : —

Wheras, by an order of Court bearin date the first of October, 1661, libertie was graunted vnto Jone Miller to make sale of a quarter p̃te of the land of Thomas Goggen, deceased, and that what it should bee sold for should bee improued for the releife of Bathsheba Coggen, att youer descretions, these are therfore to signify vnto you, that the Courts order farther is, that whatsoeuer shalbee improued of the said land sold for the releife of the said Bathsheba Coggen, that you take sufficient securitie of the said Jone Miller, in the behalfe of the Court, for the same before it be let goe out of youer hands.

The Courts order.

₽ mee, NATHANIELL MORTON, Clarke.

The Court doeth order James Walker to sellebrate marriage in the towne of Taunton vntell June, 1684.

James Walker was authorised by the Court to adminnister an oth, as occation shall require, att Taunton, as alsoe to marry p̃sons, as occation shall require, vntill the next June Court. This order was c × att June 9th, 1662, soe that the said James Walker is to giue oath & marry, as abouesaid.

[*9.]
Fine.

*Anna Bessey, for her crewell and vnaturall practice towards her father in law, Gorge Barlow, in choping of him in the backe, notwithstanding the odiousnes of her fact, the Court, considering of som̃ sercomstances, viz\, her ingeniouse confession, together with her p̃sent condition, being with child, and some other p̃ticulares, haue sentanced her to pay a fine of ten pounds, or to bee publickly whipt att some other convenient time when her condition will admitt therof.

Dorcas Bessey and Mary Bessey, for carriages of like nature towards theire said father in law, though not in soe high a degree, were both sentanced to sit in the stockes during the pleasure of the Court; which accordingly was p̃formed. The younger, viz\, Mary Bessey, was sharply reproued by the Court, as being by her disobeydience the occationers of the euill abouemencioned.

Gorg̃ Barlow and his wife were both seuerly reproued for theire most vngodly liueing in contension one with the other, and admonished to liue otherwise.

Robert Barker, for his wife and son theire changing of a gun with an Indian, fined ten pounds. 1661-2.

And for another, which hee changed with an Indian, — because the Court judgeth it was done ignorantly, — it is refered vnto the Generall Court to bee holden att Plymouth in June next, att which Court hee was fined the sume of forty shillings. 4 March. Prence, Gou^R. Fine.

John Hawes, for relateing a scandulous report, for which hee hath not produced sufficient ground for it, is fined ten shillings. Fine.

Joseph Turner, for bringing a scurrilous message vnto the major, acknowlidged his fault to the Court, and promised to satisfy the said major, and soe is cleared.

Richard Marshall, for many wicked and filthy speeches and actions, as alsoe for many other practices tending to the desturbance of naighbourhood, was sentanced by the Court to bee publickly whipt, which accordingly was executed; and his master, John Turner, of Taunton, was warned by the Court to take course that the said Richard Marshall, his servant, shall carry better amongst his naighbours, or otherwise to rid him out of the towne.

*Att the Court of Assistants held att Plymouth the seauenth Day of May, 1662. 1662.

7 May. [*10.]

BEFORE William Collyare, John Aldin, Thomas Southworth, and William Bradford, Assistants.

CONCERNING a difference betwixt Abraham Jackson and Rose, the wife of Thomas Morton, the said Abraham complaining that the said Rose, as hee came from worke, did abuse him by calling of him lying rascall and rogue, which was testified by Jonathan Prat likewise, vpon oath, the Court declared, and ordered to bee recorded, that they apprehend, that notwithstanding her soe peremptory denyall that shee called him rogue, they doe beleiue that shee soe did call him; and wheras shee owned that shee called him lying rascall, and said shee was sorry for it, and promised to bee more carfull of her words for the future, they haue for the p̄sent pased it by.

The Court haue condemned a p̄cell of tarr attached att the suite of James Cole, Seni^r, of Josepth Ramsdens, for a debt the said Ramsden owed him;

1662.
7 May.
PRENCE,
GOU^R.

and wheras it appeered to bee to little to satisfy the said debt, it being three barrells that should haue bine attached, and but a barrell and an halfe that could bee found, the said Cole and Ramsden haue agreed for the remainder betwixt themselues.

The Court doe allow vnto John Sprague three shillings for himselfe and his horse a day, imployed about the contrey seruice in goeing to Duxburrow and returning about Joshua Cockshall.

The Court condemned three barrells of tarr attached att the suite of Gyles Rickard, Junier, against Josepth Ramsden.

A paire of wheeles belonging to the said Ramsden were released, being formerly attached att the suite of John Barnes, because none appeered for the said Barnes to cleare vp the debt which they were attached to satisfy for out of the estate of Josepth Ramsden.

[*11.]

*Wee, whose names are vnder written, being impannelled on a jury to view the dead body of Thirston Clarke, Seni^r, of Duxburrow, and to enquire by what meanes hee came by his death, —

Wee find, vpon serch and enquiry, that the weather being could and snowey, hee came on that side of Joanes Riuer which is on Duxburrow side, vpon his returne from Plymouth, endeavoring to come home, and came neare home ; and by his track in the snow wee find that hee had wandered to and fro and lost himselfe, and did soe wilder that hee came vpon a flatt nygh the place called the Longe Point vpon the said flatt, which is now in the possesion of Joseph Andrews, and that hee was found. Vpon serch being made by diuers, the first thing that was found was a baskett, with diuers smale comodities, some distance from him ; and after that there was found his capp, with his staffe and one mitting, somwhat nigher to his body ; and after that his body was found, being couered with some iyce vpon him. His body was viewed by vs, and wee find the cercomstances heerof, that the iyce, with the cold and water, was the cause of his death.

This following was margined in the originall before giuen into the Court, and before the subscribsion of the names : That hee was lost, as wee conceiue, in the euening, and soe hee did bewilder himselfe, the sixt of this instant December, 1661.

Duxberry, the 8th of the 10th, (61.)

JOSEPTH ANDREWES,	JOHN ROGERS,
CHRISTOPHER WADSWORTH,	GORGE TURNER,
JOHN TRACYE,	JOHN ROBBINS,
JOHN SPRAGUE,	JOSEPTH PRIOR,
GORGE PARTRICH,	EXPERIENCE MICHELL,
JOSEPTH WADSWORTH,	SAMUELL SEABURRY.

Soe sayeth one, and soe they say all.

COURT ORDERS. 13

*The names and verdict vpon oath of the enquest impannelled by Captaine Thomas Willett, by order, for to enquire concerning the cause of the death of Robert Allin, deceased, the brother of John Allin, of Rehoboth, which said Robert Allin died the 15 day of May, 1661.

1662.

22 April.
PRENCE,
Gov^R.

[*12.]

sworne, { Mr Stephen Paine, Seni^r,
John Reed,
Robert Abell,
John Butterworth,
Robert Wheaton,
Roger Annadowne, }

sworne, { Leift Peter Hunt,
Will Sabin,
James Browne,
Richard Bullocke,
Josepth Carpenter,
Richard Whittacus. }

These, haueing viewed the dead body of the said Robert Allin, and heard the relations of those that were in the house of the said John Allin, where hee, the said Robert Allin, died, att the time of his death, doe with one consent declare, that hee came by his death by laying violent hands vpon himselfe.

THOMAS WILLETT.

Dated att Rehoboth the 22^{cond} of Aprill, 1662.

---

*Att the Generall Court held att Plymouth the third Day of June, 1662.

3 June.
[*12^b.]

BEFORE Thomas Prence, Gou, William Collyare, John Aldin, Josias Winslow,

Thomas Southworth, William Bradford, and Thomas Hinckley,

Assistants, &c.

MR THOMAS PRENCE was chosen Gou^r, and sworne.

{ William Collyare,
John Aldin,
Thomas Willett,
Josias Winslow,
Thomas Southworth,
William Bradford, and
Thomas Hinckley, } were chosen Assistants, and sworne.

1662.
3 June.
PRENCE,
GOUR.

Major Josias Winslow and Captaine Thomas Southworth were chosen comissioners; Mr Thomas Prence was the next in nomination.
Constant Southworth was chosen Treasurer, and sworne.

[*13.]

*The names of the deputies of the seuerall townes of this jurisdiction whoe serued att this Court are as followeth: —

John Dunham, Seni^r,	Mr Thõ Howes,
Robert Finney,	Richard Saeres,
John Morton,	Henery Cobb,
Ephraim Morton,	Nathaniell Bacon,
Mr Constant Southworth,	Leiftt Perrigrine White,
Wiltam Paybody,	Ensigne Marke Eames,
Leiftenant James Torrey,	Leiftt Peter Hunt,
Cornett Robert Studson,	Henery Smith,
Thomas Burgis,	Leiftt John Freeman,
Wiltam Bassett,	Josias Cooke,
Leiftt James Wyatt,	Wiltam Britt.
James Walker,	

The Grand Enquest.

sworne, {
Mr Anthony Thacher,
Mr Josepth Tildin,
Mr Allexander Standish,
Anthony Snow,
Austine Bearce,
Gorḡ Macye,
Wiltam Maycomber,
Daniell Smith,
Samuell Newman,
John Otis,
Jacob Cooke,

sworne, {
Wiltam Clarke,
Francis West,
Thomas Caswell,
Wiltam Twiney,
John Miller,
Arther Hathawey,
John Carey,
Gorge Lewis,
Jacob Burgis,
Thomas Tupper.

[*14.]

*The Constables of the seuerall Townes.

Plymouth, ...	Abraham Jackson.
Duxburrow, ...	Benjamine Bartlett.
Scittuate, ...	{ John Bryant, John Daman.

COURT ORDERS.

Sandwich,	Thomas Dexter.	1662.
Taunton,	William Witherell.	3 June.
Yarmouth,	Edward Sturgis.	PRENCE,
Barnstable,	Thomas Huckens.	Gov^R.
Marshfeild,	{ Capt Nathaniell Thomas, Thomas Little.	
Rehoboth,	Nathaniell Paine.	
Eastham,	Nicholas Snow.	
Bridgwater,	John Eames.	
Acushenah,	Samuell Jeney.	

Surveyors of the Highwaies.

Plymouth,	{ Josepth Warren, Thomas Lettice, Francis Combe.
Duxburrow,	{ Christopher Wadsworth, Moses Simonson.
Scittuate,	{ James Doughtey, Stephen Vinall.
Sandwich,	{ Thomas Burgis, Richard Chadwell.
Taunton,	{ Anthony Slocome, William Harvey.
Yarmouth,	{ Mr John Joyce, William Eldred.
Barnstable,	{ Thomas Lewis, Moses Rowley.
Marshfeild,	{ John Rouse, William Foard, Juni^r.
Rehoboth,	{ Nocholas Hyde, John Pecke.
Eastham,	{ Gyles Hopkins, Thomas Paine.

*Att this Court, Mr William Hedge was alowed and approued by the Court to bee captaine of the milletary companie of Yarmouth. [*15.]

James Leanard, of Taunton, was freed from training in the milletary companie of Taunton in reference to his calling, being a bloomer, and in respect to a former order of Court wherin hee was exempted in that respect.

1662.

3 June.
Prence,
Gou^r.

Wheras Thomas Little, of Marshfeild, hath bought a farme land in Marshfeild, which was somtimes the land of Major Willam Holmes, deceased, and hath build, fenced, and otherwise bestowed labour theron, wherby it is much bettered since hee came to improue it and inherite it, the Court haue ordered, for the securitie of the said Thomas Little, hee, his heires, exequitors, and adminnestrators, that incase any one shall come in future time and lay claime to the said lands, and cleare vp a better title then the said Thomas Little hath thervnto, that then such as soe doe shall then fully satisfy vnto the said Thomas Little, or his heires or assignes, the full worth of whatsoeuer laboure or charge hee hath bine att on the same lands as abousaid, before they enter on the posession therof.

Vpon the complaint of Edward Perrey, of Sandwich, that the marshall had attached his meddow on the account and att the suite of Henery Saunders, it being a mistake in the marshall, the Court haue ordered, that the said Saunders shall quit his claime thervnto, and surrender it to the right owner, and lett him enjoy it quietly, and that the said Henery Saunders hath libertie to take out a new execution for what is due to him in that behalfe.

Lres of adminnestration is graunted vnto Mirriam Wormall to adminnester on the estate of Joseph Wormall, deceased.

[*16.]
Att the Court held att Plymouth the fift day of October, 1664, Josias Wormall engaged to the Court for the sixt p^{te} of the estate of Josepth Wormall, deceased; and on this the Court released Mr Hatherley of the abouesaid bonds.

*Mr Timothy Hatherley is heerby engaged and stands bound vnto the Gou and Court of New Plymouth in the sume of an hundred pounds, to saue harmless the said Gou and Court from any damage that may arise by the letters of adminnestration graunted by the Court vnto Meriam Wormall, widdow, to administer on the estate of Josepth Wormall, deceased.

Leiftenant James Wyate, together with the widdow Allice Deane, of Taunton, doe both of them joyntly and seuerally stand bound vnto the Gou and Court of New Plymouth in the sume of twenty pounds, to saue harmles the Court and vndamnifyed by theire pmitting of a legacye of ten pounds to bee payed by Thomas Troubridge, of New Hauen, vnto Isacke Dean, of Taunton, the said Isacke Dean being vnder age.

Mr Hatherley is desired and deputed by the Court to adminnester an oath to the widdow Vtley, of Scittuate, for the truth of the inventory of her husbands estate, whoe is lately deceased, in regard that shee is weake and ill, and not able to make her psonall appeerance att the Court.

Lres of adminnestration is graunted vnto Mistris Allice Parker, of Taunton, to administer on the estate of Mr Willam Parker, deceased.

Lers of adminnestration is graunted vnto James Leanard, of Taunton, to adminnester on the estate of Thomas Billington, of Taunton, late deceased.

Att this Court, Tatacomuncah, an Indian, complained against Wamsitta

COURT ORDERS.

for selling away a necke of land called Saconett, which hee saith belongeth to him.

A like abuse a squa sachem, called Namumpam, complained of against Wamsutta; and the Court engaged to doe what they could in convenient time for theire releife in the p̃mises.

1662.

3 June
PRENCE,
GOUᴿ.

*Conserning a cow belonging to Jane, the daughter of Anthony Bessey, of Sandwich, the Court haue ordered Gorge Barlow, in whose hands the said cow hath bine for som̃ tim̃, to returne her to the ouerseers of the estate of the said Anthony Bessey, to bee disposed of by them for the vse and good of the said Jane Bessey.

[*17.]

The Court haue remited fiue pounds of a fine of ten pounds amerced on Robert Barker for his wife and sone theire exchanging of a gun with an Indian.

And the said Robert Barker is fined the sum̃e of forty shillings for exchanging another gun with an Indian before the abouemenchoned, hee professing ignorance and injeniously confesing the same.

Wheras it hath bine giuen forth that diuers haue bine vnsatisfied about the sale of Kenebecke, and that an oppertunitie is lately presented vnto vs for the haueing of it againe, the deputies haueing considered therof, and finding noe way presenting itselfe by theire takeing of it againe for the countreyes better advantage, haue with one consent agreed, that they desire not to meddle with it againe, but doe rattify the sale therof.

Conserning a mare killed by the Indians att Mashpe, which, vpon the best euidence that can bee had, is found to belong to John Allin, of Sandwich, Paupemamecke and Keencomsett haue engaged before the Court that the Indians shall pay the sum̃e of fourteen pounds vnto the said John Allin or his assignes betwixt this and the fifteenth day of Aprill next ensueing the date heerof, in manor and forme following, viz͡ : the one halfe of it in corn and porke, and the other halfe in oysters, att prise current att the payment therof; or incase they can kill any woulues in the intrime, the Court haue engaged to make payment in theire behalfe vnto the said John Allin for soe much as they shall come vnto according to the ordinary rate that they ‸ or payed for killing of them ; but incase they shall make payment in specye as abouesaid, that then they shall pay as much of it as they can to Nicholas Dauis, and the rest att Sandwich to the said John Allin, or his assignes in the behalfe of the said John Allin.

*In reference vnto a desire of Mʳ Collyare about his × of meddow att the North Hill, in the township of Duxburrow, the Court haue ordered Major Winslow and Mʳ Aldin to view and settle the bounds of the said meddow.

[*18.]

VOL. IV.   3

PLYMOUTH COLONY RECORDS.

1662.
3 June.
PRENCE, GOUR.
See booke of orders and passages of the Court, 1661, June.

Captaine Willett is appointed by the Court to purchase the lands of the Indians which is graunted vnto such that were servants and others that are ancient freemen, which the × thinkes meet to add to them to haue enterest in the said graunt, the tenure wherof is extant in the × of the Court.

It was further graunted by this Court, that the abouesaid servants and ancient freemen shall haue libertie, incase they can not procure Saconett Necke according to the × graunt, to looke out some other place, vndisposed of, for theire accomodation.

Theire names are as followeth : —

James Cole, Seni^r,	Willam Merricke,
+John Hanmore,+	+Gorḡ Partrich,+
Nicholas Wade,	Josepth Beedle,
Thomas Williams,	John Rouse,
Richard Bishop,	Abraham Sampson,
Gorge Vicorey,	John Vobes,
Samuell Chandeler,	John Irish,
+Roger Annadowne,+	Peter Collymore,
Willam Sherman,	John Haward,
+Walter Woodworth,+	Thomas Pope,
John Smaley,	Richard Beare,
Willam Tubbs,	Willam Shirtliffe.

Richard × as an ancient freeman, Josias Cooke as a servant and as an × freeman, John W × , Senir, as an ancient freeman and as a seruant.

Josias Cooke and John Was × are to bee considered with a × portion in reference to the condition abouemensioned, as being both ancient freemen and servants.

A tract or pcell of land is graunted to the towne of Sandwich lying alonge the herring riuer downe to Josias Standishes land att Manomett.

In answare to a petition prefered to the Court by Bridgwater, it is graunted by the Court, that the meddow land lying northward and westwards from the center within the seauen miles, is graunted to the towne of Bridgwater.

[*19.] *In reference to a petition prefered to the Court by sundry of the freemen, and in reference vnto a graunt made to some to looke out accomodations of land, as being the first borne children of this goūment, and for the

COURT ORDERS.

disposing of two seuerall tracts of land lately purchased, the one by Major Winslow and the other by Captaine Southworth, the Court, haueing viewed the seuerall lists of the names of those that desired to bee accomodated therin, haue settled it vpon those whose names follow : —

1662.
3 June.
PRENCE,
Gou^R.

Mr Prence,	Anthony Anible, for his daughter,	× dders
Mr Bradford,	Hannah Burman,	× to sell of
		× idg to be
Major Winslow,	Francis Sprague,	× oyed by
		× Winslow
Mr Aldin,	Gorḡ Soule,	× were
Wiłłam Mullins,	Nathaniell Warren,	× ×
		× ×
Mr Brewster,	Samuell Fuller, Juni^r, of Plymouth,	× both
		× due.
Mr Howland,	Andrew Ringe,	
Francis Cooke,	Francis Billington,	
Leiftenant Fuller,	Moses Simonson,	
Leiftenant White,	Resolued White,	
Wiłłam Pontus,	Wiłłam Bassett,	
Steuen Dean,	Edward Bumpas,	
Phillip Delanoy,	Samuell Eedey,	
Mr John Winslow,	Wiłłam Hoskins,	
John Adams,	Gorḡ Partrich,	
Peter Browne,	Wiłłam Nelson, by right of his wife.	
John Shaw,		

Edward Gray to haue a double share, to bee layed forth together.

It is ordered by the Court, that those to whom these lands were disposed shall come to a deuision therof within two monthes after the date heerof, and satisfy all disbursments for the purchase therof, both to the major, Edward Gray, or any others ; and incase they shall not come to a deuision within two monthes as abouesaid, that then Edward Gray may sett his house in any place within the said tract, and that thervnto hee shall haue a double portion layed out to him, and to haue libertie likewise to mow any   ×   ×   ×

Alsoe,
× by the
× that none
× enjoy
× in two
× the
× d
× othe
×   ×

*In reference vnto a former graunt to sundry ancient freemen of the towne of Taunton, to looke out lands for theire accomodation, and in answare to the request of some others that are joyned with them in desireing accomodations of land, the Court haue graunted vnto them that they shalbee accomodated on the lands on the northerly bounds of Taunton, and that the major, Captaine Southworth, and Captaine Bradford are appointed by the Court to purchase the same of the Indians in the behalfe of those heerafter named, prouided that which shalbee purchased shall not bee prejudiciall to the Indians.

[*20.]

1662.

3 June.
PRENCE,
GOVR.

Captaine Thomas Southworth,	Joseputh Warren,
Mr Wiłłam Parker,	Leift James Wyate,
Mr Henery Andrews,	John Morton,
John Parker,	Ephraim Morton,
Gabriell Fallowell,	Robert Finney,
Gyles Rickard, Senir,	Ensigne Marke Eames,
Richard Wright,	Wiłłam Paybody,
Anthony Snow,	Gorge Hall,
Nathaniell Morton,	John Deane,
Mr John Gilbert,	Walter Deane,
Captaine Poole,	John Dunham, Junir,
James Walker,	John Rogers,
Richard Williams,	Gorge Bonum,
John Wood,	Jonathan Briggs,
Henery Wood,	Dauid Briggs,
Wiłłam Harlow,	John Bundey.

It is ordered by the Court, that the abouesaid land shalbee purchased by the next June Court, and not to exceed such a proportion as is suitable in quantity to soe much as such a number as those haue that had a graunt with the major in those two graunts or tracts before mencioned in this booke.

[*21.]   *In reference vnto an order of Court bearing date the first of March, 1641, the Court haue graunted an inlargement and accomodation of land vnto the towne of Barnstable, according to theire desire expressed in that order.

A Deposition about Land appointed to bee recorded.

10 June.   Our towne appointed mee, with others, to purchase of Osamequin a tract of land about a place knowne to our towne by the name of Satuckett, which wee did from the center six miles, which center is the ware in the riuer aboue expressed, and wee paid him for it; the writing or deed expressed vnder Osamequins hand was seauen miles.

The oath of Mr Constant Southworth, Leift Nash, alsoe being deposed to the same in the Court held in Plymouth the 10th of June, 1662.

Attested p me,

NATHANIELL MORTON, Clarke.

An other Testimony about Land appointed to bee recorded, as followeth.

This testifyeth, that when Captaine Standish was there to sett out the Indians land, that then Napoietan, the sagamore, told Mr Winslow and the rest of the companie that hee gaue the one halfe of that land to Tacomacus; soe hee and his wife and children haue enjoyed it euer since.

HENERY COBB.

1662.
10 June.
PRENCE, Gou^r.

*Mr Aldin and the major are appointed by the Court to sett out the bounds betwixt Barnstable and Sandwich, and to end any difference that is betwixt them and the Indians about any graunt of lands.

[*22.]

The Treasurer is appointed by the Court to take order and agree with a workeman to repaire the house bought by the countrey of Edward Gray.

The major, Capt Southworth, and Capt Bradford are appointed by the Court to draw vp a forme of comission for milletary officers, viz$, captaines, leiftenants, and ensignes, which shalbee in a reddines to bee viewed by the councell of warr att the next generall training; and if by them, or any seauen of them, approued, then to bee established. Aded vnto these abouemensioned for advise and councell, Leiftenant Torrey, Leiftenant White, Leiftenant Nash, and Cornett Studson.

Mr Josepth Pecke is authorised by the Court to graunt a replevin to any, the owners of cattle, that shall treaspas in the liberties of Rehoboth, and are or shalbee impounded.

A deputie of euery towne in the gofment was appointed to take the account of the Treasurer, viz$, of those that were now att the Court.

Theire names are as followeth: —

John Morton,	Nathaniell Bacon,
William Paybody,	Leiftenant Peregrine White,
Leiftenant James Torrey,	Leif^t Peter Hunt,
William Bassett,	Leiftenant John Freeman,
Leiftenant Wyate,	William Britt.
Mr Thomas Howes,	

See the account in the Treasurers booke in anno 1662.

*The Treasurer, William Paybody, and William Britt are appointed by the Court to see the lands of Captaine Standish about Satuckett Pond layed forth, soe much as was graunted to him, which is about two hundred and thirty acres, if it bee there to bee had, a quarter p̃te of the first graunt being taken out, and Josias Standish haueing other lands alowed to him att Mannomett.

[*23.]

Wheras Mr Thomas Dexter, Seni^r, complaineth of abuse and wronge done him by Leiftenant Fuller, and sundry of his naighbours, by pulling vp

22   PLYMOUTH COLONY RECORDS.

1662.
10 June.
Prence,
Govr.

of his fence and turning in cattle, &c̄, and that now att Plymouth the said Thomas Dexter speaking with the said Leiftenant Fuller about that matter, hee engaged to giue him meeting before the Court, that soe the Court might haue the hearing of the case, which hee neglected to attend, the Court therfore orders and doth heerby require, that the said Leiftenant Fuller and all others that haue damnifyed him, the said Thomas Dexter as aforsaid, by pulling vp his fence and the like, doe scase from soe doeing all this p̄sent summer vntill the next October Court; and that att the said Court there may bee a hearing of the case, and such determination as the Court shall see reason.

The Court haue authorised Mr Timothy Hatherly to sollemise the ordinance of marriage in the township of Scittuate as occation shall require, and likewise to adminnester an oath to any to give euidence for the tryall of a cause, and alsoe to adminnester an oath to any that shall giue euidence to the grand enquest as occation shall require within the township of Scittuate.

The Court doe likewise authorise the said Mr Timothy Hatherly to adminnester an oath to the widdow Vtley for the truth of the inventory of the estate of her husband, late deceased.

[*24.]
Thomas Bird was whipt the first time att this Court.

*Att this Court, Thomas Bird, for com̄itting of seuerall adulterouse practices and attempts, soe farr as strength of nature would p̄mitt, with Hannah Bumpas, as hee himselfe did acknowlidge, was sentanced by the Court to bee whipt two seuerall times, viz⸗, the first time att the p̄sent Court, and the second time betwixt this and the fifteenth day of July next.

And the said Hannah Bumpas, for yeilding to him, and not makeing such resistance against him as shee ought, is sentanced to bee publickly whipt, which accordingly was pformed.

Mr Timothy Hatherley was requested and authorised by the Court to see justice done on the body of Thomas Bird by publicke whiping in Scittuate, according to the abouesaid sentance.

And likewise the abouesaid Thomas Bird hath engaged to the Court to make payment of the full sum̄e of ten pounds vnto the abouesaid Hannah Bumpas or her assignes, in p̄te of satisfaction for the wronge hee hath done her as aboues̄d.

The said Indian was whipt att this Court.

Att this Court, a sertaine Nantuckett Indian named Tetannett, allis Ned, was, for pilfering and stealing sundry thinges from John Mayo, of Eastham, centanced by the Court to bee publickly whipt, and alsoe warned, according to former order, being a stranger in our gou̅ment, to depart to his owne place att Nantuckett; and incase hee shall reside within this gou̅ment, and bee found therin any other then as a passenger on a journey or the like, that then hee shalbee taken and publickely whipt, and sent home againe.

COURT ORDERS. 23

Att this Court, a fine of forty shillings was remited to Mr John Vincent, of Sandwich, which was by him forfeited for none appeerance att the last June Court to serue as a deputy.

1662.
10 June.
PRENCE,
Gou^r.

Capt Bradford, the Treasurer, and Cornett Studson are appointed by the Court to agree with a workman to mend Joanses Riuer bridge.

*The Names of those that are appointed by the Court in the seuerall Townes of this Goûment to take the Invoice of what Liquors, Powder, Shott, and Led is brought into the Goûment.

[*25.]

Plymouth,	John Morton, William Harlow.
Duxburrow,	Mr Constant Southworth, Benjamine Bartlett.
Scittuate,	Edward Jenkins, John Daman.
Sandwich,	Nathaniell Fish, Thomas Tobey.
Taunton,	Gorḡ Macye, Francis Smith.
Yarmouth,	Mr Anthony Thacher, Robert Dennis.
Barnstable,	Nathaniell Bacon, Josepth Laythorpe.
Marshfeild,	Anthony Snow, William Maycomber.
Rehoboth,	Leift Peter Hunt, Richard Bullocke.
Eastham,	Daniell Cole, Jonathan Sparrow.
Bridwater,	William Brett, John Willis.

These are to giue a trew account of all liquors, wine, powder, shott, and ledd that comes into the collonie, and comes to thire knowlige, att the Generall Courts of the yeare, according to order.

See the law of this June, 1662.

1662.

3 June.

PRENCE, GOUr.

[*26.]

*Att the Generall Court held att Plymouth, in New England, the third Day of June, Anno Dom 1662.

Wheras, notwithstanding all former prouision made for the pfecting of the line betwixt the Massachusetts and this collonie, from Accord Pond westward, hath bine hitherto obstructed, the neglect wherof, being soe greiuious to them and vs, and soe hurtfull in sundry respects, —

This Court doth therfore order, that Major Josias Winslow, Capt Thomas Southworth, and Cornett Robert Studson bee a comittee fully impowered to acte in the pfecting of the said line, and to conclude the right therof, according to the graunt of the charter of our collonie; whoe are to giue meeting vnto a comittee being in like manor impowered by the honored Court of the Massachusetts to acte therin in theire behalfe, that soe there may bee a finall issue put to that controuersy; and what shalbee by the said comittees acted, our said comittee are to returne to our next Generall Court.

[*27.]

*Wheras many controuersies haue bine between Phillip, the sachem of Sowams, and Quiquequanchett and Namumpam, his wife, and som Narragansett Indians that are with them; and the said pties interśted haue desired vs to take notice of them, and by joynt agreement haue refered it to our determination and issue; wee, haueing fully heard theire seuerall allegations and complaints, doe find that the principall difference between them hath arisen from the abouesaid Quiquequanchett and his wife entertaining of some Narragansetts against Phillipes liking and good will after conditions broken, and haueing well minded such please as they haue made for the proprietie and royaltie to such places as they haue bine soe entertained, wee euidently see that it hath bine originally in the said Phillipes predecessers, and is acknowlidged by the other to haue bine from Phillipes father conveyed to him, and that on the condition that such as should there liue vnder him should alwaies obserue such orders and costomes as they had found amongst them, the non obseruance wherof hath bine a great cause of theire psent troubles.

Wee doe therfore giue it as our aduise, for the issue of the contestes between the pties abouenamed, that the said Quiquequanchett and his wife doe dismise such of the said Indians as are, to Phillipes offence, entertained by them, vnles by any agreement with him hee may bee made willing to theire continuance there on theire promise of better carriage; and for returne of any goods by him taken from them, wee find hee hath alsoe bine treaspased and damnifyed by them, yett would haue him returne the canooes complained of, or any thinge of that nature that is yett extant, and doe advise that all vnkindnesses may bee buried between them, and that the remembrance of this difference, ariseing from such smale begiñings, may for future make them wise to liue in peace and loue.

1662.
8 October.
PRENCE, Gouʳ.

THOMAS PRENCE, Goñ,
JOHN ALDEN,
JOSIAS WINSLOW.

Plymouth, October the 8ᵗʰ, 1663.

*Forasmuch as there hath lately many rumers gon too and frow of danger of the rising of the Indians against the English, and some suspision of theire ploting against vs to cut vs of, the councell of warr, being assembled, saw cause and reason to send vnto Phillip, sachem of Poconakett, to require his appeerance att the Court held att Plymouth the sixt of August, 1662, to make answare vnto such intergatories as should bee proposed vnto him for the clearing of the aforsaid p̱ticulares, and to deliberate and congratulate with him about such matters as might tend to a further settlement of peace, and renewall of former couenants, as hee seemed to desire, plighted betwixt our predesessors and his ancestors; and accordingly the said sachem appeered att the Court abouesaid, and after curtesy expresed on both sides, and a large and deliberate debate of p̱ticulares, hee absolutely dencyed that hee had any hand in any plott or conspiracy against the English, nor that hee knew of any such contrivance against them, and proffered his brother, vpon the Courts demaund, as an hostage to bee secured vntill the Court could haue more sertainty of the truth of his defence. Vnto which they returned, that although they had just cause to require and accept of his hostage, yett notwithstanding they doe not desire it att the present, for such reason as they then expressed vnto him. In fine, it was concluded by the Court and him mutually, that the ancient couenant betwixt his predesessors and vs should bee continued; an abstract wherof was drawne vp and agreed on both p̱tes, and subscribed both by the said Phillip, the sachem, as alsoe his vnkell and sundry other of his most considerable men; the contents of which said couenant and subscribsion is as followeth : —

[*28.]

*Att a Court of Assistants held att Plymouth on the sixt day of August, anno Dom. 1662, Phillip, allis Metacum, sachem of Pocanokett, makeing his appeerance, did earnestly desire the continuance of that amitie and frindship that hath formerly bine between this goûment and his deceased father and brother; and to that end the said Phillip doth, for himselfe and his successors, desire that they may for euer remaine subject to the Kinge of England, his heires and successors, and doth faithfully promise and engage that hee and

6 August.
[*29.]

VOL. IV. 4

1662.
6 August.
Prence,
Gouʳ.

his will truely and exactly obserue and keep inviolable such conditions as haue bine by his predecessors formerly made, and p̃ticularly that hee will not att any time needlesly or vnjustly prouoake or raise warr with any other of the natiues, nor att any time giue, sell, or any way dispose of any lands to him or them appertaineing to any strangers, or to any without our priuity, consent, or appointment, but will in all thinges indeauor to carry peacably and inoffenciuely towards the English.

And the said Court did then alsoe expresse theire willingnes to continew with him and his the abouesaid frindship, and doe on theire p̃te promise that they will afoard them such frindly assistance by aduise and otherwise as they justly may; and wee will require our English att all times to carry frindly towards them. In witnes wherof the said Phillip, the sachem, hath sett to his hand, as alsoe his vnkell, and witnessed vnto by sundry other of his cheifemen.

The marke of PHILLIP, allis METACUM,
Sachem of Pocanakett,
The marke of VNCUMPOWETT,
Vnkell to the abouesaid sachem.

Witnesse John Sasomon,
The marke of Francis, the sachem of Nausett,
The marke of Nimrod, allis Pumpasa,
The marke of Punckquaneck,
The marke of Aquetaquesh.

---

3 October.
[*30.]

**Att the Generall Court holden att Plymouth the third of October, 1662.*

BEFORE Thomas Prence, Gouʳ,   Thomas Southworth,
Wilłam Collyare,   Wilłam Bradford, and
John Aldin,   Thomas Hinckley,
Josias Winslow,
Assistants, &c̃.

Mʳ WILŁAM COLLYARE and Mʳ John Aldin are appointed by the Court to view and bound an addition of land graunted vnto Captaine Bradford, in some convenient place for him adjoyning to the land hee hath att Stonybrooke.

COURT ORDERS. 27

Mʳ John Bradford and Mʳ Josepth Bradford are to bee considered in an accomodation of land in that which Captaine Willitt hath purchased on the north bounds of Rehoboth or elswhere. Since aded thervnto Henery Sampson, Edwa: Dotey, John Whiston.

1662.
3 October.
PRENCE,
GOUʳ.

Wheras Mʳ Collyare complaineth that the records of his graunt att the north hill are lost and cannot bee found, both of the vpland and meddow, the Court hath ordered, that Mʳ Aldin and Major Winslow shall view the same land, and bring report of it to the next March Court, that soe it may bee recorded as neare as may bee according to the first graunt.

Att this Court, a tender was made vnto Samuell Hickes by the Court to come to an equall deuision with others enterested in the lands of Mʳ Robert Hickes att Accushena, Coaksett, and places adjacent; and the said Samuell Hickes hath refused the same; and therfore the Court is nessesitated to appoint some to deuide it to such as are by Mʳ Hickes his will enterested therin in such proportion as the said land will beare; and the Court haue accordingly appointed Samuell Jenney, James Shaw, and Arther Hathewey to doe the same.

Conserning a coult enquired after by John Sutton, att Rehoboth, it is ordered by the Court, that hee shall haue the said coult into his custody, with this prouiso, that if any other shall come heerafter, and make proffe that it is theires, that then hee shall haue him forth coming, to bee deliuered to them.

Nicholas Norton and John Pease, of Martins Vinyards, are authorised by the towne of the said Vinyards to answare the suite of John Doged, comenced against the said towne att this Court.
  Witnes Thomas Burcher,
    William Weekes.

Captaine Cudworth, Mʳ Josepth Tildin, Leiftenant Torrey, and Cornett Studson are appointed by the Court to make deuision of some lands in p̃tenorship betwixt John Williams, Seniʳ, of Scittuate, and his son, John Williams.

*Mʳ John Done, John Smalley, and Jonathan Sparrow to bee considered with those whoe are graunted accomodation of land on the northerly bounds of Taunton.

[*31.]

Experience Michill, Mʳ Allexander Standish, Henery Sampson, Samuell Fuller, and Thomas Cushman, Juniʳ, are nominated to bee considered in the aforsaid lands, if it bee there to bee had when those are supplyed to whom the graunt is made, if it bee there to bee had; and if not there, in some other place, if it may bee found.

1662.
3 October.
PRENCE, Govr.

The oath of Jonathan Briggs, of Taunton, taken before this Court, is as followeth : —

I, Jonathan Briggs, aged twenty-fiue yeares or theraboutes, doe testify, that about six yeares agone, as I was in the house of James Walker, of Taunton, I heard James Walker aske William Browne what hee would doe with his land if hee should not returne from England againe. William Browne answared, that if hee did not returne againe, then hee would giue all his land to his little cousen, which was Peter Walker, whoe then stood before him.

The Account of the Liquors brought into the Towne of Yarmouth since June last before the date heerof, giuen into this Court by Mr Anthony Thacher.

The 22^{cond} of the fift month, brought in by Mr Gray 18 gallons of liquors.

The 9th of the six month, brought in by Mr Hedge about fifteen gallons of liquors, ten pounds of powder, and halfe an hundred of ledd.

William Nicarson, att the same time, brought in one barrell of liquor.

The 19th of the 7th month, Mr Hedge brought in ten gallons.

The 26 of the 7th month, Elisha Hedge brought in 16 gall.

The same time, William Griffin brought in ten gallons.

Att this Court, Richard Bourne and James Skiffe were appointed by the Court to settle the bounds of Nanquatnumuks land.

Mr Hatherley is fully cleared of this bond this third of June, 1663.

Ann Allin, widdow, and Mr Timothy Hatherley, both of Scittuate, doe heerby stand bound and are engaged vnto the Gou and Court of Plymouth in the sume of foure hundred pounds, to saue harmles and vndamnifyed the said Gou and Court of Plymouth from any dammage that may arise to them by the letters of adminnestration graunted by them vnto the said Ann Allin to adminnester on the estate of John Allin, deceased.

[*32.]

*Att this Court, Captaine Willett and some other whom hee shall thinke meet, are requested by the Court to view the bounds of Taunton, wherin they desire to bee enlarged ; and if hee sees it convenient, and that it bee not prejudiciall to others, to confeirme it to them ; and incase that Captaine Willett shall neglect soe to doe, the Court haue declared that they will take some course to answare theire desires att the next March Court.

Fines and contances.

Samuell Howland, of Duxburrow, being p'sented for breach of the Sabbath in carrying a grist from the mill on the Sabbath day, is, according to the law, sentanced to pay ten shillinges or be whipt.

COURT ORDERS. 29

And Wiłłam Foard, Seni^r, is fined fiue shillings for suffering him to take it from the mill att such an vnseasonable time.

1662.

3 October.
Prence,
Gou^r.

Kanelme Winslow, Juni^r, for riding a journey on the Lords day, although hee pleaded some disappointment inforcing him thervnto, is fined ten shillings.

Timothy Hallowey, for prophaning the Lords day in triming his servant theron, is fined ten shillings.

Teage Jones, of Yarmouth, for being ouertaken in drinke, haueing bine formerly a transgressor in that kind, was fined fifty shillings.

Gorḡ Crispe, being p̃sented for receiueing into his house some liquors or such like goods illegally taken, though hee knew it not, and suffering some disorders in his house, is fined twenty shillings.

The wife of Gorḡ Crispe being p̃sented for a lye, the Court, haueing considered the matter, doe find that shee spake a falshood, but judg it not to come vnder the notion of a pnisious lye, but onely vnadvisedly, and soe require not the fine.

Wiłłam Randall, being p̃sented for diuers lyes and slaunders in defamation of John Bryant, for his lyes was fined twenty shillings.

And in reference to his p̃sentment about Thomas Ouldums cooper stuffe, hee is fined for a lye about it ten shillings.

John Palmer, Juni^r, of Scittuate, for that without cause, out of prejudice, hee did forge a slaunder against Josepth Siluester, wherin is sundry pnisious lyes, is fined fiue pounds; and Samuell Palmer, being in the same default, and now absent, is left to further consideration.

John Tompson, warned to attend this Court to serue on a jury, did absent himselfe, and soe lyable to fine, vnlese hee can satisfy the Court by his defence.

*The rates for the publicke charge of the countrey for this yeare, according as they were proportioned on the seuerall townshipes, are as followeth:—

[*33.]

Plymouth, rate to 120^{li}, ...	11 : 02 : 00
Duxburrow, ...	06 : 14 : 06
Scittuate, ...	18 : 03 : 00
Sandwich, ...	10 : 02 : 00
Taunton, ...	10 : 02 : 00
Yarmouth, ...	10 : 02 : 00
Barnstable, ...	11 : 02 : 00
Marshfeild, ...	10 : 02 : 00
Rehoboth, ...	15 : 03 : 00
Eastham, ...	08 : 02 : 00

1662.

3 October.
PRENCE,
GOVᴿ.

Bridgwater,	04 : 10 : 00
Sowamsett,	05 : 10 : 00
Cushenah and Coaksett,	03 : 10 : 00
The farmes against Road Iland,	01 : 10 : 00
	125 : 14 : 06

The officers wages being taken out of the abouesaid sume, the remainder to bee paied, the one halfe therof in wheat and barly, att 4ˢ 8ᵈ p̄ bushell, and the other halfe therof, one third of it to bee paid in wheat and barly att the prise aforsaid, and the other two thirds in Indian corne att three shillings p̄ bushell.

The 2ᶜᵒⁿᵈ of December, 1662, the sume of twenty-four shillings in money was receiued by the Treasurer from the clark, which was the money which was taken from a boy which ran away, whose name is Christopher Fowler, fiue shillinges and threpence wherof was payed by the Treasurer for the defraying of the charge of the marshall, &c̄, about the said boy ; and the Treasurer is ordered by the Court to returne the remainder to the right owner.

1662-3.

3 March.
[*34.]

*Att the Generall Court held att Plymouth the third Day of March, 1662.

BEFORE Thomas Prence, Gouʳ,   Josias Winslow,
Wiłłam Collyare,   Thomas Southworth,
John Aldin,   Wiłłam Bradford, and
Thomas Willett,   Thomas Hinckley,
Assistants, &c̄.

IN answare vnto a request made by Mʳ Hatherley vnto the Court, that a jury might bee impannelled to make deuision of the lands in p̄tenorship betwixt John Williams, Senⁱʳ, and Ensigne John Williams, his son, the Court did approue and appoint those whose names are vnderwritten to repaire vnto the house of Mʳ Anthony Eames, att the North Riuer, and there to giue meeting vnto Major Winslow ; and that a jury out of them bee impanneled to make deuision of the lands aforsaid, vizṫ : Leifṫ James Torrey, Cornett Robert Studson, Mʳ Josepth Tildin, Walter Briggs, Isacke Chettenden, John Daman, Edw̄ Jenkens, John Hollett, Jeremiah Hatch, John Ottis, John

COURT ORDERS.   31

Turner, Juni^r, Mathew Gannett, Thomas Hiland, William Tickner, and Walter Woodward.   1 6 6 2-3.

3 March.
P&ence, Gou^r.

Mr Hinckley is appointed by the Court to adminnester an oath to such as are to take theire oathes to the will and inventory of the estate of Mr Robert Linnell, deceased ; and that Josepth Laythorp and Nathaniell Bacon bee aded to the widdow Linnell to bee healpfull to her in seeing the debts payed either out of the whole or p̃te of the estate.

Letters of adminnestration are graunted vnto Jonathan Hatch and Lydia, the wife of Henery Taylor, to adminester vpon the estate of Thomas Hatch, deceased, to pay all lawfull debts owing from the said estate, and to bee reddy to giue account therof vnto the Court.

Memorand: that att the next June Court some course bee taken to settle the bounds betwixt Taunton and Secuncke, to preuent damage that might arise to the Indians by the neglect therof ; and Captaine Willett is desired to take course to prevent the English in depasturing theire cattle neare the Indians corn to theire prejudice.

Att this Court, Leiftenant Torrey, Cornett Studson, and Mr Josepth Tildin were appointed by the Court to lay out the tract of land graunted to Mr Hatherley aboue Scittuate, according to the graunt, vizt̃: to begine att the southermost end of Accord Pond, and to goe noe farther northerly least it entrench vpon the Bay line.

This to bee done betwixt this date and the 15 of Aprill next.

*Att this Court, Josias Hallott and Thomas Starr, for goeing into the house of John Done, Juni^r, att Eastham, there being no body att home, and behaueing themselues vnciuilly therin, ransacking the house for liquors and drinking therof, and for writing and seting vp a libelouse and scandalouse paper of verses in the said house, and leauing of it there, are sentanced by the Court to find surties for theire good behauior vntill the next Generall Court, to bee holden att Plymouth the first Tusday in June next, and longer time if the Court shall see cause, and to pay for a fine, each of them, the sum̃e of fifty shillinges.

[*35.]

Elisha Hedge and Samuell Sturgis, for being guilty in the said p̃ticulars, though not soe deeply as the former, as is conceiued, are sentanced to find surties for theire good behauior vntill the next Generall Court abouesaid, to bee holden att Plymouth the first Tusday in June next, and longer time if the Court shall see cause, and to pay, each of them, a fine of thirty shillinges.

Josias Hallott acknowlidgeth to owe vnto our sou lord the Kinge the sum̃e of . . . . } 20 : 00 : 00

Trustrum Hull the sum̃e of . . . . 10 : 00 : 00

The condition, that if the said Josias Hallott bee of good behauior   Released.

1662-3.

3 March.
PRENCE,
GOVᴿ.

towards our soū lord the Kinge and all his leich people, and appeer att the Generall Court to bee holden for this goūment att Plymouth the first Tusday in June next, and not depart the said Court without lycence; that then, &c.

Thomas Starr acknowlidgeth to owe vnto our soū lord the Kinge the sume of . . . . } 20 : 00 : 00

Ralph Smith the sume of . . . . 10 : 00 : 00

Released, paying his fees.

The condition, that if the said Thomas Starr bee of good behauior towards our soū lord the Kinge and all his leich people, and appeer att the Generall Court to bee holden for this goūment att Plymouth the first Tusday in June next, and not depart the said Court without lycence; that then, &c.

Elisha Hedge acknowlidgeth to owe vnto our soū lord the Kinge the sume of . . . . } 20 : 00 : 00

Robert Denis the sume of . . . . 10 : 00 : 00

These bonds are forfeited, but since ten pound fine accepted.

The condition, that if the said Elisha Hedge bee of good behauior towards our soū lord the Kinge and all his leich people, and appeer att the Generall Court to bee holden for this goūment att Plymouth on the first Tusday in June next, and not depart the said Court without lycence; that then, &c.

[*36.]

*Samuell Sturgis acknowlidgeth to owe vnto our soū lord the Kinge the sume of . . . . } 20 : 00 : 00

John Miller the sume of . . . . 10 : 00 : 00

Cleared of these bonds, paying his fees.

The condition, that if the said Samuell Sturgis bee of good behauior towards our soū lord the Kinge and all his leich people, and appeer att the Generall Court to bee holden for this goūment att Plymouth the first Tusday in June next, and not depart the said Court without lycence; that then, &c.

Att this Court, Ephraim Done, Thomas Ridman, John Knowles, and John Wilson, for trading of liquors with the Indians att Cape Codd, are fined, each of them, twenty fiue shillinges.

Ephraim Done and Thomas Ridman, for pmiting the Indians to haue liquors in theire boate, it appeering that one of the Indians was drunke therby, are fined, each of them, fifty shillings.

Conserning a rundelett of liquor found with one Peter, an Indian, none of the abouesaid owncing that they had helped the Indian to it, it is found to bee forfeited to the countrey; and for soe much of the liquor as is spent, that the said Indian bee required to make it good.

Ephraim Done acknowlidgeth to owe vnto our soū lord the Kinge the sume of . . . . } 40 : 00 : 00

John Knowles the sume of . . . . 20 : 00 : 00

Ephraim Done was freed of these bonds October 10ᵗʰ, 1663.

The condition, that if the said Ephraim Done doe appeer att the Court to bee holden att Plymouth the first Tusday in June next, to make further

answar vnto such thinges as shalbee enquired of him conserning the death of
Josias, the Indian sachem, att Eastham, and not depart the said Court without
lycence; that then, &c.

1662-3.
3 March.
PRENCE,
Gou^r.

John Knowles acknowlidgeth to owe vnto our soũ
lord the Kinge the sũme of . . . . } 40 : 00 : 00

Ephraim Done the sũme of . . . . 20 : 00 : 00

The condition, that if the said John Knowles doe appeer att the Court to bee holden att Plymouth the first Tusday in June next, to make further answare vnto such pticulares as shalbee enquired of him concerning the death of Josias, the Indian sachem, att Eastham, and not depart the said Court without lycence; that then, &c.

Abraham Sampson, for being drunke, fined ten shillings.

Thomas Lucas, for being drunke, it being the third time hee hath ben convicted and sentanced in the Court for being drunke, was sentanced by the Court to bee publickely whipt, according to the law, onely the execution therof is respited vntill hee shalbee taken drunke the next time, and then hee is to bee forthwith taken and whipt, without further psenting to the Court.

*Thomas Ridman acknowlidge to owe vnto our soũ
lord the Kinge the sũme of . . . . } 40 : 00 : 00

[*37.]

John Wilson the sũme of . . . . 20 : 00 : 00

The condition, that if the said Thomas Ridman doe appeer att the Generall Court to bee holden att Plymouth the first Tusday in June next, to make answare vnto such pticulares as shalbee further enquired of them conserning the death of Josias, the Indian sachem, att Eastham, and not depart the said Court without lycence; that then, &c.

John Wilson acknowlidgeth to owe vnto our soũ lord
the Kinge the sũme of . . . . } 40 : 00 : 00

Thomas Ridman the sũme of . . . . 20 : 00 : 00

The condition, that if the said John Wilson doe appeer att the Court to bee holden att Plymouth the first Tusday in June next, to make answare vnto what further shalbee enquired of them conserning the death of Josias, the Indian sachem, att Eastham, and not depart the said Court without lycence; that then, &c.

Att this Court, Moses Crooker and Richard Man were psented before the Court for entering into the house of Edward Williams, of Scittuate, and ployning of his money and goods, and laying of gunpowder about his hearth soe as it fiered, to the endangering of the life of the said Williams, with other pnisious practices which proued injurious to the said Williams, for which they

1662-3.

*3 March.
Prence,
Govr.*

Memorand.: that the said Thom: Hinckley hath paide fiue pounds vnto Edward Williams as of satisfaction for the wrong don him by the boyes.

were sentanced by the Court to bee both seuerly whipt, which accordingly was inflicted; and wheras the money and goods they tooke from the said Williams could not bee made good by them, nor satisfaction giuen for other injuries, the Court ordered them to bee put forth to seruice vntill each of them should attaine the age of twenty and one yeares from the date heerof, viz$, the said Moses Crooker to liue with, continew and abide with John Williams, Seni^r, of Scittuate, the full tearme of eight yeares, hee being att the writing heerof of the age of thirteen yeares; hee, the said John Williams, paying vnto the said Edward Williams the sume of fiue pounds; and incase the said John Williams shall decease before the said time bee expired, that then hee shalbee att the dispose of the said John Williams for the remainder of his time, with the consent and approbation of the Court; and likewise the Court doth dispose of the said Richard Man to bee with and abide with Mr Thomas Hinckley, of Barnstable, or his assignes, with the approbation of ye Court, after the mannor of an apprentice, the tearme of ten yeares from the date heerof, hee being att the writing heerof of the age of eleuen yeares; and incase the said Thomas Hinckley shall decease before the said time bee expired, that then the said Richard Man shalbee att the dispose of him, the said Thomas Hinckley, for the remainder of his time, with the consent and approbation of the Court.

[*38.]

The tearmes of the p'sentment was for striking and reuiling by oprobriouse speches, and thrusting ouer a boat thought Willm Walker.

*Att this Court, Ralph Smith, of Eastham, for breaking the peace in striking of William Walker, is fined 00 : 03 : 04.

And for other p̃ticulares in the p̃sentment att October Court, 1662, considering hee hath agred with the said Walker, and in p̃te made satisfaction, the Court doth heer pas it by.

And as conserning his former p̃sentment, conserning teling of a lye and other injuries done by him to the towne of Eastham about a whale, the Court haueing onely fined him for the lye, haue respeted the sensuring of him for the remainder vntill they haue further notice of his future walking.

Samuell Smith, for saying hee could find in his hart to thrust a pen into the said William Walker, was fined 00 : 03 : 04.

Nathaniel Church and Elizabeth Soule, for comitting fornication with each other, were fined, according to the law, each of them, 05 : 00 : 00.

Att this Court, this following order was directed to the towne of Taunton : —

Vpon the complaint of some of the inhabitants of Taunton, that some there haue gone about to alter the ancient way of distribution of lands in that towne formerly settled and long practised, wherby, besides many other inconveniencyes that doe arise therby, some Indians that by the leaue of the towne had libertie to plant corne in the remote p̄tes of the townshipe are disturbed in the improuement of the said lands, to theire great impouerishing, by such p̄sons theire takeing vp such great quaintities of land, which is ill resented by vs; wee doe therfore require them to desist from any such practice as that which wee feare may create much trouble and inconveniencye, vntill wee haue further inquired into the same.

1662 3.

3 March.
PRENCE,
GOVᴿ.

The Courts order.

p̄ me,   NATHANIELL MORTON, Clark.

---

*Att the Court of Assistants holden att Plymouth the fift Day of May, 1663.

1663.

5 May.
[*39.]

BEFORE Thomas Prence, Gouʳ,   Thomas Southworth,
Willam Collyare,   Willam Bradford, and
John Aldin,   Thomas Hinckly,
Josias Winslow,
Assistants, &ᶜ.

IN answare vnto the desire of Stephen Bryant and Ephraim Tinkham, that some course might bee taken about some differences amongst theire naighbourhood about the bounds of theire lands, the Court haue ordered, that Willam Crow bee aded to those whoe the towne of Plymouth haue appointed to measure and settle the bounds of lands, that hee with them may endeauor to settle the said controuersy amongst them.

In answare vnto a petition prefered to the Court by Judith, the wife of Willam Peakes, of Scittuate, in reference vnto her son Josias Leichfeild, the adopted son of John Allin, deceased, the Court haue ordered and doe heerby giue libertie vnto the said Josias Leichfeild to choose two guardians, and to p̄sent them vnto the next Generall Court.

In answare vnto a p̄ticulare in a letter directed to the Court from Mʳ Hatherley, wherin hee desired the Court would take other cecuritie for the estate of John Allin, there being noe other appeering to giue in cecuritie, doe heerby signify that they looke att him as standing bound and engaged vnto them in that behalfe, and are not willing to a release vntill some other doe appeer to bee engaged, and therfore doe aduise him to take the best course hee can to secure himselfe.

1663.

5 May.
PRENCE,
Gouʳ.

Concerning the complaint of Thomas Butler in the behalfe of his son, Daniell Butler, against Wiłłam Browne, for that the said Browne did neglect to deliuer two barrells of tarr to Mʳ John Barnes, of Plymouth, or his assignes, which said tarr the said Browne receiued of the said Daniell Butler for that end and purpose, the Court haue awarded the said Wiłłam Browne to pay vnto the said Daniell Butler two barrells of marchantable tarr with all convenient speed, and eight shillings for charges the said Butler hath bine att about the said suite.

Memorand : that Samuell Hinckley bee sumoned to appeer att the next Court, to giue oath to the will of Mʳ Samuell Hinckley, deceased.

Conserning the land graunted to Edward Gray att Namassakett, the Courts order about it is to bee vnderstood, that the said Edward Gray is to haue a double share of the said lands, both vpland and meddow, to bee layed out together ; that is to say, a double share of the said lands, to take it where hee would in the said tract, soe as hee tooke it together.

---

1 June.
[*40.]

Att the Generall Court of Election held att the Towne of Plymouth, for the Jurisdiction of New Plymouth, the first Day of June, 1663.

BEFORE Thomas Prence, Gouʳ,	Josias Winslow,
Wiłłam Collyare,	Thomas Southworth,
John Aldin,	Wiłłam Bradford, and
Thomas Willett,	Thomas Hinckley,

Assistants, &c.

Mʳ THOMAS PRENCE was chosen Gouʳ, and sworne.

Wiłłam Collyare,
John Aldin,
Thomas Willett,
Josias Winslow,   } were chosen Assistants, and sworne.
Thomas Southworth,
Wiłłam Bradford, and
Thomas Hinckley,

Mʳ Thomas Prence and Major Josias Winslow were chosen comissioners for the following yeare.

COURT ORDERS.

And Capt Thomas Southworth is the next in nomination.
Mr Constant Southworth was chosen Treasurer, and sworne.
It was ordered by the Court that a ^ ^

1663.
1 June.
PRENCE,
Govr.

*The Names of the Deputies that serued att this Court. [*41.]

Mr John Howland,	Leiftenant James Wyate,
Robert Finney,	Mr Anthony Thacher,
Ephraim Morton,	Mr Yelverton Crow,
Nathaniell Warren,	Nathaniell Bacon,
Mr Constant Southworth,	John Chipman,
William Paybody,	Ensigne Marke Eames,
Leiftenant James Torrey,	Leiftenant Peter Hunt,
Isacke Bucke,	Leiftenant John Freeman,
Thomas Tupper, Senir,	Josias Cooke,
James Skiffe,	William Britt.

One deputy from Taunton was returned backe, and one deputy from Marshfeild was returned backe againe. Mr Stephen Paine, one of the deputies chosen for Rehoboth, could not appeer by reason of weaknes.

The Grand Enquest.

John Morton,	John Russell,
Leiftenant Josepth Rogers,	Henery Sampson,
Mr James Browne,	Robert Wheaten, absent,
John Willis, absent,	John Turner, Senir,
John Dingley,	William Bassett, Junir,
Edmond Freeman,	Peter Pitts,
Ensigne John Williams,	Thomas Howes, Junir,
James Mathewes,	Thomas Tildin,
Thomas Laythorpe,	John Bryant,
Abraham Blush,	Benajah Pratt.
John Rogers,	

The Constables of the seuerall Townes of this Jurisdiction.

Plym,	Stephen Bryant.
Duxb,	John Sprague.
Scittu,	John Sutton.
Sandw,	Gorg Barlow.
Taunton,	Hezekiah Hoare.
Yarmou,	Samuell Ryder.

1663.

1 June.
PRENCE,
GOVR.

Barnst, ... Tristrum Hull.
Marshfeill, ... { Wiłłam Holmes, Justice Eames.
Rehoboth, ... Wiłłam Carpenter.
Eastham, ... Edward Banges.
Bridgw̄, ... Samuell Edson.
Acushenah, ... Wiłłam Spooner.

[*42.]

*The Surveyors of the Highwaies.

Plym̄, ... { James Cole, Senir, Josepth Warren, Samuell Sturtivant.
Duxbū, ... { Mr Samuell Sabery, Samuell Hunt.
Scitt, ... { John Cushen, Wiłłam Brookes.
Sand, ... { Thomas Burge, Senir, Thomas Launder.
Taunton, ... { James Leanord, Samuell Smith.
Yarmoū, ... { John Joyce, Wiłłam Eldred.
Marshfeild, ... { Thomas Doged, Anthony Snow.
Rehoboth, ... { John Peram, Senir, Gilbert Brookes.
Bridgwater, ... { John Willis, Junir, Samuell Allin.

Freemen admited this Court, and sworne.

Jeremiah Howes,   Wiłłam Carpenter,
John Miller,   Jonathan Sparrow,
John Reed,   Samuell Eaton.
Samuell Newman,

Att this Court, Cornett Studson was appointed by the Court to accompany the Treasurer in demanding and receiueing the moneyes due to the countrey from the purchasers of Kenebecke.

For diuers reasons and considerations, the Court haue suspended the generall training for this yeare, and that the next yeare it bee obserued att Yarmouth att the ordinary time of the yeare.

1 6 6 3.
1 June.
PRENCE,
GOUR.

Leiftenant Wyate, Nathaniell Bacon, and Robert Finney were appointed by the Court to view the lands on the north side of Secunke, and make report therof vnto the Court.

Ensigne Dexter is ordered by the Court to exersice the milletary company of Sandwich in armes vntill the Court shall see reason otherwise to order.

*The Court haue ordered, concerning the disposing of the estate of Faith Clarke, widdow, deceased, that her daughter, Faith Dotey, widdow, shall haue a quarter p̃te, or one p̃te of foure, of the goods and chattles of the said Faith Clarke, her debts being discharged ; and the remainder three p̃tes of four, or three quarters therof, shalbee equally deuided betwixt her two sonnes, Henery and Thurston Clarke ; and that Captaine Bradford and Josepth Andrewes shall make the said deuision, together with another whom the said Faith Dotey shall make choise of ; and that the said Capt Bradford and Joseph Andrewes shall take course that the debts due from the said estate bee defrayed out of the same.

[*43.]

Att this Court, Josias Leichfeild made choise of Leiftenant Torrey and Cornett Studson to bee his gaurdians, whoe were allowed and approued soe to bee by the Court.

Wheras John Allin, of Scittuate, and Anna, his wife, longe since tooke Josias Leichfeild as theire adopted child, with purpose to bringe him vp, and to doe for him as theire child, and soe faithfully pformed during the said Allin his life, and not long before his death was mindfull of him ; yett being suddainly taken away, left not his mind soe full and p̃ticulare concerning him as hee intended and might haue bine desired ; yett soe much appeered to the Court vpon oath as in theire apprehensions carryed the true intent and force of a will. The said Josias haueing chosen Leiftenant James Torrey and Cornett Robert Studson his gaurdians, it was att this Court agreed between Anna, the relict of the said Allin, and the boyes abouenamed guardians, with the Courts approbation and likeing, that the said Josias should haue twenty pounds sterling payed into the hands of his said gaurdians about Michilmus next, by them to bee improued for him, and soon after that time to bee freed & to bee put forth to a trad, and conueniently fited out with suitable apparrell and nessesarries ; and when hee shall come to the age of twenty one yeares, to bee posessed of the farme and appurtenances giuen him by the said John Allin, deceased.

Of this see more, June Court, 1665.

Of this will heer expressed see where wills and inventoryes are recorded.

*The Court doe order, that Mr Collyares meddow bee recorded lying

[*44.]

1663.

1 June.
Prence,
Govr.

about North Hill, haueing bin lately viewed by Mr Aldin and the Major Winslow, and bounded by a pine tree anciently marked standing on the north side of the brooke, and from then by a range of stakes a crosse the meddow to a marked three on the west or southwest side of the said meddow, all the meddowes lying on the southerly side of that range, and alsoe a little nooke of meddow lying downe the said brooke towards North Hill, containing about two acrees.

The Court doe acknowlidg Gilbert Winslow, deceased, whoe was one of the first comers, to haue a right to land, and doe allow his heires to looke out and propose to the Court some p̄cell of land that the Court may thinke meet to accomodate them in.

Liberty is graunted to Mr Edmond Freeman, Seni^r, to looke out a tract of land to accomodate both himselfe and the children of Mr William Paddy, deceased, vizt, Samuell and Thomas Paddy, and to make report of it to the Court, that a competency may bee confeirmed vnto them, if it may bee, about a ceder swamp, by him named, soe as it bee found not to intrench vpon other mens right; if soe, hee may looke out elsewhere where it may bee found.

Liberty is graunted vnto William Crow, of Plymouth, in respect vnto his vnkell, Mr John Adwood, of Plymouth, deceased, to looke out for accomodation of land, and to make report therof to the Court, that soe a competency may bee alowed him.

Mr Hinckley, Mr Dexter, Seni^r, and Mr Constant Southworth are appointed by the Court to settle the bounds between the townshipps of Sandwich and Plymouth as soon as conveniently they can.

It is ordered by the Court, that a rate of forty pounds bee leuied on the seuerall townes of this jurisdiction for the defraying of nessesary charges of the collonie, that they are nessesitated to expend att the p̄sent; which said rate euery one is to pay his proportion which hee shalbee rated thervnto in money, or wheat att 4^s p̄ bushell, to bee payed by the last of August next; of which rate the naighbourhood of Sowamsett is to pay thirty shillinges, the naighbourhood att Acushena 10^s, and Bridgwater thirty shillinges, in the specy aboue expressed.

Thomas Huckens is approued, and his former libertie renewed to keep an ordinary att Barnstable.

[*45.]

*Wheras there was a graunt by the Court of an adition of land vnto Mr William Bradford, Seni^r, as appeers vpon record, which was not layed out nor bounded in his life time; and wheras Captaine William Bradford, the son of the said Mr William Bradford, Seni^r, did make request vnto the Court that the same might bee pformed; the Court held att Plymouth on the third of October, 1662, did appoint Mr William Collyare and Mr John Alden, Assistants, to view and bound an addition adjoyning vnto the lands which the said William Bradford posseseth. Now, wee, the aboue named Assistants, haue, this twentyeth of May, 1663, viewed and bounded as followeth: on the north east from a smale rundelett that runeth downe to a place comonly called the Tussukes, and soe to range alonge northerley by Plymouth bounds next to the bounds of Duxburrow, and soe to the brooke that runes into black waters, to the place where the old path went to the bay, so rainging downe the brooke a mile in length.

1663.
1 June.
PRENCE, Gour.

WILLAM COLLYARE,
JOHN ALDIN.

It is ordered by the Court, that those that are sett downe att Sowamsett be accounted to belonge to the towne of Rehoboth, and those that are sett downe att Saconeesett to belonge to Barnstable, and those that are sett downe att Namassakett to belonge to the towne of Plymouth vntill the Court shall see reason otherwise to order.

The major, the Treasurer, and Cornett Studson are appointed to agree with a workeman or workemen to repaire the bridge att Joanses Riuer, or to erect a new one, as occation shall require.

The major and the Treasurer are appointed by the Court to agree with William Berstow to repaire the bridge att the North Riuer; and the charge therof is to bee leuied by rate on the seuerall townshipes of this goūment; and for the quantity and specey therof, it is to bee as they, the said p̄ties, shall agree with workmen, and to bee made knowne that it may bee leuied by rate in October next after the date heerof.

Anthony Annable and William Crocker are appointed by the Court to bee adminnestrators on the estate of Thomas Burman, and that they are to giue in cecuritie to the Court to saue the Court from all damage that may come to them by the said p̄ties theire adminestration.

Liberty is graunted vnto John Gorum to looke out some land for accomodation, and to make report therof to the Court, that soe a competency may bee graunted to him.

Ensigne Merricke is alowed and approued of by the Court to bee in the office of a leiftenant in the milletary companie of Eastham.

	li	s	d	
*Elisha Hedge acknowlidgeth to owe vnto our sou lord the Kinge the sume of	20	00	00	[*46.]
Edward Sturgis, Senir, the sume of	10	00	00	

1663.

1 June.
PRENCE,
GOUR.
Freed, paying his fees.
Sensures.

The condition, that if the said Elisha Hedge bee of good behauior towards our soñ lord the Kinge and all his leich people, and appeer att the Court to bee holden for this goũment att Plymouth the first Tusday in October next, and not depart the said Court without lycence; that then, &c̃.

The Court being enformed that Joseph Rogers, of Namassakeesett, hath frequently and from time kept companie with Mercye, the wife of Wiłłam Tubbs, in a way and after such manor as hath giuen cause att least to suspect that there hath binc laciuiouse actes cõmitted by them, the Court sees cause and haue required the said Joseph Rogers to remoue his dwelling from Namassakeesett aforsaid by the twentieth day of this instant June, and haue alsoe declared vnto him that if att any time hee shall bee taken att the house of the said Tubbs, or in the companie of the said Marcye Tubbs alone in any place, that then hee shall forth with bee taken and seuerly whipt; and the said Wiłłam Tubbs was by the Court strictly charged not to tollarate him to come to his house or where hee hath to doe att any time, as hee will answare the same att his pill.

The abouesaid Josepth Rogers, for his contentious departing from the Court held att Plymouth the last March without licence, being bound to appeer and attend the said Court to answare for matter of fact, is fined fiue pounds to the collonies vse.

Fines.

Christopher Winter, for neglecting to frequent the publicke worship of God on the Lords day, is fined ten shillings.

Timothy Hallowey, for being drunke, fined fiue shillinges.

John Shilley, for playing att cards on the Lords day, fined 20ˢ.

Nathaniell Fitsrandall, for cõmiting fornication, fined ten pounds; hee hath liberty vntill the next October Court to pay the fine, or suffer corporall punishment.

Edward Sturgis, for bringing in liquors into the towne of Yarmouth, and not giueing seasonable notice therof to the men appointed to take the invoyce therof, is fined the sũme of six pounds, wherof foure pound to the collonies vse and forty shillings to the said invoycers.

[*47.]

*The lands that Mʳ Constant Southworth and Wiłłam Paybody layed out in consideration of the graunt of lands to Captaine Myles Standish att Satuckett Pond lyeth on the north side of the mouth of Winnatucksett Riuer, the said riuer being the bounds on the south side buting vpon Satuckett Riuer, being the bounds on the west end, ruñing in length from Satuckett Riuer into the woods 160 rodds east and by north, ruñing in breadth north and by west from the abouesaid Winatucksett Riuer to a great white oake tree burnt att the bottome, and a ridd oake tree marked standing close by it; alsoe, a smale tract of meddow land lying att the head of Satuckett Pond, contaiñg about four acrees more or lesse, in p̃te of the graunt of competency to such a tract of vpland.

1663.
1 June.
PRENCE, Gouᵣ.

In answare vnto a petĩon p̃fered to the Court by Mʳ Thomas Cushman, Thomas Clarke, and Thomas Pope, the ouerseers of the estate of Mistris Sarah Jeney, deceased, in reference vnto a mare disposed of by the Treasurer in the behalfe of the countrey, the Court haue allowed them, in reference vnto the children of the said Mistris Jeney, the first horse beast, bee it horse or mare, that shalbee found to belonge vnto the countrey.

And in answare vnto a petition prefered to the Court by Mʳ Thomas Bourne, of Marshfeild, conserning a horse hee layed claime vnto, the Court haue left the case relateing to that controuersy as they found it, and see noe light to acte further in it.

Mʳ Timothy Hatherley is appointed and deputed by the Court to adminnester marriage within the township of Scittuate for the following yeare, as alsoe to adminnester an oath to any witnesses to giue testimony to the grand enquest as occation shall require, as alsoe to any witnesses to giue euidence to the Court for the triall of any cause, and likewise in his maᵗⁱᵉˢ name to issue forth warrants and summons to warne any p̃son of the towne of Scittuate p̃sonally to appeer att the Court att Plymouth to answare any suite as occation shall require this following yeare.

Mʳ John Done is appointed by the Court to adminester marriage within the township of Eastham for this following yeare, and to adminester an oath to any witnesses to giue euidence to the grand enquest, and alsoe to any witnesses to giue euidence to the Court for the tryall of a cause to any within the towne of Eastham for this following yeare.

*Gorḡ Vaugham, of Marshfeild, vpon his p̃sentment for not attending the publicke worship on the Lords day, fined, according to order, ten shillinges.

[*48.]
Fines and sensures.

William Paule, of Taunton, fined for drunkenes, it being the 2ᶜᵒⁿᵈ time, ten shillinges.

The same Paule, for breach of the peace, three shillinges and four pence, and for prophane swearing that hee bee sett in the stockes as the constable shall haue order, and for his not appeering to his summones hee is fined twenty shillinges.

John Hathewey, for his breach of the peace, fined three shillinges and four pence.

John Doged, of Rehoboth, being by Captaine Willett convicted of two lyes, is fined twenty shillinges.

1663.

1 June.
PRENCE,
Gouʳ.

It is ordered by the Court, that Edward Perrey bee called to account in convenient time for a rayling letter which hee wrote to the Court.

It is agreed and ordered by the Court, that in due and convenient time Wiłłam Nicarson bee required to make satisfaction for his breach of the law prohibiting any to buy or hier any lands of the Indians without lycence and by order of the Court.

It is ordered by the Court, that a letter shalbee drawne vp as from the Court, and sent to Road Iland, in answare to theires, and likewise the Court haue declared themselues that they see noe cause to admitt of a treaty with them concerning our lands claimed and pretended by them to bee purchased, it being but to make a dispute in matters that are cleare and out of controuersy.

[*49.]

*It is ordered by the Court, that a convenient, hansome rome bee aded to the Goũnors house, and that the chargͥ of the building therof bee defrayed out of the pay for Kenebecke, if that kind of pay will doe it; and if not, then a p̃te of those goods, and the rest to bee raised by rate; and that the major, the Treasurer, and Cornett Studson are impowered to take course for the procureing of the thinge done, on such conditions as they can.

The sũme of thirty pounds is allowed to the Goũ for his extreordinary charges this yeare, in the best pay that wee can make it.

It is ordered, that the Treasurer bee requested to prouide for the majestrates table, as formerly.

4 August.
[*50.]

*Att the Court of Assistants held att Plymouth the fourth Day of August, 1663.

BEFORE Thomas Prence, Gouʳ,   Josias Winslow,
Wiłłam Collyare,   Thomas Southworth, and
John Aldin,   Wiłłam Bradford,
Assistants, &c̃.

VPON the motion of Mʳ Hatherley and Mʳ Tildin, in the behalfe of the widdow, Mistris Lydia Garrett, of Scittuate, to haue libertie to sell stronge liquors, in regard that sundry in that towne are oft times in nessesitie therof, this Court doth giue libertie vnto the said Lydia Garrett to sell liquors, alwaies prouided that the orders of Court concerning selling of liquors bee obserued, and that shee sell none but to house keepers, and not lesse than a gallon att a time.

Libertie is graunted vnto Thomas Leanard, of Taunton, Seni^r, to sell stronge liquors and wine in the said towne betwixt this date and the Court to bee holden att Plymouth in June next, and that hee obserue the orders of Court as are extant about selling of liquors and wine, and that hee keep good order in his house with them to whom hee sels any.

1663.
4 August.
PRENCE, GOU^R.

Josepth Andrews fined fiue shillings for refusing to serue on a jury for the laying out of highwaies att Duxburrow, being sumoned thervnto.

Memorand: that John Sutton bee summoned vnto the next Generall Court, to giue an account of the deuision and disposall of the estate of Samuell House, deceased, incase Mr Tildin and hee doe not end it in the interem; and that notwithstanding hee bee sumoned to giue in cecuritie for the said estate and the disposall therof vnto the Court.

Richard Bourne and Myles Blacke were appointed by the Court to purchase the land of the Indians that Mr Freeman hath graunted vnto him and the children of Mr Paddy by the Court, and likewise to sett apart such a portion of the ceader swampe that is therin as shalbee behoofefull and by them thought competent for the naighbourhood residing att Mannomett.

---

*_Att the Generall Court held att Plymouth the fift of October, 1663._

5 October.
[*51.]

BEFORE Thomas Prence, Gou,   Thomas Southworth,
        Wiltam Colyare,   Wiltam Bradford, and
        John Aldin,   Thomas Hinckley,
        Josias Winslow,

Assistants, &c.

THE inhabitants of the towne of Taunton haueing seuerall times, for diuers yeares, complained of the straightnes of the bounds of theire towne, and haueing petitioned the Court for some enlargment, the Court, haueing desired some to take a view of what they haue desired, and finding that it is not likely to bee prejudiciall to any, they graunt as followeth, vizt: that the path which goeth from Namassakett to Assonett Riuer bee theire bounds on the southeast, and soe by a line from thence to Baiting Brooke, and from Baiting Brooke a north line till it meet with theire opposite line called the Longe Square, prouided that it come not within two miles of Tetacutt; alsoe, it is graunted that the inhabitants of Taunton that haue interest in the

1663.

5 October.
PRENCE,
GOVʳ.

iron workes there shall haue free libertie to cutt wood on those lands for the vse of theire iron workes, but not any foraigner excepting Richard Church, of Hingham.

Letters of adminnestration is graunted vnto Lydia Rawlins, widdow, to adminnester on the estate of Nathaniel Rawlins, deceased.

Captaine Willett is requested to adminnester an oath to the widdow Abell, of Rehoboth, for the truth of the inventory of the estate of Robert Abell, deceased.

Memorand: that the Court doe consider of the condition of Naomy Siluester, widdow, her deceased husband haueing by his last will and testament left, in an absolute way, but a smale, inconsiderable p̃te of his estate vnto her; that the Court take some prudent course that shee bee considered with that wʰ may bee thought convenient in that respect, shee haueing approued herselfe, as appeers by the testimony of some of her naighbours, to bee a frugall and laborious woman in the procuring of the said estate.

In answare to a complaint made by Gorge Allin, of Sandwich, about the straightnes of a way from his house to the com̃on, the Court haue ordered Benjamine Nye, Edmond Freeman, Juniʳ, and Thomas Tobey to lay out the said way, which is to bee thirty foot wide, and with as little p̃judice as can bee vnto any.

The Court doth allow vnto three Indians that came to the Court to answare the complaint of Ephraim Done, the said Done not appeering att the last Court to prosecute his complaint, to each of them fiue shillinges.

[*52.]

*Leiftenant Torrey, John Bryant, and Willam Barstow are appointed by the Court to lay out a certaine tract of land, formerly graunted to Mʳ Hatherley, aboue Scittuate bounds, next Accord Pond, which said land is to bee layed out according to an order of Court bearing date March, 1662.

The Court certifyed to the towne of Scittuate, that they require them to appoint two men whoe they shall thinke meet to be aded to Leiftenant Torrey, John Bryant, and Willam Barstow, to run the line of Scittuate betwixt Indian Head Riuer Pond and Accord Pond; and incase the towne shall neglect to choose two men, then the Court appoints the said Leiftenant Torrey, John Bryant, and Willam Barstow to run the said line, and this to bee done by the 26 of this instant October.

Marcye Tubbs acknowlidgeth to owe vnto our soū lord the Kinge the sume of . . . . } 20 : 00 : 00

Willam Tubbs the sume of . . . . 10 : 00 : 00

Cleared.

The condition, that if the said Marcye Tubbs bee of good behauior towards our soū lord the Kinge and all his leich people, and appeer att the

COURT ORDERS. 47

Court to bee holden att Plymouth the first Tusday in March next, and not depart the said Court without lycence ; that then, &ᶜ.

Josepth Rogers acknowlidgeth to owe vnto our soū lord the Kinge the sume of . . . . } 20 : 00 : 00

Wiłłam Randall the sume of . . . . 10 : 00 : 00

1663.
5 October.
PRENCE, Govʳ.
Released.

The condition, that if the said Josepth Rogers bee of good behauior towards our soū lord the Kinge and all his leich people, and appeer att the Court to bee holden att Plymouth the first Tusday in March next, and not depart the said Court without lycence ; that then, &ᶜ.

The abouesaid Marcye Tubbs and Josepth Rogers, for theire absean and laciuous behauior each with other, cleared against them by the trauers of a p̄sentment against them, were centanced by the Court to find sureties for theire good behauior as abouesaid, and fined each fifty shillings for the vse of the collonie.

Wiłłam Norkett, for comitting fornication with his now wife, fined fiue pounds.

Nehemiah Bessey, for drinking tobacco, att the meeting house att Sandwich, in the time of exercyse on the Lords day, was fined fiue shillings.

Thomas Ingham, vpon his p̄sentment for detaining yerne from sundrey psons whoe brought it to him to bee wove, is fined ten shillinges.

Ralph Earle, for drawing his wife in an vnciuell manor on the snow, is fined twenty shillings.

Richard Berry, and Wiłłam Griffin and his wife, and Richard Michell and his wife, for playing att cards, fined each of them forty shillings, according to the law, to the vse of the collonie.

These fines are since remited by the Court held in March, 1663.

Abraham Peirce, Junʳ, to bee sumoned to appeer before the major and Mʳ Aldin to answere for his abusiue speeches vsed to his father, and if they shall see cause, to bind him ouer to answere it att the Court.

*The Rates that were leuied on the seuerall Townshipes of this Jurisdiction for the Charge of the Majestrates Table and of the Comissioners and other nessesary Charges of the Collonie, viz, the Officers Wages, &ᶜ.

[*53.]

	li s d
Plymouth, ...	10 : 03 : 06
Duxborrow, ...	05 : 15 : 00
Scitteatt, ...	16 : 12 : 09
Sandwich, ...	09 : 06 : 02
Taunton, ...	09 : 06 : 02
Yarmouth, ...	09 : 06 : 02
Barnstable, ...	10 : 03 : 06

1663.

5 October.
PRENCE,
Gouʳ.

Marshfeild,	. . . .	09 : 06 : 02
Rehoboth,	. . . .	13 : 17 : 09
Eastham,	. . . .	07 : 08 : 06
Bridgwater,	. . . .	04 : 02 : 06
Sowamsett,	. . . .	06 : 17 : 00
Coaksett and Cushenett,	. . . .	02 : 10 : 00

The abouesaid p̃ticulars were ordered by the Court to bee payed in wheat att 4ˢ 6ᵈ p̃ bushell, or in mault att 4ˢ 6ᵈ p̃ bushell, soe much therof as respects the charge of the majestrates table, with other nessesary charges of the collonie, excepting the officers wages, which is to   payed in Indian corne at three shillings p̃ bushell.

---

1 December.
[*54.]

**Att the Court of Assistants held att Plymouth the first Day of December, 1663.*

BEFORE Thomas Prence, Gouʳ,   Thomas Southworth,
   Wiłłam Collyare,   Wiłłam Bradford, and
   John Aldin,   Thomas Hinckley,
   Josias Winslow,

      Assistants, &c.

IN answare to Richard Chadwell his complaint of wronge done vnto him by the laying out of a way through his ground, through a wronge enformation giuen vnto the Court by Gorge Allin, of Sandwich, the Court haue ordered, that the way formerly layed out by Mʳ Vincent, Mʳ Freeman, and Richard Bourne shall stand as formerly, onely that the place att the turning, where it was so straight, shalbee made wider; and those men abouenamed shall further order matters about that way as occation shall require.

Vpon the complaint of Samuell Chandeler, that the range of the land is not sett betwixt Moses Simons & himselfe, the Court haue ordered Wiłłam Paybody, Phillip Delanoy, and Leiftenant Nash to run the range of the said land, according to theire best intelligence and with the best care they can.

Att this Court, Thomas Pope and Gyles Rickard, Seniʳ, for breaking the Kinges peace by striking each other, were fined each three shillinges and foure pence; and concerning the said Pope his takeing away a certaine p̃cell of wood from the said Rickards dore, which was the occation of the abouesaid

COURT ORDERS.

breach of peace, the Court haue ordered, that the said Pope shall returne the said wood againe; and for the said Thomas Pope his striking of the said Rickards wife, and for other turbulent carriages in word and deed, the Court haue centanced him to find surties for his good behauiour vntill the Generall Court to bee holden for this goũment the first Tusday in March, and for longer time if the Court shall see reason.

1 6 6 3.

1 December.
PRENCE,
Gouʳ.

Thomas Pope acknowlidgeth to owe vnto our soũ lord the Kinge the sũme of . . . . } 20 : 00 : 00 [11]

Samuell Dunham the sũme of ten pounds.

The condition, that if the said Thomas Pope bee of good behauior towards our soũ lord the Kinge and all his leich people, and doe appeer att the Generall Court to bee holden for this goũment att Plymouth the first Tusday in March next, and not depart the said Court without lycence; that then, &ᶜ.

Freed of these bonds.

Att this Court, Wiłłam Nicarson, Senjʳ, being summoned, appeered to answare for his purchasing of land of the Indians att Mannamoiett, contrary to order of Court, and owned the same, but sayed that hee had done the same of ignorance, &ᶜ, and intreated the mercye of the Court in that behalfe.

---

*.*Att the Generall Court holden att Plymouth the first Day of March, Anno Doɱ 1663.*

1 6 6 3-4.

1 March.
[*55.]

BEFORE Thomas Prence, Goũ,
John Aldin,
Thomas Willett,
Josias Winslow,

Thomas Southworth,
Wiłłam Bradford, and
Thomas Hinckley,

Assistants, &ᶜ.

ATT this Court, a bill of inditment was prefered against Samuell Howland, of the towne of Duxburrow, in the jurisdiction of Plymouth, in New England, in America, for that by discharging of a fowling peece on the body of Wiłłam Howse, late of Sandwich, in the jurisdiction aforsaid, on the twenty fift of October, anno Doɱ 1663, att a place comõnly called the High Pyne, on the Salt House Beach, in the said jurisdiction, wherby the said House was wounded, languised, and ymediately died.

And the said Howland, being demaunded by whom hee would bee tryed, answared, by God and the countrey.

The names of the jury that went on this tryall are as followeth : —

1663-4.

1 March.
PRENCE,
Govr.

sworne,
{ Mr Josias Winslow, Senr,
Edward Jenkens,
Mr Nicholas Pecke,
Isacke Chettenden,
Thomas Burge, Senr,
James Walker, }

sworne,
{ John Tisdall,
Samuell Fuller,
Josepth Bedle,
Wiłłam Swift,
Myles Blacke,
Wiłłam Barstow. }

The verdict of the said jury is as followeth, verbatim: —

Not guilty of wilfull murder; yett wee find that the said House receiued his deadly wound by Samuell Howlands gun goeing of as it lay on his shoulder.

Vpon the receiueing the said verdict, the said Samuell Howland was openly cleared and sett att liberty, hee discharging all nessesary charges of his imprisonment.

[*56.]

*John Briggs, Senr, of Taunton, for breakeing the Sabbath, fined ten shillings, according to order.

Timothy Hallowey, of Taunton, for misdemenor in frequent kising the wife of John Hathewey, and for being att the house of the said Hathewey att vnseasonable time, and for neglecting to appeer att Court according to sumons, fined twenty shillings.

Ensigne Wiłłams and John Bayley, for breakeing the peace by striking one another, fined each 00 : 03 : 04.

Richard Willis and Josepth Sauory, for breaking the peace by striking one another, fined each 00 : 03 : 04.

These two wee-men were cen-tanced either to sit in the stockes during the pleasure of the Court or to pay the fines heer mencion-ed, and they chose to pay the fine.

Ann, the wife of Wiłłam Hoskins, for speaking most laciuiouse and filthy language to Hester Rickard, fined twenty shillings.

Hester, the wife of John Rickard, for most abcean and filthy speeches, fined twenty shillings.

Richard Willis and Francis Baddow, for breach of the Sabbath, fined each ten shillinges.

Robert Ransome, for breach of the Sabbath, fined ten shillings; the said Ransom, for his turbulent and clamorvs carriage in the Court, was comitted to ward during the pleasure of the Court.

Henery Green, of Taunton, for breach of the peace by striking Phillip Leanard, fined 03 : 04.

In reference to Anthony Annables p̄sentment the Court orders, that it bee signifyed to him that they looke att it as a rash acte of him, worthy of blame, yett soe as judging that it was not any wilfull intension of his to remoue any land markes, properly soe called, and therfore passe it by, yett withall conceiue the grand enquest might see cause, by reason of theire oath, to p̱sent it.

1663-4.
1 March.
PRENCE,
Gouᴿ.

Att this Court, fiue Indians, for abusing Robert Shelley, of Barnstable, by coming one euening into his house and afrighting his family, and other abuses att that time by them offered, were all sentanced to sit in the stockes on some publicke day of meeting, att the discretion of Mʳ Hinckley; and likewise they are to pay vnto the said Robert Shelley, each of them, fiue shillings in worke or otherwise.

*Concerning Robert Harper, for his intollorable insolent disturbance both of the congregation of Barnstable and Sandwich, and for his abusiue and causles railing vpon Mʳ Walley and Mʳ Wiswell, the Court haue sentanced him to bee now publickly whipt, which accordingly was inflicted.

[*57.]

Richard Willis, for rebaldry speeches by him spoken, was sentanced to site in the stockes, which accordingly was p̱formed.

Abraham Hedge, for pound breach, fined fifty shillinges.

An Indian was complained on, att this Court, for abusing of Humphery Tiffency; this was refered to Capt Willett to heare and determine.

Att this Court, Thomas Lucas was publickly whipt for being drunke the third time. Hee was sentanced formerly for being drunke the third time; neuertheles the execution therof was respected vntill hee should bee found drunke againe, which accordingly was witnessed against him, and soe the said punishment was inflicted on him as aforesaid.

Att this Court, Isacke Gurney, for pilfering and other disorderly liueing, was sentanced by the Court to bee whipt, which according was inflicted.

An Order of Court directed to the Townsmen of Scittuate concerning the said Gurney.

To the Townsmen of Scittuate.

These may certify, that Isacke Gurney, whoe was complained against by some of youers for pilfering and other disorderly liueing, hath for the same receiued such punishment as wee judged hee was capeable of beareing; and not finding that hee doth soe properly belonge to any other place as to youer towne, wee can doe noe lesse then send him backe vnto you, with order that hee bee prouided for according to his condition, and that such as you shall place him with doe soe order and goūn him as that soe farr as hee is able hee may bee made to worke for his liueing; and that wheras some extreordinary charge hath arisen by his imprisonment, that it bee by you repayed.

1 6 6 3-4.   And accordingly the said Gurney was by warrant returned from constable to constable backe to Scittuate.

1 March.
Prence,
Gouᴿ.

Att this Court, Wiłłam Maaz, of Taunton, for swearing profanely, sentanced to sitt in the stockes att Taunton on some publicke meeting day; an order to bee sent vp about it.

[*58.]   *A Note of the p̃ticulares of the Liquors that haue bin brought into the Towne of Yarmouth since May, 1663, and envoyced.

Item, Edward Sturgis, Seniʳ, & Mʳ Hedge, one anker.
Item, Edward Sturgis, one anker in June, (63.)
Item, Edward Sturgis, 10 gallons of sacke & 12ˡˡ of lead.
Item, Mʳ Hedge, a quarter caske of liquors, and one barrell of powder, and 100ˡˡ of shott, and 50ˡˡ of ledd.

December, (63.)

Item, Samuell Sturgis, 10 gallons.
Item, Edw̃ Sturgis, Seniʳ, 10 gallons.
Item, Edw̃ Sturgis, Juniʳ, 10 gallons.
Item, Elisha Hedge, 10 gallons.
Item, Mʳ Hedge, 10 gallons & fiue cases.
Item, Samuell Sturgis, 86ˡˡ of shott, & 14ˡˡ of powder & an halfe.
Item, Elisha Hedge, 8 pound of powder.
Item, Mʳ Hedge, 20ˡˡ of powder, & 100ˡˡ of shott, & 40 or 50ˡˡ more.
Item, Robert Eldred, 8 pound of shott.
Item, Mʳ Thacher, 3 cases.

January, (63.)

Mʳ Hedge, Edw̃ Sturgis, Seniʳ, & Samuell Sturgis, 17 gall.
Nathaniell Couell, 10 gallons.
Teage Jones, 10 gałł envoyced, and one case forfeite to the country.
Richard Michell, 10 gall.

ANTHONY THACHER,
ROBERT DENIS

The Account of the Wine, Liquors, Powder, and Shott that hath bine giuen in to mee, that hath bin brought into Barnstable.

The first of Aprill, (63.)

Thomas Huckens, for himselfe, 4 or 5 and 30 gałł of wine and 9 gallons of brandy.

COURT ORDERS. 53

For Josepth Laythorp, 10 gallons of rum; and another time, for Nicholas Dauis & his man, 4 gallons of liquors; the next time hee brought a case of liquors and halfe a hundred of shott.

1 6 6 3-4.

1 March.
FRENCE,
GOUᴿ.

Trustrum Hull, the 4ᵗʰ of June, (63,) 100 gallons of liquors; and in Nouember, (63,) six cases of liquors, and a barrell of powder, & 200 waight of shott, for Mʳ Thomas Clarke; hee brought about 20 gall of rum.

February 29, (63.)   ℞ me,   JOSEPTH LAYTHORP.

*In reference to the longe and troublesome controversye between John Jacob and John Sutton, now att length comeing before vs in a way of chancery, wee, haueing seriously considered the case both as formerly att large posessed of it and as now it stands, see cause to remitt of the bonds forfeited the sōme of twenty three pounds; and doe adjudge that John Sutton doe pay, or cause to bee payed, vnto John Jacob, between this and the 29ᵗʰ day of the next September, in current pay, att a current prise, att the house of Gorge Russell, of Scittuate, the sume of twenty seauen pounds, which incase hee doe not, that then the said Jacob shall haue an execution to bee forthwith leuied on his estate for the abouesaid sume of twenty seauen pounds; and that the said John Sutton is to giue the said John Jacob sufficient notice of the time of the deliuery of the said sume att the place abouenamed.

[*59.]

In reference vnto the complaint of Richard Tayler, of the Rocke, against Thomas Starr, that hee had taken a peece of timber a way from him, the Court haue ordered the said Thŏ Starr to returne vnto the said Rich Tayler another peece of timber as good as that hee tooke away by the 22ᶜᵒⁿᵈ of this instant March, and to pay all damages the said Tayler hath bine att about the recouery of the said peece of timber; which if hee shall neglect to doe, hee shall pay vnto the said Rich Tayler three pounds, out of which sume hee is to take his said charges.

                                                       li   s   d

The charge comes in all vnto . . . . 01 : 09 : 06

Forasmuch as great wronge hath bin don by diuers of the inhabitants of the towne of Plymouth, for want of bounds of the first lotts towards Plain Dealing, the Court doth order, that the want of measure in the breadth of the lotts on the south side of the lotts of Mʳ John Winslow shall haue theire measure on the south side vpon the comon aboue the acrees, and that Sarjeant Morton and Gorge Bonum lay them forth att the first oppertunity, and giue in to the clarke what bounds they make, to prevent trouble for the future.

*Concerning the complaint of John Allin, of Sandwich, against Keencomsett, that hee hath not satisfyed an agreement, bearing date June 3, 1663, about the killing of a mare, the Court hath ordered, that wheras the said

[*60.]

1663-4.
1 March.
Prence,
Gouʳ.

Keencomsett, by his agents, hath left three barrells of oysters with Nicholas Dauis, by the said Allins former order, that hee shall accept of them as p̃te of pay for the said mare, att prise current.

This Court, takeing notice of such euidence as hath bin produced for the clearing of a controuersy between John Tompson, plaintiffe, and Richard Wright, in reference to a p̃cell of land att Namassakett, doe allow an agreement between the said p̃ties, which was ordered heer to bee entered, as followeth, vizṣ: that the said p̃ties shall haue equall share of the land allotted to Francis Cooke att Namaskett aforsaid, prouided that they bee equall in bearing the charge about the said land.

In regard of much abuse of liquors in the towne of Yarmouth, this Court doth call in any lycence formerly giuen to Edward Sturgis, Seniʳ, and doe require that hee forbeare to draw wine or liquors for the future without further order from the Court.

And likewise, vnderstanding that James Leanard, of Taunton, haueing buryed his wife, and in that respect not being soe capeable of keeping a publicke house, there being alsoe another ordinary in the towne, doe call in the said Leanard his lycence.

Richard Bullocke, of Rehoboth, is alowed by the Court to keep the ferrey there, soe that hee make a horse boate to ferrey ouer horses, and is alsoe lycenced to sell liquors to strangers and passengers, but not to towne dwellers.

Concerning the complaint of the sachem, Phillip, that some of the English of Rehoboth haue felled some quantity of timber in a swamp belonging to him, the Court haue refered the hearing and determining of the said case to Capt Willett.

In reference to the complaint of Thomas Greenfeild against Henery Saunders, for killing of the said Greenfeilds cow, the Court doth order him to returne as good a cow, or the vallue therof.

‡In reference vnto the complaint of Humphrey Tiffeney, of Rehoboth, that an Indian there hath offered him some abuse, this ⌃ refered to Captaine Willett to heare and determine.‡

[*61.]
*Capt Willett is appointed by the Court to take securitie of Mistris Newman, in the behalfe of the Court, for adminnestration on the estate of Mʳ Samuell Newman, decesed.

Łres of adminnestration graunted vnto the said Mistris Newman, together with her son, Mʳ Samuell Newman, Juniʳ, to adminnester on the said estate.

Łres of adminnestration graunted vnto the widdow, Joannah Abell, to adminnester on the estate of Robert Abell, deceased.

COURT ORDERS. 55

Capt Willett is likewise ordered by the Court to take securite of her, in 1663-4.
the Courts behalfe, for her true and faithfull adminestration on the said estate.
Łres of adminnestration graunted to Mr Nicholas Pecke and Samuell 1 March.
Pecke to adminnester on the estate of Mr Josepth Pecke, deceased. PRENCE, Gou^R.

Łres of adminnestration graunted to John Ensigne to adminnester on
the estate of Thomas Ensigne, deceased.

Att this Court, Thomas Rogers, of Eastham, was pmitted and authorised
by the Court to adminnester vpon the estate of Josepth Rogers, Juni^r, deceased, as his heire.

Mr Thomas Walley, Juni^r, and Mr Wright, are allowed by the Court to
retaile stronge liquors att Barnstable, soe that they sell not lesse then a gallon
to any, and that they giue in an account therof, and the psons to whom sold.

Mr Hinckley is appointed by the Court to adminnester an oath to the
widdow Lewis for the truth of the inventory of the estate of Gorge Lewis,
deceased, and to take securitie in the Courts behalfe for her true and faithfull
adminnestration on the said estate.

And likewise Mr Hinckley is authorised by the Court to adminnester an oath
to the witnesses of the last will and testament of Mistris Jone Swift, deceased.

The 30th of March, 1664. Thomas Lucas acknowlidg- } 20 : 00 : 00   1664.
eth to owe vnto our soû lord the Kinge the sume of }
Stephen Bryant the sume of . . . . 05 : 00 : 00   30 March.
And Gorge Bonum the sume of . . . . 05 : 00 : 00

The condition, that if the said Thomas Lucas bee of good behauior Released June
towards our soû lord the Kinge and all his leich people, and appeer att the 11th, 1664.
Generall Court to bee holden for this goûment att Plymouth the first Tusday
in June, 1664, and there bee reddy to answare for his abusing of his wife to
her danger and hazard, as alsoe for his railing and reuiling others, to the desturbance of the Kings peace, and not depart the said Court without lycence ;
that then, &ĉ.

*Aprill 7th, 1664. Wiłłam Witherell acknowlidgeth to }^{ll} 20 : 00   [*62.]
owe vnto our soû lord the Kinge the sume of . . . . }   7 April.
Hezekiah Hore the sume of . . . . 10 : 00

The condition of the abouesaid obligation is, that if Wiłłam Witherell Released.
bee of good behauior towards our soû lord the Kinge and all his leich people,
and especially to keep from libelling, and appeer att the Generall ^ to
bee holden att Plymouth the first Tusday in June next, and not depart the
same without lycence ; that then, &ĉ.

Gyles Gilbert acknowlidgeth to owe vnto our soû lord the } ^{ll} 20 : 00
Kinge the sume of . . . . }
Gorḡ Watson the sume of . . . . 10 : 00

56   PLYMOUTH COLONY RECORDS.

1664.

7 April.
PRENCE,
Govr.
Released.

The condition of the abouesaid obligation is, that if Gyles Gilbert bee of good behauior towards our sofl lord the King and all his leich people, and especially to keep from libelling, and appeer att the Generall Court to bee holden att Plymouth the first Tusday in June next, and not depart the said Court without lycence; that then, &c̄.

The cause of the bonds aboue written is, that wheras James Walker, being a p̄tenor in the saw mills att Taunton, complained of great hurt done to the said saw mill by som̄ psons that came in the night in a fellonious manor and stole away seuerall thinges, and did great spoile, and left a libellous paper behind them; and it being suspected that the abouebounden Wil̄lam Witherell and Gyles Gilbert were the psons, or some of them, that haue done the said mischiffe, they, the said Wil̄lam Witherell and Gyles Gilbert, being sum̄oned, appeered att Plymouth before the Gofl and Captaine Southworth, on the day and yeare first aboue written, and being examined, it appeered that they were guilty in the aforsaid p̄ticulares, and therfore the said majestrates saw cause to take the said bonds of them for theire good behauior, &c̄.

---

3 May.
[*63.]

Att the Court of Assistants held att Plymouth the 3^d Day of May, 1664.

BEFORE Thomas Prence, Gofl,   John Aldin,
Josias Winslow, and
Assistants, &c̄.

Released.

ATT this Court, Josepth Gray and Samuell Linkorn, being sum̄oned, appeered to answare for being p̄tenors in doeing great hurt to the saw mill att Taunton, coming in the night in a fellonious manor, and leaueing a libellous paper behind them, &c̄; and being examined about the p̄mises, owned that they were guilty therin, and therfore for the p̄sent were sentanced to find surties for theire good behauior.

    Josepth Gray acknowlidgeth to owe vnto our sofl lord   } ^{li}
        the King the sum̄e of . . . . } 20 : 00 : 00
    Gorge Watson the sum̄e of . . . . 10 : 00 : 00

Released.

The condition, that if the said Josepth Gray bee of good behauior towards our sofl lord the King and all his leich people, and especially to keep from libelling, and appeer att the Generall Court to bee holden att Plymouth the first Thursday in June next, and not depart the said Court without lycen̄; that then, &c̄.

Samuell Linkorn acknowlidgeth to owe vnto our soū lord the King the sume of . . . . } ^{li} 20 : 00 : 00

Thomas Leanard the sume of . . . . 10 : 00 : 00

1664.

3 May,
PRENCE,
Gov^R.
Released.

The condition, that if the said Samuell Linkorn bee of good behauior towards our soū lord the Kinge and all his leich people, and especially keep from libelling, and appeer att the Court to bee holden att Plymouth the first Thursday in June next, and not depart the said Court without lycence; that then, &c.

Wheras, att this Court, the aboue bounden Joseph Gray and Samuell Linkorne, together with Gorge Watson, complained of great wrong, sustained not onely by them, but by the whole towne of Taunton, by James Walker his neglecting, according to engagement, to leaue a sufficient passage for the herrings or alewines to goe vp in the riuer on which the saw mill standeth, the Court directed an order to the constable of Taunton to require him to signify vnto the said James Walker that hee speedily take course that a free passage bee left for the goeing vp of the alewiues in the said riuer whiles yett some p̄te of the season remaines of theire goeing vpp.

*Att this Court, vpon the complaint of Wilłam Browne against Henery Saunders, for non payment of a debt of thirty shillinges in butter and 3^s 6^d in other pay, the Court awarded the said Saunders to pay or cause to bee payed to the said Browne, with all conuenient speed, the sume of 40 shilł in current comoditie att money prise; and incase this bee not done within one month after the date heerof, that the constable of Sandwich shall leuy and take soe much of the goods or chattles of the said Saunders as will satisfy the said sume of 40^s to the said Browne.

[*64.]

Att this Court, a judgment of fifteen shillings, wanting a peney, was graunted vnto James Cole, Seni^r, against Henery Saunders, for none payment of a debt due to the said Cole from the said Saunders.

Att this Court, James Shaw complained against an Indian, called Wawanquin, for killing a cow of his in a trapp; and forasmuch as it appeered to the Court that the said Shaw had taken and disposed of the said cow, viz$\}$, the flesh and hyde of her, and that the said Indian had none of it, the said Indian is awarded by the Court to pay vnto the said Shaw the sume of thirty shillings, in good and considerable pay, with all conuenient speed.

Concerning a controversye betwixt John Rushell, of Acushena, and an Indian, about a pretended cure wrought by him on the said Indian, whoe had bin sicke, the said Rushell afeirming that the Indian had giuen him his gun in satisfaction for the said cure, hee complaining that sundry Indians, to the number of fiue, came into his house, and in an hostile manor tooke away the

1664.

3 May.
PRENCE,
GOVR.

said gun, the Court ordered, that for his charge and paynes with the said Indian as towards his cure, that hee, the said Indian, shall pay vnto the said Rushell the sume of twenty shillings, and his gun to bee deposeted in the constables hands till the said 20ˢ is payed; and that the said Indians, viz͠, Woomham, Pagenatowin, Weesunka, Sucquatamake, and Chacapaquin, for theire said hostile and insolent carriage in takeing away the said gun, bee fined to the vse of the collonie fiue pounds, viz͠, twenty shillinges a peece; and wheras the said Rushell was found blame worthy, in takeing vp of an axe, and indeauoring to improue it against the said Indians in a turbulent and dangerous manor, the Court reproued him for his soe doeing, and admonished him to take heed of doeing noe more soe, as hee will answare it att his p̃rill.

[*65.]

*Att this Court, Hannah Churchill, widdow, desired that the one halfe of the land graunted to William Pontus, being in the diuision of lands att Namassakett and places adjacent, might bee confeirmed vnto her and her heires and assignes for euer: the Court, considering of her request, and serching the records conserning both the will of the said deceased William Pontus and the manor of the graunt of the said lands, haue, with the consent likewise of Phillip Delanoy, whoe was then p̃sent, and with the consent of Mary, his wife, the other daughter of the said William Pontus, settled the one halfe of the whole intire share of land lying and being att Namassakett or places adjacent, with all and singulare the meddows and all other appurtenances thervnto belonging, vpon and vnto the said Hannah Churchill, widdow, to her and her heires and assignes for euer.

Att this Court, Mr Constant Southworth requested conserning a smale p̃cell of vpland ground lying neare vnto his meddow, being alreddy his by graunt and purchase, might bee settled and confeirmed vnto him; and wheras there is some controversy between some of the naighbors about the bounds and ranges of theire lands lying neare vnto the said lands of the said Constant Southworth, the Court haue appointed Phillip Delanoy, Leiftenant Nash, and William Paybody to settle the bounds of the said p̃cell of vpland vnto the said Constant Southworth.

Ɫers of adminnestration was graunted, att this Court, vnto Syselia Fish, widdow, to adminnester on the estate of Mr John Fish, deceased.

March the 4, 1663. Wheras, att the Court of Assistants holden att Plymouth the first day of December, 1663, William Nicarson, being summoned, appeared to make answare for his eregulare purchaseing of land of the Indians, contrary to the order of Court bearing date anno 1643; and after much patience and forbearance of the Court, hee, the said Nicarson, retaineing, posessing, and improueing of the said land, contrary to the aforsaid order, the Court saw cause to issue out warrants, in his ma^ties name, to the cheife marshall, in reference thervnto, the tenure wherof followeth in the next page : —

1664.
3 May.
[PRENCE, GOVERNOR.]

*The Coppy of a Warrant directed to the Cheife Marshall of the Jurisdiction of New Plymouth, as followeth.

[*66.]

To the Cheife Marshall of the Jurisdiction of New Plymouth, greet.

Wheras, att a Generall Court holden att Plymouth, anno 1643, it was enacted by the Court that noe psons whatsoeuer should purchase or buy any land of the Indians within this goũment but such as the Court should authorise thervnto, vpon the penaltie of forfeiting fiue pounds to the collonie for euery acree of land soe eregularly bought or purchased ; and wheras it hath bin abundantly manifested that Wilłam Nicarson, somtimes of Yarmouth, within this jurisdiction, hath, contrary to the said order of Court, purchased or bought a very large tract of land of the Indians of Mannomoiett, to the prejudice of many the more ancient inhabitants and freemen of this jurisdiction, and that the Court hath vsed great indulgency towards the said Nicarson by sundry tenders and much patience, if happily hee might apply himselfe to them for his owne indempnitie either in whole or in p̃te, which haueing bine by him, the said   ̭   , obstinately refused, and resolued to carry on his owne eregulare way in contempt of authoritie, to the great detriment of the whole, the Court finds themselues nessesitated att the last to put forth in a regulare way to giue some checke to his vnsufferable insolencyes by leuying some p̃te of the penaltie att present, and soe to proceed further afterwards as they shall see just cause. These are, therfore, in his ma^ties name, to will and comaund you, on receipt heerof, to leuy the sume of two hundred pounds of the goods or chattles of the said Wilłam Nicarsons, or soe much therof as shalbee found within this goũment, as p̃te of the penaltie due for the breach of the aforsaid order, and see that they bee duely prised according to order of Court, and make returne heerof and of youer doeings heerin vnto the Treasurer.

THOMAS PRENCE, Goũ.
JOHN ALDIN,
THOMAS WILLETT,
JOSIAS WINSLOW,
THOMAS SOUTHWORTH,
THOMAS HINCKLEY.

Dated att Plymouth the 4th of March, 1663.

1664.

8 June.
PRENCE,
Gov^R.
[*67.]

*Att the Generall Court of Election holden att Plymouth the eight of June, 1664.

BEFORE Thomas Prence, Goft,   Thomas Southworth,
John Aldin,   Wiltam Bradford, and
Josias Winslow,   Thomas Hinckley,
Assistants, &c.

MR THOMAS PRENCE was chosen Gou^r, and sworne.

Wiltam Collyare,
John Aldin,
Thomas Willett,
Josias Winslow,   } were chosen Assistants, and sworne.
Thomas Southworth,
Wiltam Bradford, and
Thomas Hinckley,

Major Josias Winslow and Captaine Thomas Southworth were chosen comissioners for the following yeare, and Mr Thomas Hinckley is the next in nomination.

Mr Constant Southworth was chosen Treasurer, and sworne.

The names of the deputies that serued att this Court and the adjournments therof are as followeth:—

John Dunham, Senr,   Edward Sturgis,
Robert Finney,   James Mathews,
Ephraim Morton,+   Nathaneell Bacon,+
Nathaniell Warren,+   John Chipman,+
Mr Constant Southworth,   Ensigne Eames,+
Leiftenant James Torrey,   Anthony Snow,+
Isacke Bucke,+   Mr Stephen Paine,+
Richard Bourne,   Leiftenant Hunt,+
James Skiffe,   Leiftenant Freeman,
Wilt Harvey,   Josias Cooke,
‡Leiftenant Wyatte,‡   Wiltam Britt,+
Richard Williames,+   John Willis.

COURT ORDERS.

*The Grand Enquest.

1664.

8 June.
PRENCE,
Gou^r.
[*68.]

sworne, { Wiłłam Sabin,
John Hollett,
John Allin,
Nicholas Biram,
Henery Bourne,
John Hall,
John Ottis,
John Tracye,
Mr Josias Standish,
Thomas Little,
John Tompson,

sworne, { Wiłłam Harlow,
Samuell Dunham,
Stephen Winge,
Josepth Holly,
Samuell Williames,
John Deane,
John Burgis,
John Caruer,
Thomas Paine,
Arther Hathewey.

The Constables of the seuerall Townes.

Plym̃, ... Samuell Sturtivant.
Duxb̃, ... Josepth Andrews.
Scittũ, ... { Isake Chettenden,
Wiłłam Curtis.
Sand̃, ... Thomas Burgis, Seni^r.
Taunton, ... Francis Smith.
Barnst̃, ... Josepth Laythorp.
Yarmouth, ... Samuell Hall.
Marshfeĩ, ... { John Thomas,
Francis Crooker.
Rehob̃, ... Samuell Newman.
Eastham, ... Daniel Cole.
Bridgw̃, ... Samuell Packer.
Dartmouth, ... James Shaw.

Surveyors for the Highwaies.

Plym̃, ... { Mr Barnes,
Jacob Cooke,
Thomas Morton.

*Att this Court, Mr Thomas Walley, Seni^r, Mr Keith, Benajah Dunham, and Samuell Hunt were admitted to bee freemen of this corporation, and sworne. [*69.]

Mr Thomas Crosbey and Thomas Rogers stand propounded.

1664.

8 June.
PRENCE,
GOVR.

Att this Court, the body of the freemen of this corporation being assembled, it was agreed and voated by them that an adresse shalbee made vnto his ma^tie for the further confeirmation of our pattent with as much conveniency as may bee; and for the management and ordering of matters concerning it, both for the raiseing of moneyes and appointing of men to bee imployed therin, the countrey haue refered the same to the Court of Majestrates and Deputies.

The body of the freemen of this corporation, being assembled in Court, haue ordered, and doe heerby declare theire resolution to maintaine theire just rightes, which for many yeares they haue binc posessed of, in all those lands from Cape Codd to Saconett Point, with Pochasett, Causumsett, and the lands about Rehoboth to Patuckett Riuer, and as farr vp the said riuer till wee meet the Massachusetts line, which crosses the said riuer, and thence to Coahassett as the line runs.

And that incase any pson or psons bee seated, or shall seate themselues, within any the said lands, or cause any cattle to bee brought within the said bounds, or otherwise acte to our treaspas without leaue from this goûment, and not withdraw after warning giuen them, that then some effectual course bee taken for the remouall of them.

And for that end, it was likewise voated that letters should bee directed from this Generall Court to the Goû and Councell of Road Iland, for the asserting of our just rights as aforsaid, and that they would imploy theire interest ouer such to reclaime them as haue thrust in vpon vs neare to Pochassett or elswhere.

It is ordered by the Court, that if comissioners shall come out of England, and incase, by the prouidence of God, they shall either ariue in this harbour or come by land, that some psons bee deputed to bee in a reddines to accomodate them in a ciuill manor behoofull to theire condition; and for that end that the Treasurer bee prouided with nessesaries for theire intertaīment; and that incase there shalbee such occation, that a generall rate bee made to defray the charge therof.

[*70.]   *It was ordered by the Court, for the supply of our honored Goû, that it bee graunted to giue out of the oyle, if it come in, the sume of twenty pounds, and likewise twenty pounds more out of that which appertaineth to the countrey, for Keñebecke, and this to bee ordered for this p̃sent yeare; but if the oyle shall fayle, then to make the supply out of that which is to come to the countrey for Keñebecke.

Forasmuch as the countrey is indebted to the Treasurer in money fifteen pounds, and likewise money to bee provided for the comissioners, wee judge

COURT ORDERS.

it nessesary that there bee a leuy of sixty pounds, the one halfe in money, the other halfe in wheat or pease, and the money to bee payed in the month of July next ensueing, for the defraying of the aformensioned charge and other charges that appeers to vs that will ensue, and the other halfe to bee payed in wheat or pease in the month of October next.

1664.
8 June.
PRENCE,
Govr.

The Proportions of the seuerall Townes as they are rated to the said Sume.

Plymouth,	05 : 11 : 00
Duxburrow,	03 : 00 : 00
Scittuate,	09 : 01 : 06
Sandwich,	05 : 01 : 00
Taunton,	05 : 01 : 00
Yarmouth,	05 : 01 : 00
Barnstable,	05 : 11 : 00
Marshfeild,	05 : 01 : 00
Rehoboth,	07 : 11 : 06
Eastham,	04 : 01 : 00
Bridwater,	02 : 10 : 00
Dartmouth,	01 : 00 : 00
Sowamsett,	02 : 05 : 00

The Acount of the Charges expended att the Runing of the Line betwixt the Jurisdiction of the Massachusetts and ours.

This was allowed by the Court.

Item, money expended by the Treasurer,	07 : 06 : 06
Item, for ourselues and horses 9 daies, att 5 shilli p day,	06 : 15 : 00
Item, for a horse and a man of Major Winslowes, 6 dayes,	01 : 00 : 00
Item, for William Barstow 9 dayes, att thre shill p day,	01 : 07 : 00
	16 : 12 : 06

Besides a horse and a man that went on our account, and was forgotten to bee reconed by them; and the halfe of the charge of a surveyor, both now and formerly, att 20 shillings p day.

*The Court haue ordered the sume of six pounds vnto Captaine Southworth and Captaine Bradford, viz$, to each of them three pound, for and

[*71.]

1 6 6 4.

8 June.
Prence,
Govr.

towards theire time & paines in theire late journey to Conecticott on the countreyes busines.

The Court haue allowed vnto Nathaniell Bacon and Robert Finney, for being imployed in the countreyes busines in viewing land, each of them twenty shillings.

Concerning a controuersy betwixt sundry Indians, vizt, Mattaquason, sachem of Mannomoiett, and John Quason, his son, on the one p̃te, and Wil̃am Nicarson, on the other p̃te, about bounds of lands bought by the said Nicarson of the said Indians, the Court, haueing heard what can bee said on both p̃ties, haue ordered that some psons bee deputed by the Court to giue meeting to the said Nicarson, to take knowlidge of the bounds of the said lands, and make report therof to the Court.

Wheras Wil̃am Nicarson, of Yarmouth, hath for some time since illegally purchased a certaine tract of land att Mannomoictt, contrary to the order of Court, and that, notwithstanding great patience and forbearance of the Court, hee still psisteth on in his way of posession and improucing of the said land; and haueing nothing to bee found to answare the penaltie of the law, the Generall Court of freemen, being assembled, haue voated that the said land shalbee put to sale, and improued to the vse of the collonie, onely that the said Nicarson shall haue a portion therof allowed vnto him, accordingly as the Court or the psons deputed in the behalfe of the countrey to make sale therof shall thinke meet; which said psons are Mr Hinckley, Mr Bacon, Leiftenant Freeman, and Wil̃am Bassett, they or any three of them; and the Goᵣ is appointed by the countrey to affix the common seale of the goᵣment vnto such deeds as shall ^ made to any for the sale therof.

It was alsoe voted by the Court of Majestrates and Deputies, that the said Nicarson shalbee wholly dispossessed of the said lands before it bee sold or otherwise desposed of.

Cornett Studson and Nathaniel Warren are appointed by the Court to lay out a certaine tract or pcell of land graunted to Mr Browne, lying neare Patuckett Riuer, northward of Mr Blackstones.

Mr Hinckley, in the behalfe of John Coggen, sollicited the Court to haue libertie to make sale of the land of Henery Coggen, his father, deceased: the Court, haueing certaine inteligence that hee, the said John Coggen, is heire apparent vnto the said Henery Coggen, and that hee is of age, haue giuen leaue to him, the said John Coggen, to make sale of the lands as hee shall see cause.

It is ordered by the Court, that the generall training shalbee the first Wensday in July next, and to bee att Yarmouth this yeare.

[*72.]

*Leiftenant Josepth Rogers is reestablished in to the office of a leiftenant of the milletary companie of Eastham.

COURT ORDERS.

Serjeant Ephraim Morton is appointed and approued of by the Court to bee leiftenant of the milletary companie of Plymouth.

Mr Josepth Bradford is appointed and approued of by the Court to bee ensigne bearer of the milletary companie of Plymouth.

Henery Smith is appointed and approued of by the Court to bee ensigne bearer of the milletary companie of Rehoboth.

John Marchant is appointed and approued of by the Court to bee ensigne bearer of the milletary companie of Yarmouth.

It is ordered by the Court, that the generall training shalbee this yeare the first Wensday in July next.

Att this Court, all that tracte of land comonly called and knowne by the name of Acushena, Ponagansett and Coaksett is allowed by the Court to bee a townshipe; and the inhabitants therof haue libertie to make such orders as may conduce to theire comon good in towne consernments; and that the said towne bee henceforth called and knowne by the name of Dartmouth. <small>Dartmouth made a towne.</small>

Josias Cooke is deputed and appointed by the Court to make contracts of marriage in the township of Eastham, and likewise to adminnester an oath to giue euidence to the grand enquest as occation may require, and likewise to adminnester an oath to witnesses for the tryall of a case as occation may require, as alsoe, incase any stranger shall haue occation to comence a suite against any pson, it shalbee lawfull for the said Josias Cooke to issue out warrants in his maties name to bind ouer the said pson to answare the suite att the Court att Plymouth by attachment or summons as occation may require. <small>This is otherwise ordered by the Court.</small>

‡Leiftenant James Torrey is authorised by the Court to make contracts of marriage in the towne of Scittuate as occation may require, and likewise to adminnester an oath to witnesses for the tryall of a case as occation may require, and likewise to adminnester an oath to giue evidence to the grand enquest as occation may require; and alsoe, in case any stranger shall haue occation to comence a suite against any pson, it shalbee lawfull for the said Leiftenant Torrey to issue out warrants in his maties name to bind ouer the said psons to answare the suit att the Court att ⁁ by attachment or summons as occation may require.‡ <small>‡And otherwise to supena wittnesses to giue euidence in any case to appeer att the Court at Plyms.‡ This is otherwise ordered.</small>

*Mr Stephen Paine is authorised by the Court to make contracts of marriage in the towne of Rehoboth as occation may require, and likewise to adminnester an oath to giue euidence to the grand enquest as occation may require, and likewise to adminnester an oath to any witnes for the tryall of a case as occation may require; and incase any stranger or forraigner shall haue occation to comence a suite against any pson, it shalbee lawfull for the said Stephen Paine to bind ouer the said pson to answare the said suite by issue- <small>[*73.] This is otherwise ordered by the Court.</small>

1664.

8 June.
PRENCE,
Govʳ.

ing forth warrants in his maᵗⁱᵉˢ name to cause them to appeer att the Court att Plymouth to answare the said complainant.

In reference to the complaint of sundry of the inhabitants of the towne of Taunton against James Walker and others, for the restraining of the alewiues from goeing vp according to theire vsuall manor by reason of a sawmill in thire herring riuer, by which obstruction of the said fish the said towne hath and is in danger to suffer much damage, this Court hath ordered, that betwixt this date and the next season of the fishes goeing vp, they, the said owners of the mill, shall make or cause to ^ made a free, full, and sufficient passage for the goeing vp of the said fish, or otherwise, vpon the further complaint of the towne, the Court will take an effectuall course that the same shalbee done.

Wilłam Paybody, for makeing a writing for the seperating of Wilłam Tubbs from Marcye, his wife, in reference vnto theire marriage bond, is fined by the Court the summe of fiue pounds; and Leiftenant Nash and John Sprague, for subscribing as witnesses to the said writing, are fined each three pounds.

Att this Court, a protest was openly published, att the request of Wilłam Tubbs, against Mercye, his wife, as disowneing all debts that shee shall make vnto any from this time forward, as not intended to pay any of them to any pson whatsoeuer.

Att this Court, Wilłam Witherell, Mʳ Gyles Gilbert, Josepth Gray, and Samuell Linkhorne, were sentanced by the Court to pay each a fine of twenty shillinges for an abuse done to a saw mill att Taunton belonging to James Walker and others, by coming in the night and breaking downe some p̃te of the said mill, and for takeing away seuerall thinges from the same.

In reference vnto the complaint of an Indian called Josepth, liueing neare Taunton, that Mʳ Gyles Gilbert had killed one of his hoggs, the Court, haueing heard the complaint and defence, haue some ground to suspect that the said hogg was killed by the said Gyles Gilbert, haue therfore ordered, that incase the said Gilbert shall and doe pay vnto the said Indian twenty shillings att his demaund, that then the said case shalbee soe issued; but if otherwise, vpon the further complaint of the said Indian of neglect heerof, the said Gilbert is responsable to answare his complaint att Plymouth, and for that end that Thomas Jacus, the servant of the said Gilbert, bee warned to appeer the next Court to giue testimony in the × ×

These fines are both remited.

‡Thomas Lucas, for swearing, sentanced to sit in the stockes during the pleasure of the Court, according to order, which accordingly was pformed.‡

Dorcas Presberry, for comitting fornication, fined fiue pounds. Gorge Barlow stands engaged in her behalfe to see it payed.

COURT ORDERS.

*The p̃sons nominated to take vp the Excise in the seuerall Townshipes of this Goũment, whoe are likewise to take notice of what Liquors, &c̃, are brought into the Goũment. See the Orders in the Booke of Lawes.

1 6 6 4.

8 June.
Prence, Govr.
[*74.]

Plymouth,	{ John Morton, William Harlow.
Duxbur̃,	Benjamine Bartlett.
Scittuã,	{ Edward Jenkens, John Daman.
Sand,	{ James Skiffe, Thomas Tobey.
Taunton,	{ James Walker, Francis Smith.
Yarmouth,	{ Mr Hawes, Richard Tayler.
Barnstable,	{ Henery Cobb, Nathaniell Bacon.
Marshfeild,	John Bourne.
Rehoboth,	{ Leiftenant Hunt, Richard Bullocke.
Eastham,	{ John Done, Juni^r, William Walker.
Bridgwater,	John Willis.

Libertie is graunted vnto Robert Finney to looke out a p̃cell of land for accom̃odation about Sepecan or elsewhere, and to make report of it to the Court, that soe a competency may bee graunted vnto him.

The Court giues libertie to Josias Cooke, Leiftenant Josepth Rogers, Gyles Hopkins, Henery Sampson, and Experience Michell to looke out a p̃cell of land lying betwixt Bridgwater and the Bay line for theire accom̃odation.

The Court haue graunted vnto John Cooke fifteen acrees of meddow lying som̃where neare the bounds of Dartmouth; and hee hath libertie to purchase it of the Indians, soe as it be not meddow alreddy graunted to any other.

Anthony Snow, Ensigne Marke Eames, Josepth Warren, Richard Wright, William Harlow, Nathaniell Morton, Ephraim Morton, William Paybody, John Dunham, Juni^r, John Rogers haue libertie to looke out land for accom̃odations, and to make report therof to the Court, that soe a competency may bee allowed to them. [*75]

*Att this Court, sundry of the towne of Hingham appeered, and desired to buy a p̃cell or tract of land of the countrey lying betwixt the Bay line and

See records of sale of lands, 1664.

1664.

8 June.
PRENCE,
GOVᴿ.

This land was layed out afterwards, by order of the Court, by John Whitmarsh and John Jacob, and is att the path that leads from Waymouth to Bridgwater, as it is said, a little brooke running through the same.

Accord Pond and the land graunted to Mʳ Hatherley ; and the Court declared themselues willing to sell it, and pitched a prise, and refered the agreement to the Treasurer in the countreyes behalfe.

In reference vnto the request of Phineas Pratte and the Elder Bates, in the behalfe of the children of Clement Briggs, that wheras they, the said Phineas Pratt and Clement Briggs, haue not had theire proportions of land with others of this jurisdiction formerly called purchassers or old comers, that they might haue some consideration of land in that respect in a p̃cell or tract of land lying neare vnto the line betwixt the Massachusetts jurisdiction and vs, neare vnto Waymouth, the Court doth graunt vnto the said Phineas Pratt and vnto two of the said Clement Briggs his sonnes, viz§, Dauid Briggs and Remember Briggs, three hundred and fifty acrees of the said lands, with all and singulare the appurtenances thervnto belonging, vnto them and theire heires and assignes for euer, viz§, vnto the said Phineas Pratt two p̃tes of three of the said three hundred and fifty acrees, and the remainder therof vnto the two sonnes of the said Clement Briggs afornamed ; and this to bee layed forth for them by John Jacob, of Hingham, and John Whitmarsh, of Waymouth ; and incase any Indian or Indians shall heerafter lay claime vnto the said lands, that the said Phineas Prat and the Elder Bates stand bound to the Court to answare the charge of the purchase therof and all other nessesary charges about the said land.

11 June.

An Order sent downe to Sandwich, as followeth.

To Mʳ Freeman, Richard Bourne, Mʳ Dexter, James Skiffe, and William Bassett, greet, &c̃.

Wheras Nanquatnumacke hath complained of wrong done to him in his corne by horses of Sandwich, these are to request you to take some serious and effectuall course that the poor man may haue his corne preserued from the horses, either by keeping of them away or some other course, this sommer, or otherwise wee shalbee in some straight what to doe in the case.

This is the Courts desire and order.

              p̃ me,   NATHANIELL MORTON, Clark.

Plymouth, June 11ᵗʰ, 1664.

[*76.]
27 July.

*Witnesseth these p̃sents, that I, William Barstow, Senिʳ, of Scittuate, haue bargained, couenanted, and agreed, and doe by these p̃sents fully and absolutely bargaine, couenant, and agree, with Mʳ Constant Southworth and Major Josias Winslow in the behalfe of this colloney of New Pymouth, concerning the repaireing and maintaining of a certaine bridge, com̃only called

COURT ORDERS. 69

Barstowes Bridge, standing vpon the North Riuer, as followeth, viz͡t : that in consideration of twenty pounds sterling of them in hand receiued, I shall forthwith repaire the aforsaid bridge, and shall from the day of the date heerof, during the full and compleate tearme of twenty whole yeares, maintaine and keep or cause to bee maintained in good and sufficient repaire, to serue the countrey for transportation of passengers, horses, chattle, and all such vse as they shall ordinarily put it to ; for the true pformance wherof, I, the said Barstow, doe bind and make ouer the house and land on which I now dwell, a smale tract alreddy disposed vnto my son, Moses Simons, excepted, vnto the said Major Winslow and Constant Southworth abouesaid, in the behalfe of the said collonie of New Plymouth, as securitie for my true and faithfull pformance of the abouemencioned agreement. In witnes wherof I haue heervnto sett my hand and seale this 27th day of July, 1662.

1664.
27 July.
Prence,
Gouʳ.

      WILLAM BARSTOW, and a seale.

In the presence of
 Sarah Standish,
 Penelope Winslow.

 This Court, begun the 8th of June, 1664, is adjourned vntill the last Tusday in September next, vnlesse the majestrates shall see cause to summon a Court sooner.

 Concerning two p̃sentments, the one against Samuell Sabin, of Rehoboth, and Mary Billington, and the other against Mary Marriho, of Yarmoth, the former, viz͡t, that of Rehoboth, is refered to Captaine Willett to heare and determine ; the latter, viz͡t, of Yarmouth, is refered to Mʳ Hinckley to heare and determine.

---

*Att the Court of Assistants held att Plymouth the 2cond of August, 1664.

2 August.
[*77.]

Before Thomas Prence, Goů, Thomas Southworth,
   John Aldin,   Willam Bradford, and
   Josias Winslow,   Thomas Hinckley,
      Assistants, &c.

IN reference vnto a gun attached by James Cole, Senir, belonging to Joseph Billington, the Court haue ordered, that the said gun shalbee returned,

1664.
2 August.
Prence,
Govr.

forasmuch as it doth appeer that all that the said Billington had was bound ouer vnto John Barnes before the said attachment was layed on the said gun.

Att this Court, an acquittance was shewen in the Court, wherby it appeered that the portion belonging to Sarah Andrews, the daughter of Mr Henery Andrews, of Taunton, deceased, is fully payed and satisfyed; which said acquittance was signed with Jared Talbut, and witnessed by Gorḡ Macye and William Harvey, whose names were subscribed thervnto with theire owne hands.

Att this Court, Mr Thomas Dexter, Seni^r, complained of sundry injuryes against the towne of Sandwich about rights and titles to meddowes, &ā, concerning which controversye, by mutuall consent of both p̄ties, it was desired that the Goū, Mr Aldin, Mr Hinckley, and the Treasurer would repaire in convenient time to Sandwich, to haue the hearing and determination of the said controuersyes; and accordingly the Court haue ordered, that the time for the hearing and determination therof, as aforsaid, shalbee soḿetime in October next, by the p̄ties and att the place aboue named; and that for this p̄sent summer, Mr Dexter, Juni^r, and others of Sandwich as haue formerly improued the said meddowes, shall still improue them.

And wheras there is a controversye betwixt the towne of Barnstable and the Indians about bounds of lands, the Goū with the other aboue named are appointed by the Court to haue a hearing and determination therof before theire returne.

This Court hath ordered, in reference vnto the purchase of some meddowes, belonging to sundry of the towne of Plymouth, called the South Meddowes, &ā, lately purchased by the Goū, the major, and William Bassett, that notice shalbee giuen to all such as posesse the said meddowes that they may meet together and appoint some, in the behalfe of the rest, to treat and compound with those that haue bought it of the Indians, as aforsaid; which if they shall neglect to doe, that it bee refered, for the determination of the same, to the next session of the Court, to bee holden att Plymouth the last Tusday in September next.

This Court, receiueing sufficient intelligence by late testimony produced in Court that Nehemiah Bessey, of Sandwich, is of full age to enter vpon the posession and enjoyment of such lands as his father left him, haue ordered and doe heerby giue libertie vnto the said Nehemiah Bessey forthwith to enter vpon the full enjoyment and posession of his fathers inheritance, according to the bequeast of his deceased father, Anthony Bessey, as appeers by his last will and testament.

[*78.]

*July the fift, Anno Doḿ 1664.

The names of the jury summoned by the constable of Taunton vpon the

COURT ORDERS. 71

occation of the death of Leiftenant James Wyatt, on the day aboue written, Walter Deane, Jonas Austine, Hezekiah Hoare, John Cobb, Wiłłam Harvey, Peter Pitts, Aron Knap, Richard Stacye, James Leanard, Christopher Thresher, Samuell Williams, and John Deane, being sumoned, found, that on the fift of July abouemencioned, Leiftenant James Wyatt road to a meddow of his to cutt grasse, a seruant of his, an Indian boy, following him, and when hee came to the meddow hee found his master dead, as it is testifyed by him, who, returneing to the towne, reported that his master was dead. John Hall, Thomas Deane, and James Bell rode to the meddow, and there found that hee had cutt some grasse, and was gone out of the meddow, and there was fallen downe dead; and vpon search, the said jury finds not any cause of any violent death, butt the ymediatt hand of the Lord; and this is the agreement of vs all whoe haue heer subscribed.

1664.

5 July.
PRENCE,
GOVR.

WALTER DEANE,
The marke A of JONAS AUSTINE,
HEZEKIAH HOARE,
JOHN COBB,
WIŁŁAM HARVEY,
PETER PITTS,
The mark ◯ of ARON KNAPP,
The mark ⓢ of RICHARD STACYE,
The ⚡ marke of JAMES LEANARD,
The ⚘ marke of CHRISTOPHER THRESHER,
SAMUELL WIŁŁAMS,
JOHN DEANE.

**Att the 2cond Session of the Generall Court begun in June last, now held the 27th of September.*

27 September.
[*79.]

THE majestrates and deputies being assembled, it was ordered and enacted as followeth:—

Viz§: that the sume of one hundred pounds should bee leuied by rate on the seuerall townes of this jurisdiction, according to theire proportions, for the entertainment of his maties comissioners, the one halfe therof to bee payed in money vnto the Treasurer att or before the one and twentieth day of Nouember next, and the other halfe to bee payed in weat, pease, barly, or Indian

1664.
27 September.
PRENCE,
GOUR.

corn, soe as the barly exceed not in proportion one third p̃te of the said halfe, the wheat to bee payed att foure shillings and sixpence the bushell, the barly att four shillings, the pease att three shillings and sixpence, and the Indian att three shillings the bushell; the said graine to bee deliuered to the Treasurer att his house att Duxburrow, or to his order, by the sixteenth day of March next, good and marchantable, and the charge of transportation defrayed.

The proportions of the seuerall townes to the said rate are as followeth :—

Plymouth, to one hundred pound, is	09 : 05 : 00
Duxburrow (Bridgwater being encluded) is	08 : 08 : 03
Scittuate,	15 : 02 : 06
Sandwich,	08 : 08 : 06
Taunton,	08 : 08 : 06
Yarmouth,	08 : 08 : 06
Barnstable,	09 : 05 : 00
Marshfeild,	08 : 08 : 06
Rehoboth,	12 : 12 : 06
Eastham,	06 : 15 : 00
	95 : 02 : 09
Sowams,	03 : 15 : 00
Dartmouth,	02 : 10 : 00
Sum̃a totalis,	101 : 07 : 03

The Court haue ordered and agreed, that incase his ma^ties com̃issioners shall see cause to send for any of the majestrates of our jurisdiction to haue speech with them, that the major and Captaine Southworth, being deputed by the Court, shall bee in a reddines to goe, if such occation shall require.

The sum̃e of six pounds is allowed by the Court vnto Major Winslow and Captaine Southworth, viz§, to each of them three pounds, for and towards theire expence of time and other troubles and inconueniencyes by them sustained in theire late journey to Conecticott as com̃issioners of our jurisdiction.

It was ordered by the Court, that the towne of Rehoboth and the naighborhood of Sowamsett, in all leuies for publicke rates, shalbee considered as one intire township vntill such time that the said naighborhood shalbee in a capassitie and desire to bee a township of themselues.

[*80.]   *The towne of Scittuate is allowed by the Court to make sale of a certaine p̃cell of land belonging to Gorge More.

Ten acrees of meddow is graunted vnto Mr Allexander Standish, lying att Satuckett Riuer, if it bee there to bee had.

1 6 6 4.

27 September.
PRENCE,
GOU^R.

This Court did allow and approue of Thomas Haward, Juni^r, to bee leiftenant of the millitary companie of Bridgwater.

And of John Haward, Seni^r, to bee ensigne of the said companie.

In reference vnto the request of diuers desireing land att Namassakett in the last purchase, the Court haue refered the graunting of the said lands vnto the next sessions of this Court; and that then there shalbee a finall issue put thervnto, and in the interem a due observation bee taken by such as it consernes of such psons vnto whom most fitly it ought to bee distributed.

Memorand: that att the next sessions of this Court sume way and course bee thought on for proportioning of sume charge on lands lying dormand.

The majestrates and deputies doe thinke meet, and accordingly this Court is adjourned vntill the 2^{cond} Tuesday in May next, vnlesse by some nessesary occation falling out in the interem, the Goū and Assistants shall thinke meet to summon the next meeting of this Court sooner.

*Septem̃ 27th, 1664.

[*81.]

Mr Stephen Paine is authorised by the Court to make contracts of marriage in the towne of Rehoboth, and likewise to adminnester an oath to giue euidence to the grand enquest, and likewise to adminnester an oath to any witnesses for the tryall of a case as occation may require; and incase any pson resideing in this goūment shall haue occation to com̃ence a suite against any stranger or forraigner, it shalbee lawfull for the said Stephen Paine to issue out warrants in his ma^{ties} name to bind ouer any such pson or psons to answare the said suite att the Court of his ma^{tie} to bee holden att Plymouth att any time by attachment or summons as occation shall require, and likewise to graunt subpenaes as occations shall require.

[This paragraph is duplicated and cancelled on the preceding page.]

Septem̃ 27th, 1664.

Leiftenant James Torrey is authorised by the Court to make contractes of marriage in the towne of Scittuate, and likewise to adminnester an oath to giue euidence to the grand enquest, and likewise to adminnester an oath to any witnesses for the tryall of a case as occation may require; and incase any pson resideing within this jurisdiction shall haue occation to com̃ence a suite against any stranger or forraigner, it shalbee lawfull for the said Leiftenant Torrey to issue out warrants in his ma^{ties} name to bind ouer any pson or psons to answare the said suite att the Court of his ma^{tie} to bee holden att Plymouth

1664.
27 September.
PRENCE,
GOVᴿ.

att any time by attachment or summons as occation shall require, and likewise to graunt subpenaes as occation may require.

Septem̃ 27ᵗʰ, 1664.

Josias Cooke, of Eastham, is authorised by the Court to make contracts of marriage in the towne of Eastham, and likewise to adminnester an oath to giue euidence to the grand enquest, and likewise to adminnester an oath to any witnesses for the tryall of a case as occation may require; and incase any pson or psons resideing in this jurisdiction shall haue occation to com̃ence a suite against any stranger or forraigner, it shalbee lawfull for the said Josias Cooke to issue out warrants in his maᵗⁱᵉˢ name to bind ouer any pson or psons to answare the said suite att the Court of his maᵗⁱᵉ to bee holden att Plymouth att any time by attachment or summons as occation may require, and likewise to graunt subpenaes as occation may require.

4 October.
[*82.]

*Att the Generall Court held att Plymouth the 4ᵗʰ of October, 1664.

BEFORE Thomas Prence, Goũ, Thomas Southworth,
John Aldin, William Bradford, and
Josias Winslow, Thomas Hinckley,
Assistants, &c̃.

JAMES LOUELL, of Waymouth, produceing a deed of sale from the heires of Mʳ Nathaniel Souther for a sertaine tract of land long since graunted by this collonie to Mʳ Souther abouesaid, and alsoe propounding a place where hee desired to take it vp, viz§, neare the place where Phenias Prat and the sonnes of Clement Briggs were accom̃odated, between theire land and the line of the pattent, this Court, takeing notice of the former graunt, doe accordingly allow vnto the said James Louell two hundred acrees of land in the place abouemencioned, and haue appointed Leiftenant Torrey and Cornett Studson, if hee may bee obtained, to view it and lay it out vnto him, hee paying them for theire paines; and incase Cornett Studson cannot, then William Barstow is desired to doe it; and that they reporting to the Court on theire returne what meddow theire may bee, or swamp land that may goe in consideration of meddow, the Court will graunt him what is meet in that respect, hee paying the Indian purchase, if any shalbee justly demaunded.

This Court haue likewise graunted vnto John Hanmore and Walter Woodward, of Scittuate, (who haue a right as servants,) vnto each of them is graunted sixty acrees of land neare about the place abouemencioned, prouided it intrench not vpon former graunts, and alsoe that they pay the Indian purchase for it if any bee justly demaunded; and haue impowered the same psons that lay out James Louells to lay out theires alsoe, they satisfying them for theire paines.

1664.
4 October.
PRENCE,
Gou^r.

By a suite comēnced by Edward Jenkens, of Scittuate, against John Williams, Juni^r, conserning the impropriateing of lands that are comōn to the propriators of Conihassett, and alsoe of an ancient highway that goeth to the harbour, by fenceing the same, both which seemed to bee well cleared to vs to bee injuriouse, this Court haue therfore appointed and desired Mr Timothy Hatherley, Captaine James Cudworth, Leiftenant Torrey, Cornett Studson, and John Turner, Juni^r, to take a view of the fence sett vp by the said Williams; and except hee shall otherwise satisfy, doe impower the aboue named Mr Hatherly, &c̄, to throw vp the abouemencioned fence, that the highway and comōn lands bee not vnjustly impropriated.

*Mr Josepth Tilden haueing complained to this Court that Edward Bumpas, Juni^r, is indebted vnto him in the sumē of eight pounds and odd mony, as will appear by bill vnder his hand, and a considerable p̃te of the debt lyeth vnder attachment in Goodman Holmes his hand, this Court doth desire that Anthony Snow, Leiftenant White, Josepth Bedle, and Thomas Doged, whoe haue bine by the towne of Marshfeild impowered to acte for the said Bumpas, or some of them, with the said Edward, to treat and issue with Mr Tilden in reference to his debt, that soe any further suites may bee preuented; and the men aboue named, or such of them as shall acte in it, haue power to see such goods as are yett vnder attachment released for payment of the debt, and it shalbee the constables discharge.

[*83.]

Att this Court, Josias Wormall appeered in Court, and engaged vnto the Court for the sixt p̃te of the estate of Josepth Wormall, deceased, which is the portion of Hester Wormall; and when this engagement was taken, Mr Hatherley was cleared of his bonds for the adminnestration graunted vnto Mirriam Wormall, of which see orders of Court, June, 1662.

Wheras John Wheston, late deceased, dyed intestate, and soe the lands of the said Wheston falls by right of law vnto Josepth Wheston, the heire apparent vnto the said John Wheston; and that it doth likewise appeer to the Court that the estate of the said John Wheston is but little, the lands excepted, and that there are diuers smale children to bee brought vp out of the said estate, therfore, vpon the free will and condecendensy of the said Josepth

1664.

4 October.
Prence,
Govr.

Wheston, hee is content and hath by these p̃sents taken the house and land that his father liued on and died in, in the towne of Scittuate, for his full and intire portion of his fathers estate both of lands and goods, freely allowing that the profitt and benifitt of the said house and land shall redound vnto his mother, Susanna Wheston, for the full tearme of six yeares from the date heerof, for and towards the bringing vp of the other children of the said John Wheston, they keeping the said house and land in repaire. Morouer, conserning the said John Wheston his p̃te or share of Conihassett land, bee it more or lesse, both vpland and meddow, hee, the said Josepth Wheston, hath freely resigned, made ouer, and allianated the same from him and his heires vnto the rest of his brothers and sisters, the children of the said John Wheston, to bee by them or in theire behalfe improued or sold as occation shall require; onely that incase the said lands or any of them shall att any time bee sold, that the said Josepth Wheston shall haue the first proffer for the buying of them.

[*84.]

*Att this Court, Captaine James Cudworth, Leiftenant Torrey, Ensigne Eames, Isacke Chettenden, and John Bryant are appointed and deputed by the Court as a com̃ittee to settle a controuersy conserning a p̃cell or tract of land lying on the east side of the North Riuer, between the lands of Daniell Hicke and Robert Sprout, the said p̃sons to meet about the said expedition on the first Munday in the next month next after the date heerof; and incase they can not settle the said controuersy to the satisfaction of the propriators, that then they make report of theire proceeding therin vnto the Court, and that Walter Hatch and John Siluester are to take course for the satisfaction of the said p̃sons for theire paines about the same.

Att this Court, Christopher Winter, being summoned, appeered to make answare, being suspected to haue killed a horse of Josepth Bedles; the Court, not resting satisfyed in his p̃sent defence, saw cause to bind him ouer to further appeerance att the Court as followeth : —

Christopher Winter acknowlidgeth to owe vnto our soũ lord the King the sum̃e of . . . . } $\overset{li}{20 : 00 : 00}$

These are come to an agreement, and soe declared to the Court in March 7th, 1664.

The condition, that if the said Christopher Winter doe appeer att the Court of his ma^{tie} to bee holden for this goũment att Plymouth the first Tusday in March next, to make further answare conserning the killing of a horse of Josepth Bedles, and not depart the said Court without lycence; that then, &c̃.

Att this Court, Gyles Ricard, Seni^r, for swearing by the wounds of God, was sentanced to bee com̃itted to prison, and there to bee in durance the space of twenty foure houres.

COURT ORDERS. 77

Ruhamah Turner, for comitting fornication, fined 05 : 00 : 00.

William Maze, of Taunton, for sweareing, sentanced to sit in the stockes dureing the pleasure of the Court, which was accordingly executed.

James Bell, of Taunton, for strikeing John Eedey, fined 00 : 03 : 04.

*The rates of the countrey, vizt, for the officers wages, for the charge of the majestrates table, and for the charge of the comissioners men and horses, — the pticulares of each townes proportion therin is as followeth : —

1664.

4 October.
Prence,
Govr.
Seuerall of the naighbours of Sandwich engaged to pay this fine in the behalfe of Ruhamah Turner.

Plymouth,	08 : 06 : 06
Duxburrow,	04 : 01 : 04
Scittuate,	13 : 12 : 03
Sandwich,	07 : 11 : 04
Taunton,	07 : 11 : 04
Yarmouth,	07 : 11 : 04
Barnstable,	08 : 06 : 06
Marshfeild,	07 : 11 : 04
Rehoboth,	11 : 07 : 03
Eastham,	06 : 01 : 06
Bridgwater,	03 : 10 : 00
Sowams,	03 : 07 : 06
Dartmouth,	02 : 05 : 00
	91 : 03 : 02

[*85.]

The 8th of Aprill, 1664.

These few lines doe witnes, that I, John Coggen, doe from this day forward discharge and free my loueing frinds, James Cudworth, of Scittuate, and Isacke Robinson, of Barnstable, from being my guardians, acknowlidging myselfe to bee fully satisfyed ; whervnto I haue sett my hand.

This was p^rsented to the Court of Assistants held in Plym in February, 1664.

JOHN COGGEN.

Witnes, John Finney.

*A Writing appointed to bee recorded.   [*86.]

These witnesseth, and this bill of our hand bindeth vs, Thomas Morton, of the towne of Plymouth, in the jurisdiction of Plymouth, in New England, in America, yeoman, and John Andrews, of the towne aforsaid, in the said jurisdiction, planter, wee, our heires, exequitors, adminnestrators, and assignes, joyntly and seuerally, to pay or cause to bee payed vnto Nathaniel Warren, of the towne aforsaid, in the jurisdiction aforsaid, yeoman, to him or

1664.

4 October.
Prence,
Govr.

his heires, exequitors, adminnestrators, or assignes, the full sume of twenty and fiue pounds, to bee payed in mannor and forme following, viz§ : the one halfe in corne, English and Indian, and the other halfe therof in tarr ; that is to say, the first payment of the said twenty fiue pounds, which is foure pounds and eleuen shillinges, is to bee payed in tarr att or before the fifteenth day of June next ensueing the date heerof; and the second payment, which is foure pounds and eleuen shillings, is to bee payed in corne att or before the first day of December, 1665 ; and the third payment therof, which is foure pounds and eleuen shillinges, is to bee payed att or before the fifteenth day of June, 1666, in tarr; and the fourth payment, being foure pounds and eleuen shillinges, is to bee payed in corn att or before the fifteenth day of June, 1667 ; and the last payment, which is forty and fiue shillings, is to bee payed att or before the first day of December, 1667, which sume of forty and fiue shillinges, being the last payment of the abouesaid twenty and fiue pounds, is to bee payed in corne : all which seuerall payments are to bee payed in that which is good and marchantable both of the corn and the tarr, and att prise current as the prises shalbee att the times of the deliuery of the seuerall payments to bee deliuered, viz§ : the tarr att the towne of Plymouth, and the corne att the house of the said Nathaniel Warren att the Eelriuer, in the towneship of Plymouth aforsaid. In witnes of the true pformance of the pmisses, and of euery pte therof, wee, the said Thomas Morton and John Andrews, haue heervnto subscribed our hands and affixed our seales, this tenth day of October, anno Dom 1664.

The marke ᘒ of THOMAS MORTON,
and his seale.

The marke ᘒ of JOHN ANDREWS,
and his seale.

Signed, sealled, and deliuered in the psence of
    Thomas Southworth,
    Robert Fuller,
    Nathaniel Morton.

The sumes aboue menconed to bee payed by the pties aboue menconed, viz§, Thomas Morton and John Andrews, is to bee payed for the remainder of the time vnserued out, which the said Andrews should haue serued with the said Nathaniel Warren, hee haueing alsoe, vpon the sealing heerof, surrendered vp the said John Andrewes his indenture for the said time ; these pticulares were aded in the originall agreement in writing before the ensealing therof.

These seuerall payments are all payed by Thomas Morton and John Andrew to Nathaniell Warren and his assignes.

Testa me,   NATH: MORTON, Secre^y.

1664.
4 October.
PRENCE, Gou^r.

---

*Att the Court of Assistants held att Plymouth the seauenth Day of February, 1664.

1664-5.
7 February.
[*87.]

BEFORE Thomas Prence, Gofi,   Thomas Southworth,
John Aldin,   William Bradford, and
Josias Winslow,   Thomas Hinckley,
Assistants, &c.

IN reference to a controuersy betwixt William Shirtliffe, plaintife, against Thomas Little, defendant, for vnjust molestation to the damage of forty shillings in forcable carrying away certaine timber trees by him felled and squared, as hee supposeth, on his owne land, and for refusing to lay out and bound the land according to order, the Court hath appointed Mr Alden, the major, and Josepth Bedle in due and convenient time to settle the bounds of the said lands in controuersy between them according to theire best light, either from the records or otherwise; and in reference to the said timber trees, that Thomas Little is to returne them to the place from whence hee tooke them within ten daies from this present Court; and that the said Shirtliffe hath libertie to improue the said trees, prouided hee bee responsable to make good the vallue of them incase they shall proue heerafter to belonge to Thomas Little.

In reference to a complaint of John Smith, Juni^r, of Marshfeild, against Stephen Tilden, of Scittuate, for that the said Tilden neglected to pay vnto the said Smith the sume of twelue shillings due vnto him for the makeing of a cart, forasmuch as it appeered to the Court that the said Tilden was legally summoned, and did not appeer, nor any for him, to answare the said complainant, the said Smith owning before the Court fiue shillinges of the twelue receiued, the Court awarded the said Tilden to pay vnto the said Smith seauen shillings more, in all twelue shillings, besides twelue sh: charge.

In reference vnto diuers complaints amongst some of the naighbours of Plymouth, in p̃ticulare John Barnes against Thomas Pope, and the said Pope against Gyles Rickard, concerning bounds of land wherof they complained

1 6 6 4-5.

7 February.
Prence,
Govr.

each of other of encroāhment and treaspas by cuting of wood and makeing of hiewaies ouer the said Barnes his land, the Court haue ordered Leiftenant Morton and Gorge Bonum, with the healp of some other for a third man, to measure and bound the said lands in controuersy, the ancient bounds being lost, that soe all controuersyes about the same might sease for the future.

Att this Court, Mr Isacke Robinson was allowed and approued by the Court to keep an ordinary att Saconeesett for the entertainment of strangers, in regard that it doth appeer that there is great recourse to and fro by trauellers to Martins Vinyards, Nātuckett, &c̄.

Benjamine Bartlett appeered att this Court, and demaunded some land which was formerly belonging to Mr William Brewster, lying in Alcarmus Feild; but for as much as the p̄ticulare place cannot bee found, it is refered to the next Generall Court to determine.

[*88.]

*In answare vnto the desire and motion of Henery Wood and Thomas Pope, that for as much as it doth appeer by the last will and testament of Mistris Sarah Jenney, deceased, that did att her death giue and bequeath vnto the eldest daughters of Samuell Jenney, Henery Wood, and Thomas Pope a mare coult; and that Sarah, the eldest daughter of the said Samuell Jenney, is deceased before shee came to age, that therfore the surviuers of the said daughters might haue the p̄te of the deceased, the Court, takeing notice of the tearmes of the will, &c̄, adjudged it the right of the survivers, viz§, Sarah Wood and Sussanah Pope; but forasmuch as Samuell Jenney was not p̄sent, and that his plea about it hath not bine heard, it was refered to the Generall Court to bee holden in March next, att which time the said Samuell Jenney is to bee p̄sent, and to make his plea, if hee hath any thinge to speake in the case.

Wheras a motion was made to this Court by Richard Bourne in the behalfe of those Indians vnder his instruction, as to theire desire of liueing in some orderly way of goûment, for the better preventing and redressing of thinges amisse amongst them by meet and just meanes, this Court doth therfore, in testimony of theire countenanceing and incurraging to such a worke, doe approue of those Indians proposed, viz§, Pavpmunnucke, Keencomsett, Watanamatucke, and Nanquidnumacke, Kanoonus, and Mocrust, to haue the cheife inspection and management therof, with the healp and aduise of the said Richard Bourne, as the matter may require; and that one of the aforsaid Indians bee by the rest instaled to acte as a constable amongst them, it being alwaies prouided, notwithstanding, that what homage accostomed legally due to any superior sachem bee not heerby infringed.

This Court doth order, that if the Nātuckett Indians suspected for murther bee to bee found within this goũment, that serch may bee made by the majestrates, that they may bee found out and secured vntill they bee sent to the goũment of the Massachusetts, that they may doe with them as the case may require; and in p̃ticulare, that Mr Hinckley take care that those people about the southeren p̃tes or south sea, where they were lately knowne to bee, may giue intelligence whether they bee gon or noe out of the goũment, that it may bee knowne whether that the psons soe much concerned in it may bee enformed therof, that they may looke after them as they see cause.

1664-5.
7 February.
PRENCE,
Gou^r

Concerning some p̃ticulares which passed in this Court in reference to Mr Thomas Cushman, conserning an assignement made ouer to him by Mr Isacke Allerton, see more in orders and passages of the Court, 1648.

**Att the Generall Court of his Matie held att Plymouth the 7th of March, 1664.*

7 March.
[*89.]

John Aldin, Deputie Goũ,   Wil{l}am Bradford, and
Thomas Southworth,   Thomas Hinckley,
         Assistants.

ATT this Court, libertie was giuen vnto Barnard Lumbert, of Barnstable, to adminnester on the estate of one Cornelious More, an Irish man, late deceased, to pay all debts owing from the said estate soe farr and by equall proportions as the said estate will amount vnto, and to keep a just account of his said adminnestration, and to bee reddy to giue in a true account therof when thervnto required by the Court.

Ł^res of adminnestration was graunted by the Court vnto Joyce, the wife of Thomas Lumbert, deceased, and vnto Jedediah Lumbert and Caleb Lumbert, to adminnester on the estate of the said deceased Thomas Lumbert.

Ł^res of adminnestration were likewise graunted vnto Stephen Vinall and John Vinall, to adminnester on the estate of Ann Vinall, deceased.

Ł^res of adminnestration were likewise graunted vnto Timothy White and Josepth White to adminnester on the estate of Gowin White, deceased.

Mr Micael Peirse came before this Court, and desired that an order pased by the Court in reference vnto the desposing of the estate of John Allin, deceased, with speciall reference vnto the portion of Josias Leichfeild, might bee considered by the Court, and amended in respect that some detriment is

1664-5.

7 March.
Prence,
Govr.

likely to acrew vnto him by the said order, it standing as it doth ; in answare whervnto the Court returned, that forasmuch as diuers of the majestrates were absent, whose help is very requisett for the right regulateing therof, it is refered vnto a more full Court for the doeing of it.

James Louell, of Waymouth, came before this Court, and requested to haue a supply of meddow or swampe, that may bee hopefull, to make meddow, bordering or appertaineing to a certaine tract of land which hee bought of the heires of Mr Nathaniell Souther; hee was ordered by the Court either to come or send to the Generall Court to bee holden the begiñing of June next ensueing the date heerof, att which time the Court wilbee in a capasitie to answare his desire in some *some* suitable measure, according to a former order about it, if it may bee had.

Att this Court, it was made knowne to the Court that Elisha Hedge did breake bulke of goods before notice giuen of what liquors hee had brought into the towne of Yarmouth, and therby forfeited 16 gallons of liquor.

[*90.]

*In reference vnto a controuersy between Gorḡ Allin and Richard Chadwell about a highway, the Court haue ordered and doe request Mr Edmond Freeman, Seni^r, Edmond Freeman, Juni^r, Thomas Tobey, and Benjamine Nye, or any three of them, to settle the said differĕce with the first convenient speed they can, that soe there may bee a finall end of the said controuersy.

In reference vnto the desire of sundry, that the lands of Wilłam Randall, of Scittuate, may bee layed out and orderly bounded, the Court haue requested and appointed Captaine James Cudworth and Mr Joseph Tilden in due and convenient time to lay out and bound the said lands att the North Riuer according to theire best descretions and such euidence as they can procure, to the intent that thence forth all suites and contensions may bee preuented, and a finall end of all controuersyes relateing to the bounds of the said land.

The Court, takeing notice that sundry Indians haue manifested some willingnes to make sale of some land within the bounds of Barnstable, haue giuen libertie and doe depute and appoint Mr Thomas Hinckley, Nathaniel Bacon, and John Gorum, or any two of them, to purchase the same ; and whatsoeuer land shalbee soe purchased, they are to make report therof to the Court, that soe they may dispose of it as they shall see cause.

In reference to a cow and a steer belonging to Gabriel Fallowell that were taken in the trapps of Harry the Indian and his son, called Samuell Harry, which said cattle were soe hurt as the owner was constreyned to kill them, and therby were greatly damnifyed, the Court haue ordered, that they, the said Indians, shall pay to him, the said Gabriell Fallowell, or his assignes, the sume of foure pounds, viz§, forty shillings the next Indian haruest, and the remaining forty shillings Indian haruest come twelue month, in good and current pay. 1664-5.

7 March. PRENCE, Gou^r.

Thomas Cushman, for comitting carnall coppulation with his now wife before marriage but after contract, is centanced by the Court to pay fiue pounds, according to the law; and for the latter p̃te of the law, refereing to imprisonment, is refered to further consideration.

Thomas Totman appeered att this Court, to answare his p̃sentment for haueing carnall coppulation with his now wife before marriage, and affeirmed that it was after contract; which being not cleare to the Court, hee was centanced to pay a fine of ten pounds, if not cleared by further testimony; but if soe cleared, to pay but fiue pounds.

Wiłłam Randall, for breakeing the Kings peace by poakeing or strikeing Jeremiah Hatch with a ho pole, is sentanced to pay a fine of three shillings and four pence.

Thomas Sumers, for being drunke, fined fiue shillings.

Thomas Linkorne, Seni^r, for breaking the Kings peace, fined 3^s 4^d.

*Rehoboth, the 14th July, 1664. [*91.]

Wee, whose names are heervnder subscribed, doe heerby signify to all psons whome it may concerne, that, according to our best light and apprehension, Rebeckah Sale, the late wife of Edward Sale, was her owne executioner, viz$\S$, shee hanged her selfe in her owne hiered house.

      JOHN READ, Seni^r,
      PETER HUNT,
      JOHN PERREN, Seni^r,
      JAMES REDWAY,
      ROGER ANNADOWN,
      WIŁŁAM SABIN,
      HENERY SMITH,
      JOHN FITCH,
      THOMAS COOPER, Juni^r,
      JOHN PECKE,
      NICHOLAS PECKE,
      SAMUELL PECKE,
      DANIELL SMITH.

    Rehoboth, the seauenth of August, 1664.

Wee, whose names are subscribed heerto, doe heerby signify to all psons whom it may conserne, that Elizabeth Walker, the daughter of Phillip

1664-5.

7 March.
Prence,
Govr.

Walker, of the towne of Rehoboth, was accedentally drowned; shee, being sent to scoole, was found alsoe accedentally in the riuer first by two youthes; and they makeing knowne the same to two wemen, the wife of Nicholas Jyde and the wife of Roger Annadowne, and then to Willam Sabine, whoe forth with came and drew her out of the water, as hee saith. From the testimony of the afor specifyed psons, together with other concurring cercomstances, wee, the subscribers, conceiue that the child, which was two yeares and an halfe old, before specifyed, came accedentally to her end.

         STEPHEN PAINE, Seni^r,
         THOMAS COOPER,
         JOHN READ, Seni^r,
         PETER HUNT,
         JOHN PERRAM,
         ROBERT FULLER,
         ANTHONY PERREY,
         NICHOLAS PECKE,
         JOHN FITCH,
         HENERY SMITH,
         JOHN BUTTERWORTH,
         DANIELL SMITH.

March the 1, 1664. This jury gaue in this verdict vpon oath before Josias Winslow, Assistant.

The seauenth of March, 1664.

Ruhamah Turner, of Sandwich, for comitting fornication with John Ewen, was fined the sume of fiue pounds to the vse of the collonie.

[*92.]

*The Deposition of Richard Handy, aged about 19 Yeares.

This deponant saith, that hee being att worke about the mill dam the 19th of August with Thomas Fish, the banke being vndermined and dangerous, this deponant saith hee spoke to Thomas Fish and Edward Craggs, saying, "Lett vs knoke downe the banke." They being not willing to goe, this deponant said hee would goe; and then Thomas Fish said, "I will saue one," takeing his barrow in his hands; the banke fell downe vpon him while this deponant was goeing to knoke downe the banke, being got the halfe way or theraboutes; and this deponant saith, that ymediately after the banke was fallen downe Thomas Fish, they hastened to take the clods from him; and being bruised therby, hee was gott to bedd and dyed in about four daies and an halfe after; and further hee saith not. Edward Craggs testifyeth the same.

1664-5.
7 March,
PRENCE,
Govr.

The Deposition of Richard Church, aged about 56 Yeares.

This deponant saith, that hee, being att worke about the mill the 19th of August, hearing of a cry that the man was killed, hasted p̱sently and healped to remoue the earth from Thomas Fish, whoe, being much bruised therby, was gott to bedd, and in four dayes and an halfe dyed; and further saith not.

The Testimony of Nathaniel Fish, aged about forty-six Yeares.

This deponant saith, that hee was not willing his son should goe to worke about the dam that day that hee was hurt; and further this deponant saith, that hee heard his son say, not long before hee dyed, that Thomas Dexter said to Thomas Fish, " It is to late to goe to worke to day to Goodman Burgis."

The Names of the p̱sons warned by the Constable of Sandwich to view the Corpes of Thomas Fish, the Son of Nathaniel Fish, deceased, this 25 of August, in the Yeare 1664.

Thomas Tupper, Seni^r,	Francis Allin,
Richard Bourne,	Lodowicke Haukes,
Wilłam Bassett,	Obadiah Eedey,
Benjamine Nye,	John Gifford,
Richard Smith,	John Gibbs,
Thomas Tupper, Juni^r,	Robert Rollocke.

These twelue men before expressed, takeing into serious consideration according to the best euidence, doe find the instrumentall of the death of Thomas Fish to bee, the vnderminding and falling of the bankes vpon him, the wheelbarrow being between him and the ground, and soe bruiscing of his body that hee dyed about four dayes and an halfe after that hee was thuse bruised.

*The Propositions made by his Maties Com̃issioners to the General Court of his Matie held att Plymouth for the Jurisdiction of New Plymouth the 22^{cond} of February, Anno Dom̃ 1664.

[*93.]

1. That all houshoulders inhabiteing in the collonie take the oath of allegience, and that the adminnestration of justice bee in his ma^{ties} name.

2. That all men of competent estates and ciuell conversation, though of

1664-5. different judgments, may bee admited to bee freemen, and haue libertie to choose and bee chosen officers both ciuell and milletary.

7 March.
PRENCE,
Gov^R.

3. That all men and weomen of orthadox opinions, competent knowlidge, and ciuell liues, not scandalous, may bee admitted to the sacrament of the Lords supper, and theire children to baptisme, if they desire it, either by admiting them into the congregations alreddy gathered, or pmitting them to gather themselues into such congregations where they may enjoy the benifit of the sacraments, and that difference in opinion may not breake the bonds of peace and charitie.

4. That all lawes and expressions in lawes derogatory to his ma^{tie}, if any such haue bine made in these late troublesome times, may bee repealled, altered, and taken of from the file.

1665. The Answare of the Generall Court held att Plymouth for the Jurisdiction of New Plymouth the 2^{cond} of May, Anno Dom̄ 1665, to the aboue written Propositions, as followeth.

2 May.

To the first wee consent, it haueing bine the practice of this Court in the first place to ensert in the oath of fidelitie required of euery housholder to bee truely loyall to our sofi lord the Kinge, his heires and successors; alsoe, to adminnester all actes of justice in his ma^{ties} name.

To the second wee alsoe consent, it haueing bine our constant practice to admitt men of competent estates and ciuell conversation, though of different judgments, yett being otherwise orthodox, to bee freemen, and to haue libertie to chose and bee chosen officers both ciuell and milletary.

To the third, wee can not but acknowlidge it to bee an high fauor from God and from our soū that wee may enjoy our consiences in point of Gods worship, the maine end of transplanting ourselues into these remote corners of the earth, and should most hartily rejoyce that all our naighbours, soe quallifyed as in the proposition, would adjoyne themselues to our societie according to the order of the gospell for enjoyment of the sacraments to them and theires; but if, through different pswasions respecting church gou̅ment, it cannot bee obtained, wee would not deney a libertie vnto any, according to the proposition, that are truely consiencious, although differing from vs, especially where his ma^{tie} com̄aunds it, they maintaining an able preaching minnester for the carrying on of publicke Sabbath worship, which wee doubt not is his ma^{ties} intent, and withdraw not from paying theire due proportions of maintainance to such minnesters as are orderly settled in the places where they liue vntill they haue one of theire owne, and in such places as are capable of maintaining the worship of God in two distinct congregations; and wee being greatly incurraged by his ma^ties gracious expressions in his letter to vs, and youer honors further assurance of his royall purpose to continew our liberties, that where places by reason of our pausette and pouertie are vncapable *of two, it is not intended that such congregations as are alreddy in being should bee rooted out, but theire liberties preserued, there being other places to accomodate men of different pswasions in societies by themselues, which by our knowne experience tends most to the pseruation of peace and charitie.

1665.
2 May.
Prence, Gou^r.
[*94.]

To the fourth, wee consent that all lawes and expressions in lawes derogatory to his ma^tie, if any such shalbee found amongst vs, (which att psent wee are not consious of,) shalbee repealled, altered, and taken of from the file.

By order of the Generall Court for the jurisdiction of New Plymouth.

    p mc,   NATH: MORTON, Secr^ty.
Plymouth, May the 2^cond, 1665.

   An Acknowlidgment ordered to bee entered.
    To the honored Court psented.

3 May.

Forasmuch as the Court judges that I haue broken order, I ame sorry I haue giuen them offence; and if I had knowne that the order would haue bine soe vnderstod, I should not haue done it; and wherin I haue giuen the Court offence, I humbly craue theire fauorable judgment therin, and that the Court would bee pleased to pase by my weaknes and remite my offence.

        WILLAM NICARSON.
The third of May, 1665.

All the Court of Assistants held att Plymouth for the Jurisdiction of New Plymouth, 1665.

1665.
May.
[*95.]

Before Thomas Prence, Gou^r, Thomas Southworth,
   John Alden,   William Bradford, and
   Josias Winslow, Thomas Hinckley,
      Assistants, &c.

WHERAS William Newland standeth bound vnto this Court in the sume of three hundred pounds sterling faithfully to pay and make good vnto the children of Josepth Holley, deceased, the sume of six score pounds sterling, the Court, takeing notice and being sertifyed by seuerall writings

1665.
May.
PRENCE,
Govr.

vnder the hands of the said children and otherwise that they, the said children of the said Josepth Holley, Seni^r, deceased, viz$, Josepth Holley, Juni^r, Mary, the wife of Nathaniell Fitsrandall, Sarah, the wife of Josepth Allin, Experience Holley, and Hopestill, the wife of Samuell Worden, haue receiued theire seuerall ptes and portions of the said sume, viz$, euery of them twenty foure pounds, doe therfore fully and absolutely discharge the said William Newland, hee, his heires, exequitors, and adminnestrators, from the abouesaid bond and obligation, haueing fully paied the said sume vnto the said children aboue expressed.

Wheras Robert Ransome hath fenced in a peece of land att Lakenham that is comon, that hath occationed much trouble, the Court haue ordered, that the said fence bee throwne downe, and the land to lye open, and not to bee fenced by the said Ransome vntill hee can proue his title; and the Court haue ordered the naighborhood of Lakenham to see the same pformed by the sixt of this instant May.

James Cole, Juni^r, for breaking the Kinges peace in strickeing of Robert Ransome, is fined 00 : 03 : 04. And wheras hee spake vnaduisedly in saying, "Kill the rogue," meaning the said Robert Ransom, hee takeing notice of his great ouersight in soe speaking, and it being spoken when hee was in a great pasion, seeing his brother much abused by the said Ransom, and that hee, the said Cole, hath bine obserued otherwise to haue bine of a peacable disposition, the Court saw cause with admonition to remitt the fault.

Ephraim Tilson, for breaking the Kinges peace in strickeing Robert Ransome, is fined 00 : 03 : 04.

Att this Court Gorge Barlow appeered, being summoned to answare for attempting the chastity of Abigaill, the wife of Jonathan Pratt, by aluring words and actes of force, being to the affrighting and much wronging of the said Abigaill in the house shee dwells in, being then alone; the said Barlow bee examined, deneyed the said acusation in all the ptes of it; notwithstanding, the Court saw cause to require bonds of him for his good behauior vntill the Generall Court to bee holden att Plymouth the first Tusday in June next after the date heerof as followeth : —

Gorg̃ Barlow acknowlidgeth to owe vnto our sou lord the Kinge the sume of . . . . } 20 : 00 : 00

Thomas Sauory the sume of . . . . 10 : 00 : 00

Released.

The condition, that if the said Gorge Barlow bee of good behauior towards our sou lord the Kinge and all his leich people, and appeer att the General Court of his said ma^{tie} to bee holden att Plymouth the first Tusday in June next, and not depart the said Court without lycence; that then, &c.

COURT ORDERS. 89

Att this Court, Ralph Smith, of Eastham, was fined, for telling of a lye, 00 : 10 : 00.

In reference vnto the complaint of John Barnes against Thomas Pope, for treaspasing vpon his land in carting ouer it, and the complaint of the said Pope against the said Barnes for violently oposing the children of the said Pope in the cart way when they were about theire honest labour, and for beating the horse of the said Pope, and in strikeing of the horse struck his boy, the Court ordered, that forasmuch as these controversyes arose rather out of prejudice then out of any reall cause, that they should address themselues to the healp of naighbours for the settleing of those matters, and that the said Pope should goe noe more through Barnes his land.

1665.
May.
PRENCE,
Gou^R.

---

*Att the Generall Court holden att Plymouth the 9th of June, 1665.

9 June.
[*96.]

WHERAS there was an agreement made between the Court and Leftenant James Torrey and Cornett Robert Studson, as gaurdians vnto Josias Leichfeild and Anna, soffitimes the wife of John Allen, bearing date June, 1663, and stands vpon record p̃ticularly to bee seen, wee doe heerby declare and testify, that the said agreement wee did and doe clearly vnderstand was for a full and finall issue and settlement of what p̃tained vnto the said Leichfeild from Goodman Allens estate.

THO: PRINCE, Gou.
JO^N ALDEN,
JOS: WINSLOW,
THO: SOUTHWORTH,
THO: HINCKLEY,
WILL BRADFORD.

Nouember the 5th, 1663.

Receiued by vs, Cornett Robert Stetson and James Torrey, of Scittuate, of Micaell Peirse, of Hingham, the full and just sume of twenty pounds, for the vse of Josias Leichfeild, of Scittuate aforsaid ; which twenty pounds the said Micaell Peirse was appointed to pay vnto vs for the vse of Josias Leichfeild aforsaid by the Court holden att N. Plymouth in New England in the month of June last past. In witnes wee haue heervnto sett our hands the day and yeare first aboue written.

The marke 𝕄 of Cornett ROBERT STETSON,
JAMES TORREY.

1 6 6 5.   *Att the Generall Court of Election holden att Plymouth, for the Jurisdiction of New Plymouth, the seauenth Day of June, 1665.

7 June.
PRENCE,
Gouʀ.
[*97.]

BEFORE Thomas Prence, Gou ʳ, Josias Winslow,
   William Collyare,   Thomas Southworth,
   John Alden,   William Bradford,
       Assistants, &c.

Mʀ THOMAS PRENCE was chosen Gou, and sworne.

Mʳ William Collyare,
Mʳ John Alden,
Major Josias Winslow,
Capt Thomas Southworth,
Capt William Bradford, and
Mʳ Thomas Hinckley,
} wer̃ chosen Assistants, and sworne.

Likewise, Mʳ James Browne was chosen Assistant, but not sworne.

Major Josias Winslow and Captaine Thomas Southworth were chosen Com̃issioners, and Mʳ Prence next in nomination.

Mʳ Constant Southworth was chosen Treasurer, and sworne.

The names of the deputies of this yeare chosen to serue att this Court and the seueral adjournments therof are as followeth : —

Ephraim Morton,   Mʳ Edmond Howes,
Nathaniel Warren,   Nathaniel Bacon,
Mʳ Constant Southworth, John Chipman,
+Leiftenant Josias Standish, Anthony Snow,
Leif: James Torrey, deceased, Ensigne Marke Eames,
Isacke Bucke,   Mʳ Stephen Paine,+
Isacke Chettenden,   Leiftenant Peter Hunt,+
Richard Bourne,   Leiftenant John Freeman,
James Skiffe,   Richard Higgens,
Richard Williams,   Will Britt,+
William Harvey,   John Russell.
Mʳ Anthony Thacher,

COURT ORDERS.

The Constables of the seuerall Townes.

1665.
7 June.
PRENCE,
GOUR.

Plym̄,	Mr Wilḻam Crow, for Plymouth.
Dux.,	{ Mr Samuell Saberry, { Walter Briggs.
Scittū,	Gorḡ Russell.
Sandwī,	Richard Chadwell.
Taunton,	Josepth Wilbore.
Yarm̄,	Josepth Howes.
Barnst̄,	Thomas Laythorpe.
Marshfeī,	{ Nathaniell Thomas, { Josepth Siluester.
Rehobō,	Anthony Perrey,
Eastham,	Josepth Harding.
Bridgw̄,	Nathaniell Willis.
Dartmouth,	Daniell Wilcockes.

*The Grand Enquest.

[*98.]

sworne,
{ John Morton,
 Mr Josepth Tilden,
 Edward Jenkens,
 Phillep Delano,
 John Bourne,
 John Smalley,
 Trustrum Hull,
 Robert Denis,
 John Dingley,
 John Joyce,
 Hezekiah Hore, absent,
 Josepth Warren,

sworne,
{ Samuell Hickes,
 John Pecke,
 John Woodcocke,
 Leift Thō Haward,
 Samuell Smith,
 Stephen Skiffe,
 John Washbourne, Junir,
 James Allin,
 John Smith, of Barnstable,
 for p̄sent respetted,
 John Howland.

It was order̄, agreed, and voated by the Generall Court now assembled, that the sum̄e of one hundred and fifty pounds bee leuied by rate vpon the seuerall townes of this jurisdiction, accordinge to theire proportions, for and towards the carrying on the publicke affaiers of the collonie for this p̄sent yeare, the charge of the majestrates table being encluded in the said sum̄e, and the officers wages excepted; of which said sum̄e of one hundred and fifty pounds, forty therof to bee payed in money to bee leuied by rate forth with, and the warrants to goe out for the same with all convenient speed, soe as the said sum̄e of forty pounds is to bee payed to the Treasurer by the last day of

1665.
7 June.
PRENCE,
GOVR.

July next; and the hundred and ten pounds remaining to bee payed, one third p̃te therof in wheat, and the other two thirds in either wheat, pease, barly, or Indian corne.

Vpon consideration of diuers p̃ticulars proposed and largly agitated by the freemen of this jurisdiction assembled, concerning the proposition made by his ma^ties com̃issioners in reference vnto the manor of choise of the goũnors of this jurisdiction, and in reference vnto an adresse to bee made to his ma^tie for the renewall of our pattent, the Court haue ordered and voated, that the said p̃ticulares bee refered to future consideration.

Likewise, as conserning sending a p̃son for England as agent in behalfe of the countrey, to sollicit his ma^tie for the establishment of the bounds of our jurisdiction accordingly as they were lately sett by his ma^ties com̃issioners, it was concluded by the Court, that the said com̃issioners bee solicited to improue theire best enterst in our behalfe to the vtmost for the obtaining therof; and soe to com̃itt the case to God and vnto his ma^tie for the succes, in regard of our p̃sent incapasitie otherwise to send.

In reference vnto the question concerning the continuance of the confedaration of the Vnited Collonies, the Court haue ordered, that a loueing, curteous letter bee directed to the goũment of the Massachusetts collonie, therin declaring that wee see not light to p̃sist on therin, and that yett notwithstanding, that if vpon further enformation and consideration of any returne from them or otherwise, wee shall see cause to send to another meeting in reference vnto a more ciuell and orderly breakeing of that, wee soe doe.

[*99.]

*In reference vnto the complaint of John Hathewey, of Taunton, against two Indians, the one named Tobey and the other Phillip, for stealing some swine from him, the said charge appeering to the Court to bee true, the Court haue ordered, that speedily they shall satisfy vnto the said Hathewey a swine as good as his other swine hee hath att home, that were fellowes to the swine soe stollen; and likewise, that for asmuch as the said Hathewey is not prouided att p̃sent with euedences conserning other swine in probabillitie stollen by them, that they, the said Indians, put in cecuritie to appeer att the next Generall Court of his ma^tie to bee holden att Plymouth the first Tusday in October next, to answere his further complaint on that behalfe.

Phillip acknowlidgeth to owe vnto our soũ lord the Kinge the sum̃e of . . . . } 20 : 00 : 00
Tobey the sum̃e of . . . . 20 : 00 : 00
Daniell, allies Paquaho, the sum̃e of . . . . . . 10 : 00 : 00
Napames the sum̃e of . . . . 10 : 00 : 00

The condition, that if the said Phillip and Tobey doe appeer att the

COURT ORDERS. 93

Generall Court of his ma:tie to bee holden att Plymouth the first Tusday in August next, to answare the farther complaint of John Hathewey, of Taunton, against them for stealing of his swine, and not depart the said Court without licence ; that then, &c.

1665.
7 June.
PRENCE,
GOUR.

Ensigne Macey is approued by the Court to bee leiftenant of the milletary companie of Taunton, and Thomas Leanard for ensigne.

The remainder of the time that Moses Crocker is yett to serue from the date heerof, the Court alowes that hee shall serue it out with Thomas Hiland, Junir, of Scittuate, prouided that the said Hiland shall not dispose of him to any other without the Courts consent.

Vpon the earnest request of Phillip, the Indian sachem of Pocanacutt, for to haue libertie to buy a horse within our jurisdiction, the Court haue bestowed a horse on him, as judging it meeter then to giue him libertie to buy one; the horse is that which ^ prouided for the trumpeter belonging to the troop of horse which is spared from the said seruice on condition that another bee prouided to bee in his rome.

In reference vnto diuers complaints made conserning John Williams, Junir, his disorderly liueing with his wife, and his abusiue and harsh carriages towards her both in words and actions, in speciall his sequestration of himselfe from the marriage bed, and his accusation of her to bee a whore, and that especially in reference vnto a child lately borne of his said wife by him denied to bee legittimate, the Court saw cause to require bonds for the appeerance of the said Williams att this psent Court, and likewise sent for his wife to this Court ; and after the hearing of seuerall thinges to and frow betwixt them, the said Williams being not able to make out his charge against her, they were both admonished to apply themselues to such waies as might make for the recouering of peace and loue betwixt them ; and for that end the Court requested Isacke Bucke to bee officious therin, and soe dismised them from the Court for that time.

Notwithstanding the law prohibiting the selling of horses to Indians, the Court aloweth Keencomsett, an Indian att Barnstable, to buy a horse to bee for his vse in husbandry, to bee done by the aduise and direction of Mr Hinckley, Mr Gorum, and Nathaniell Bacon.

It is enacted by the Court, that the naighborhood of Sowamsett bee accounted to bee within the township of Rehoboth and within that constablericke, and the constable to pforme his office within the said naighborhood for the gathering of rates, &c, as in any other pte of his liberties.

Said naighborhood is to pay to the
× pound rate
× shillings
× yeare.

1665.

7 June.
PRENCE,
Govr.

[*100.]

These lands were graunted to the p^rsons heer named with all and singulare the appurtenances belonging thervnto, to them and theire heires and assigns for euer.

*The Names of those that haue Lands graunted vnto them by the Court, vizt, the Land which is purchased on the westerly Side of Namasskett Riuer, which is to bee equally deuided amongst them, and being soe deuided, is conceiued it will amount vnto thirty Acrees a Share of good Land, as alsoe Comoning adjoyning thervnto proportionable.

Imp^rmes, to the towne of Plymouth for a minnester, one share.
To Namasskett, for a minnester, ... one share.
To the Elder Cushman for his children, ... one share.
To Henery Sampson for his children, ... one share.
To Experience Michell for his children, ... one share.
To Edward Gray ten acrees, to lye in a square.
To Gabriell Fallowell, ... one share.
To Captaine Bradford, ... one share.
To James Cole, Seni^r, ... one share.
To Gyles Rickard, Seni^r, ... one share.
To Mr Josepth Bradford, ... one share.
To Anthony Snow, ... one share.
To Nathaniell Morton, ... one share.
To John Morton, ... one share.
To Ephraim Morton, ... one share.
To Edward Dotey, ... one share.
To Gorge Bonum, ... one share.
To Wiltam Harlow, ... one share.
To John Wood, ... one share.
To Henery Wood, ... one share.
To John Dunham, Juni^r, ... one share.
To Samuell Dunham, ... one share.
To Josepth Warren, ... one share.
To John Jourdaine, ... one share.
   In all 24 shares.

It was ordered by the Court, that the charge of the purchase of the said land shalbee equally bourne by all those which haue lands there, euery one a like proportion; and that none shall posesse aboue two shares of that land either of the p̃tenors or any other; and that if any one shalbee found to posesse aboue two shares therof, it shalbee forfeit to the countrey.

COURT ORDERS.

The Names of such as are graunted Land in that Tract of Land comonly called the Majors Purchase, whoe are to haue thirty Acrees appeece out of the best of it, and Comoning proportionable.

Wiłłam Clarke, of Duxburrow,	one share.
Jonathan Dunham,	one share.
Benjamine Eaton,	one share.
Josepth Dunham,	one share.
Thomas Sauory for his children,	one share.

1665.
7 June.
Prence, Gouᴿ.
These lands graunted with all and singulare the appurtenances belonging thervnto, to them and theire heires and assignes for euer.

It was ordered likewise by the Court, that wheras the lott of Mʳ Howland and the lott of Wiłłam Nelson, with two others, which are judged very meane, that they bee alowed twelue acrees apeece att the heads of theire said lotts.

The Court haue graunted vnto Zacary Eedey a smale gussett of land lying betwixt his land and the brooke, from his house below the path to Namasskett vnto the aforsaid brooke, vnto a bridḡ or way neare vnto a path that turnes out of the old way vnto Wiłłam Nelsons house; the said p̄cell of land, soe bounded as aforsaid, is graunted vnto the said Zacary Eedey, to him and his heires for euer, with all and singulare the appurtenances belonging thervnto, on condition that the said Zacary Eedey doe continue a bridge neare his house in the place wher it is needed for horse and cart, for the vse of the countrey, for the full tearme of twenty yeares from the date heerof.

*The Court haue graunted vnto Major Josias Winslow a farme of two hundred acrees of vpland, with meddow suitable and answarable thervnto, in regard of his extreordinary and emergent charges by him expended on the countreyes occations; the which farme lands hee is to looke out for in any p̄te of this goūment; and vpon his choise therof, to bee and appertaine, with all and singulare the appurtenances belonging thervnto, to him and his heires and assignes for euer; and the Court haue appointed Mʳ Constant Southworth and Cornett Robert Studson to lay it out for him.

[*101.]

A competency of land is graunted vnto Mʳ John Alden, Captaine Thomas Southworth, and Mʳ Constant Southworth in any land that may bee found and purchased att or about Namasskett or elswhere; which when it is sought out and purchased, and report therof made to the Court, to bee further confeirmed to them and theire heires & assignes for euer.

In reference vnto a former libertie graunted by the Court vnto Cornett Studson, two hundred acrees of land is graunted vnto him on the southerly side of the three mile square of land formerly graunted vnto Mʳ Hatherly, the said two hundred acrees of land, with all and singulare the appurtenances

Sence the death of Leiftenant Torrey, the major and the Treasurer are appointed by the Court to lay it out.

1665.

7 June.
PRENCE,
GOUᴿ.

belonging thervnto to appertaine vnto the said Cornett Robert Studson, to him and his heires and assignes for euer, to bee layed forth for him by Leiftenant James Torrey.

The Court haue graunted vnto Wiłłam Brett, Thomas Haward, Seniʳ, Arther Harris, Richard Williams, John Willis, and John Carey, to each of them, threescore acrees of land lying betwixt the lands of Taunton and Tcticutt; but incase these lands shall any of them fall within the last graunt of Taunton, these lands being before graunted to these men, notwithstanding it shall not make the former graunt void, but that the said lands shalbee and remaine, with all and singulare the appurtenances belonging vnto them, to the said Wiłłam Brett, Thomas Haward, Seniʳ, Arther Harris, Richard Williams, John Willis, and John Carey, to them and theire heires and assignes for euer.

Leiftenant Freeman and Leiftenant Rogers are appointed by the Court to view a certaine iland petitioned for by Richard Higgens, and to purchase it if they shall see reason, and to make report therof to the Court, that if they shall see cause they may despose of it to him, the said Richard Higgens.

Fifty acrees of land is graunted vnto Roger Annadowne, lying att a place called the Ten Mile Riuer, being a p̃te of that land which Captaine Willett bought, lying on the bounds of Rehoboth; the said fifty acrees of land, with all and singulare the appurtenances belonging thervnto, to appertaine to him, the said Roger Annadowne, to him and his heires and assignes for euer.

[*102.]

*Wheras Wiłłam Nicarson hath illegally purchased a certaine tract of land att Mannamoiett of the natiues, and hath noe visible estate to satisfy the breach of order, yett hath lately submitted himselfe vnto the clemency of the Court, this Court sees good to alow him, the said Wiłłam Nicarson, one hundred acrees of that land att or neare his house, to bee layed out according to the best descretion of Barnard Lumber, Marshall Nash, and Joseph Howes; and the rest of the said land att Mannamoiett this Court graunts vnto Mʳ Thomas Hinckley, Mʳ John Freeman, Mʳ Wiłłam Sarjeant, Mʳ Anthony Thacher, Nathaniel Bacon, Edmond Hawes, Thomas Howes, Seniʳ, Thomas Falland, Seniʳ, Leiftenant Joseph Rogers, to them and theire heires for euer, by equall proportions to bee aloted to them, prouided the said Wiłłam Nicarson haue an equall proportion of the meddow lands there with them; and these lands to bee proportioned between the said Mʳ Hinckley, Mʳ Freeman, and the rest aboue named, and the said Wiłłam Nicarsons portion of land to bee layed out to him before the first day of December next; and the Court orders, that the said Mʳ Hinckley, Mʳ Freeman, and the rest aboue named, alow in marchantable countrey pay theire equall proportions vnto him, the said Wiłłam Nicarson, of that pay as hee shall make apeer vpon just account that hee payed for the purchase of the said lands; and this Court orders and impowers the said Barnard Lumbert, Marshall Nash, and Josepth Howes, in the name of the Court, to put Mr Hinckley, Mr Freeman, Mr Sarjeant, and the rest, into full posession of the said lands att Mannamoiett; and the Court doth graunt libertie vnto Mr Hinckley, Mr Freeman, and the rest, to purchase the tract of land att Mannamoiett adjacent as are not purchased, and equally to proportion them amongst themselues, soe that it exceed not aboue one hundred acrees apeece; and this Court ordereth, that none of them shall sell or allianate his p̃te or proportion of his lands thervnto any p̃son or p̃sons whatsoeuer but with the consent and approbation of his associates or of the Court; and the Court orders all the said lands att Mannamoiett to appertaine and bee within the liberties of the township of Yarmouth, as the lands between Bound Brooke and Stony Brooke are, vntill the Court shall see cause to order otherwise.

1 6 6 5.
7 June.
PRENCE,
Gou^r.
Of this see another order 5 pages forward in this booke.

The Court haue ordered, conserning the land att Saconett, in reference vnto the petitioners for it called the ancient seruants, that none shall purchase the said lands soe as to bee any meanes to hinder them from any oppertunitie that may p̃sent for an orderly purchase therof, in order to a supply of such of them as are vnsupplyed; the p̃sons alowed by the Court to purchase it for them, if any opertunitie may bee had, are the major and the Treasurer.

A certaine p̃cell of meddow, or such swampy ground as tendeth towards meddow, is graunted by the Court vnto Pheneas Pratt and James Louell, lying on the westerly side of Phenias Pratts land that was graunted vnto him the last June Court, neare vnto the line betwixt the Massachusetts and this jurisdiction, the said p̃cell being about foure or fiue acrees, bee it more or lesse, to bee equally denided betwixt them, the said Pheneas Pratt and James Louell, to them and theire heires and assignes for euer.

Mr Hinckley, Richard Bourne, and Nathanell Bacon are appointed by the Court to purchase some land of the Indians in the behalfe of the towne of Yarmouth.

Richard Bourne and Wiłłam Bassett are appointed by the Court to view and purchase some lands desired by Edmond Freeman and Thomas Butler lying towards Saconeesett, if they find it worth the purchasing, and to make report of it to the Court.

*The Court haue ordered, that the sume of fifty pounds bee settled vpon and payed to the Gou̅ for this p̃sent yeare, to bee payed out of the treasury.

[*103.]

It is enacted and ordered by the Court, that notwithstanding the majes-

1665.

7 June.
Prence,
Govr.

trates bee rated to the charge of theire table and the officers wages, that the Treasurer shall take it of from them and place it on the countreyes account.

It is ordered by the Court, that Yarmouth and Marshfeild bee for the future rated ten shillings apeece in a forty pound rate, and that it bee charged on Dartmouth.

Conserning a highway to bee layed out att Yarmouth, it is ordered by the Court, that the jury that shalbee impannelled to lay out the said highway shall alsoe judge of the damage done to the marsh that the said way must goe through.

A Deposition appointed to bee recorded, as followeth.

Ann Hinde, the wife of William Hoskins, aged 25 yeares or therabouts, being examined and deposed before Mr Edward Winslow in a case between John Darbey and John Chipman, afeirmeth vpon oath as followeth :—

That the said Ann liued in the house of Mr Darbeyes father with the said John Chipman att such time as the said John Chipman came from thence to New England to serue Mr Richard Darbey, his brother ; and that the said Ann came afterwards likewise ouer to serue the said Richard Darbey, when old Mr Darbey requested this deponant to comend him to his cozen Chipman, and tell him if hee were a good boy hee would send him ouer the money that was due to him when hee saw good ; and further, wheras this deponant heard the said John Darbey affeirme that his money was payed to John Chipmans mother, shee further deposeth that his said mother was dead a quarter of a yeare or therabouts before her old master sent this message to his cozen Chipman ; all which this deponant sweareth, and further knoweth not.

Before mee,   EDWARD WINSLOW.

Taken the 2^{cond} of March, 1641.

An Order sent to Taunton from the Court prohibiting bad Iron to bee made there, as followeth.

To the clarke of the iron workes att Taunton, greeting.

These are to acquaint you that the Court requires you to signify vnto the owners that are p̄tenors in the iron workes att Taunton, that wheras there is great complaint of bad iron made there, that the Court requires them to take course with the workmen that hence forth the iron that shalbee made there bee good and marchantable, that soe the countrey bee noe more wronged on that behalfe.

The Courts order p mee,   NATH: MORTON, Clarke.

COURT ORDERS. 99

It is ordered by the Court, that Yarmouth is to pay a barrell of oyle to the Treasurer for the countrey for some whale they had; likewise John Ellis to pay for a whale hee had the sume of twenty shillings.

The Treasurer is allowed out of the countreyes stocke the sume of thirty shillings, by him disbursed about Capt Scott.

A fine of three pounds was remitted vnto John Sprague this Court.

Fifty shillings of Ruhamah Turners fine was remited vnto her this Court.

1665.
7 June.
Prence,
Gov^R.

*Wee, James Torrey, and Wiłłam Barstow, and John Bryant, being appointed by the Court to lay out a tract of land graunted to Mr Hatherley by Accord Pond, which p̃cells of land was to bee layed out three mile square on the head line of the towne of Scittuate, wee, James Torrey and Wiłłam Barstow, attending to our order for the time and place appointed, haue measured the aforsaid land, which begines att the vtmost southerly p̃te of Accord Pond, and runs west on a third p̃te of a point southerly three miles, then turning with a square line south and a third p̃te of a point easterly to the end of three miles, then turning with another square line east and a third p̃te of a point northerly three miles, then turning with another square line north and a third p̃te of a point westerly in the head line of the township of Scittuate three miles, which said line ends att Accord Pond, att the place where it began.

[*104.]

           P me,   JAMES TORREY,
                           WIŁŁAM BARSTOW.

Wee, Robert Studson and James Torrey, being appointed by the Court to lay out two hundred acrees of land for James Louell, of Weymouth, which said land was graunted to Mr Nathaniell Souther, wee, accordingly to our order, haue layed out the said land vpon the south west p̃te of the land graunted to Mr Hatherley by Accord Pond, ruñing two hundred rodd south and a third p̃te of a point easterly in the line of the said land graunted to Mr Hatherley; then turning with a line ruñing one hundred and sixty rodds west and a third p̃te of a point southerly, then turning on a square line north and a third p̃te of a point westerly two hundred rodd, then turning with another square line east and a third p̃te of a point northerly one hundred and sixty rodd to the place where wee began.

                         The marke ⟨mark⟩ of ROBERT STUDSON,
    P me,   JAMES TORREY.

1665.

9 June.
Prence,
Gov{{r}}.

An Order directed to the Townsmen of Scittuate, as followeth.

The Court hath bine enformed of youer reddines to appoint some of youer townsmen to the healping about the settleing of the bounds of some lands of William Randall, which hath bine hindered of accomplishment of that worke by some vnworthy speeches of the said Randall; yett being very desirouse of youer peace as our owne, therfore wee request that you would againe nominate some other psons for that worke, and desire with youer leaue that you would request Cornett Studson to bee healpfull to the aforsaid Humphrey Turner and Walter Woodward to doe the same. This is the desire of the rest of the majestrates, as youer frind acquaints you.

THOMAS SOUTHWORTH.

Plymouth, the 9{{th}} of June, 1665.

[*105.] *An Account of the Liquors brought into the Towne of Eastham, as followeth.

The 28{{th}} of the 9 month, 1664.

Thomas Paine, 5 quarts of liquor.

Josepth Harding, 2 gallons, twenty pound of shott, and 3 pound of powder.

M{{r}} Crosbey, 1 gallon of liquor, six pound of shott, and three of powder.

Gorḡ Crispe, 2 gallons of liquor.

Daniell Done, one gallon of liquor, and 3 pound of powder, and 20{{lli}} of shott.

M{{r}} John Freeman, two gallons of liquor.

Edward Banges, six gallons of liquor.

Aprill, 65. Thomas Paine, 1 gallon of liquor, and 2 gallons of Gorge Crispe.

Nicholas Snow, 1 gallon and an halfe of liquor.

Josepth Harding, one gallon and an halfe of liquor.

The 23 of the 10{{th}}, 64. Ralph Smith, 2 gallons of liquor, 35 pound of shott, and fiue pound of powder.

Stephen Hopkins, 2 pound of powder, 1 gallon of liquor.

Aprill, 65. Ralph Smith, 2 gallons of liquor, and bought for Josias Hubbert, of Hingham, fifteen gallons of liquor.

Richard Higgens, 1 gallon of liquor.

John Mayo, two gallons of liquor.

John Smalley, one gallon of liquor.

Trustrum Hull, of Barnstable, brought a barrell of rum to the towne of

Eastham, and sold it, but gaue noe account of it to either of vs, and wee thought it good to giue the Court notice of it.

1665.
9 June.
PRENCE, GOUR.

WILŁAM WALKER,
JOHN DONE.

	li	s	d
Thomas Little, for not keeping secret, but discloseing, the proceedings of the grand enquest, being one of them, was fined	01 : 10 : 00		
Samull Norman, being convicted of telling of a lye, .	00 : 10 : 00		

Gyles Rickard, Seni^r, for swearing the 2^{cond} time, being proued by two witnesses according to law, was centanced to bee imprisoned twelue houers, which alsoe, with the former sentance of the same kind for the like, were both att this Court inflicted; his punishment for the latter had not bin soe eazey but that the Court considered some matteriall cercomstance about the case respecting the witnesses, which occationed the mittigation of the punishment.

Thomas Lucas, for swearing by the wounds of God, was sentanced to bee imprisoned 24 houres, which accordingly was inflicted.

	li	s	d
John Rushell, of Acushena, allis Dartmouth, acknowlidgeth to owe vnto our soū lord the Kinge the sume of	20 : 00 : 00		
Edward Gray the sume of	10 : 00 : 00		

The condition, that if the said John Rushell shall and doe appeer att the Generall Court of his ma^{tie} to bee holden att Plymouth the first Tusday in October next, to answare to any thinge that may bee further objected against him conserning attempting the chastitie of Hannah, the wife of Wiłłam Spooner, &c̃, and in the interem of time bee of good behauior towards our soū lord the Kinge and all his leich people, and not depart the said Court without lycence; that then, &c̃.   Released.

Att this Court, fifty shillings was abated of Ruhamah Turners fine.

*Wheras Wiłłam Nicarson, of Yarmouth, stood convicted diuers yeares about eregulare purchaseing of lands att Mannamoiett, the penaltie wherof is fiue pounds for euery acree soe purchased, which amountes to much more then all hee hath is able to satisfy, and that warrants haue bine issued out for the leuying of the same in part; and that before the execution therof, the said Nicarson made some applycation to his ma^{ties} comissioners att Plymouth, February the 22^{cond}, 1664, and that the said his ma^{ties} comissioners were pleased to moue the Court on his behalfe, incase the said Nicarson should submitt himselfe to the Court; and that the said Nicarson then did acknowlidge his mistake of the said order; this Generall Court, takeing notice of and willing to

[*106.]

1665.

9 June.
Prence,
Govr.

Of this see another order in the actes of this Court 4 pages backwards in this booke.

gratify the said comissioners theirein, and not to procecute thinges to extreamities, doth therfore order the remiting of his fine, and alsoe alow him one hundred acrees of the said land, to bee layed most conveniently to his house there, with a convenient portion of meddow ground, to him and his heires for euer; and alsoe what moneyes hee hath giuen to the Indians as for that eregulare purchase of the lands shalbee repayed vnto the said Nicarson by the psons to whom the Court hath disposed of the rest of the lands there according to theire seuerall proportions; the psons are as followeth, viz: Mr Thomas Hinckley, Mr John Freeman, Mr William Sarjeant, Mr Anthony Thacher, Mr Thomas Howes, Senir, Nathaniell Bacon, Leiftenant Joseph Rogers, Mr Edmond Hawes, and Thomas Falland, Senir; this Court therfore authoriseth Marshall Nash, Barnard Lumbert, and Joseph Howes, in the name of the Court, to measure out the said proportions of land vnto William Nicarson, as alsoe to the other psons abouenamed, and to giue them posession therof in the name and behalfe of the Generall Court, to haue and to hold to them and theire heires for euer.

‡Propositions made by the Court to the seuerall Townshipes of this Goûment, refered to Consideration vntill the next Adjournment of this Court.

Concerning dormant lands, that the psons bee rated in such townshipps as the psons that ownes them inhabites.

‡1. That all psons lyable to bee rated, in euery towne of this goûment, bee rated according to theire vizible estates and faculties, that is, according to theire goods, faculties, and psonall abillities, whether they are in lands, both meddow lands, improued lands, or dormant lands appropriated, or in cattle, goods, or stocke imployed in trading, in boates, barques, &c, mills, or other visible estate; but for the incurragement of trafficke that it bee ordered, that barques, catches, and bigger vessells may not bee rated aboue halfe theire vallue; dormant lands, both vpland and meddow, out of townships, to bee rated for euery hundred acrees according to 40s estate; and if any pson lay downe any pte of his proprietie to the comonage of the companie then associated togather, hee shalbee rated but for what quantitie hee keepes his propriety in; and concerning stockes imployed in trading att home in and about the townshipes where hee liues, shalbee rated onely for two thirds of such stockes soe improued, as thuse: 120ll stocke to bee imployed in trading shalbee rated onely for 80ll, and soe proportionable.

‡Proposition 2cond. That the Goûnors that for the future shalbee chosen bee allowed fifty or sixty pounds p annum; and that there bee but fiue majestrates chosen yearly, and they to haue, each of them, twenty pounds p annum, and they to beare theire owne charges.

COURT ORDERS.

‡And if not soe, that there bee a standing councell chosen; and that there bee three in number besides the Goū alwaies of that councell, it being alwaies att the libertie of the Court to renew the choise of that councell as often as they shall see cause, alowing vnto the councell ‡sixty pounds a yeare,‡ ‖twenty pounds a peec.‖

1665.
9 June.
Prence,
Gou^R.

‡And if soe, that the countrey doe make choise of two or more yearly for majestrates to bee aded vnto them, and the countrey to beare onely the charge of theire table att the seuerall Courts.

‡This Court is adjourned vntill the 2^{cond} Tusday in October next.‡

Att the Court of Assistants holden att Plymouth the first Day of August, 1665.

1 August.
[*107.]

Before Thomas Prence, Gou^r, Thomas Southworth, and
Wiłłam Collyare,   Wiłłam Bradford,
Josias Winslow,
Assistants, &c.

ATT this Court, Edward Williams, att the request of the Court, engaged to pay vnto Ann Crooker, widdow, the sume of forty shillinges in good cloth, att a reasonable rate, which hee giueth vnto the said widdow, to bee forth with deliuered vnto her or her assignes att his returning home; which hee doth in consideration of her poor condition, and that it bee a finall end of all controuersyes between the said Ann Crooker and the said Williams conserning her sonne, Moses Crooker.

In reference vnto a horse in controuersy between Major Winslow and Ephraim Tinkham, the Court haue ordered, that the said horse bee forthwith deliuered vnto the said major, and to run vpon his ground vntill the next October Court to bee holden att Plymouth aforsaid, causualties excepted, and then to cause him to bee brought to the Court, and that then all such euidences as can bee procured bee produced for the clearing vp of the right owner.

Memorandum: that Mr Eames, Senr, Nathaniell Warren, James Clarke, and Edward Williams had the sight of the said horse, and did affeirme, that, according to theire judgments, he was then three yeares and advantage.

In reference vnto John Dunham the younger, for his abusiue carriage

1665.

1 August.
PRENCE,
GOVR.

towards his wife in continuall tiranising ouer her, and in p̃ticulare for his late abusiue and vnciuill carryage in endeauoring to beate her in a deboist manor, and for affrighting of her by drawing a sword and pretending therwith to offer violence to his life, hee, the said Dunham, is sentansed by the Court to bee seuerly whipt; but through the importunitie of his wife, the execution of the said centence was respeted for p̃sent vntill the Court shall take further notice of his future walking, and then to doe therin as occation shall require; and for the preuension of future euill in the like kind, the Court sees cause to require securite for his good behauior vntill the next Generall Court, and soe from Court to Court vntill the Court shall see cause otherwise to order.

John Dunham the younger acknowlidgeth to owe vnto our soū lord the Kinge the sume of . . . . . } $\overset{\text{li}}{20:00:00}$

Gorge Bonum the sume of . . . . 06 : 13 : 04

Benajah Pratt the sume of . . . . 06 : 13 : 04

Jonathan Dunham the sume of . . . . 06 : 13 : 04

Released.

The condition, that if the said John Dunham bee of good behauior towards our soū lord the Kinge and all his leich people, and in p̃ticulare towards his wife in reforming his former abusiue carryage towards her both in word and deed, and appeer att the Generall Court of his matie to bee holden att Plymouth the first Tusday in October next, and not depart the said Court without lycence; that then, &c̃.

Att this Court, John Arther appeered, according to summons, to answare for abusiue speeches and for entertaining of the wife of one Talmon and the wife of Wiłłam Tubbs; but the said Arther pretending hee could procure euidence to cleare him in some of the p̃ticulares charged, hee, engageing to appeer att October Court, is for the p̃sent released.

The Major Winslow, Anthony Snow, John Bourne, and Wiłłam Paybody are appointed by the Court to rectify a difference and controuersy between Moses Simons and Samuell Chandeler in reference vnto the bounds of theire lands where they now inhabite in Duxburrow.

COURT ORDERS. 105

*Att the Court held att Plymouth the third Day of October, 1665.   1 6 6 5.

BEFORE Thomas Prence, Gou^r,   Thomas Southworth,   3 October.
William Collyare,   William Bradford, and   PRENCE, GOU^R.
John Alden,   Thomas Hinckley,   [*108.]
Josias Winslow,
Assistants, &c.

THIS Court haue appointed John Pecke, John Allin, and John Woodcocke, of Rehoboth, to adminnester on the estate of Richard Ormsbey, late deceased att Rehoboth, to pay all due debts due and owing vnto any pson or psons from the said estate, soe farr and by proportion as the estate will amounte vnto, and to bee reddy to giue in a just account therof vnto the Court when required by them.

The Court doth alow vnto Sarah Ormsbey, widdow, the best bed that shee hath, with a boulster and a paire of pillowes, a paire of sheets, a paire of blanketts, and the best rugg or couerlidd that was left, and curtaines and vallence to the bed, and all her owne wearing apparrell. Att this Court, open proclamation was made, that if any can lay any claime to any due debt from the estate of Richard Ormsbey, they are to come in betwixt this date and the first of October next.

Mr Josepth Tilden and Jeremiah Hatch are alowed and appointed by the Court to bee guardians vnto Nathaniell Man; and John Cowine is required by the Court to surrender him vp to theire dispose as his guardians.

A judgment of eight shillings and the charges of the summons is awarded by the Court to bee payed by Abraham Jackson to William Nelson, in reference and for the ending of a controuersy betwixt the said pties about the keeping of two cattle some time the latter end of the last winter.

In reference vnto a controuersy betwixt John Smith, Morris Truant, and Richard Child, conserning a bargaine about the building of a house, the Court haue ordered, that the said Smith shall finish the said house according to his bargaine, and that the said Child doe prouide diett for him dureing the time hee is about it; and wheras the said Truant, by a wronge attachment serued on the said Smith, and by detaining of his tooles, and by neglecting to supply him with boards and nailes suitable to the finishing of the said worke, and diet when hee was about it, and that hee, the said Smith, hath bine att considerable charge for witnesses in reference vnto the said controuersy, the occation of which trouble and charge hath mainely arisen by the said Morris Truant his meanes, the Court haue awarded him to pay vnto the said John Smith the summe of forty shillings.

Mr Thacher, Mr Hawes, and Robert Denis are appointed by the Court to receiue the excise on liquors, &c, att Yarmouth, this yeare.

VOL. IV.   14

1665.

3 October.
Prence,
Govr.

Lres of adminnestration are graunted vnto Thomas Roes, of Scittuate, and his wife, to adminnester on the estate of Jonas Pickles, deceased.

These p̄sents witnesses, that the abouenamed Thomas Roes engageth before the Court, that if incase God giue him any children, that when hee dieth hee will leaue that estate which God giues him to bee equally deuided amongst the children of Jonas Pickles and his in equall proportion; and incase hee die without any child of his owne before his wife, hee will leaue his estate vnto his wife to bee disposed of by her; and likewise hee doth engage, that if his wife die before him, that hee will dispose of a considerable p̄te of his estate to the children of the said Jonas Pickles as the Court shall thinke meet.

‡Lres of adminnestration are graunted vnto , the wife of Leift̄e James Torrey, deceased, to adminnester on his estate, and hath giuen securitie to the Court for her true adminnestration thereof.‡

[*109.]

*‡Att this Court Ensigne John Williams appeered, being sum̄oned to answare the complaint of Mr Barnabas Laythorp, in the behalfe of his sister, the wife of the said Williams, whoe complaned of the said Williams of vnkind, churlish, and vnworthy behauior in seuerall respects towards his wife; shee being alsoe in Court, appeering according to sum̄ons, and pleaded her innosensy in such thinges as were by him layed to her charge, especially in reference vnto the child lately borne of her body, affeirming before her and vnto him in the Court that the said child was his, begotten by him, the Court being‡

John Shelley, for ployning a quantitie of liquors from Mr Barnabas Laythorp aboard his barque, is centanced to sitt in the stockes att Barnstable on a training day for the space of three houres; and for his telling a lye in his examination about it, hee is sentanced, according to the law, to pay ten shillings to the vse of the collonie.

James Cudworth, Juni^r, for com̄iting carnall copulation with his wife before marriage, is fined, according to the law, fiue pounds to the vse of the collonie.

Sarah Ensigne, for com̄iting whordome agreuated with diuers cercomstances, was centansed by the Court to bee whipt att the cartstaile; and that it bee left to the descretion of such of the majestrates as shall see the said punishment inflicted for the number of stripes, but not to exceed twenty, which accordingly was inflicted this Court.

John Barnes, being lately detected of being twise drunke, is fined twenty shillings.

Gyles Rickard, Seni^r, for suffering John Barnes to bee drunke in his house, is fined fiue shillings.

Thomas Lucas, for being drunke, fined ten shillings.

Thomas Phelpes, for telling of a lye, fined ten shillings.

COURT ORDERS. 107

James Cole, Senⁱʳ, for suffering Richard Dwelley to bee drunke in his house, fine fiue shillings.

Mʳ Paine, Leiftᵗ Hunt, and Wiltam Brett, for none appeerance as deputies att this Court, fined each twenty shillings.

Samull Edson, for none appeerance att the Court, being summoned to serue on a jury, fined

Ordered by the Court, that Thomas Huckens and Josepth Laythorp bee required either to pay theire excise or to repaire to the Court to giue a reason of theire refusing to doe it.

In reference vnto the p̃sentment of Edward Sturgis, Senⁱʳ, for swearing falsly, the Court, considering the invalliditie of one of the witnesses, doe not see reason to judge him guilty of swearing falsly, although they conceiue hee might haue bine more considerate in his apprehensions, as deeming the boat might bee affloat, and hee not see it.

*Wheras John Williams, Junⁱʳ, appeered before the Court held att Plymouth the seauenth of June last past before the date heerof, to answare for his disorderly liueing with his wife, and his abusiue carriages towards her both in words and actions, in speciall his sequestration of himselfe from the marriage bedd, and that notwithstanding the Court then tooke such order about it as was judged meet for p̃sent, yett the said Williams not attending that due reformation expected from him, wherby Mʳ Barnabas Laythorpe hath seen cause, in the behalfe of his sister and those related to her, to reuiue the former complaint, with some aditionall charges; to which the said Williams, though seeming to desire the tryall of such his guiltines or not guiltines might bee put on a jury of his peers, yett afterwards refused it when graunted to him by the Court; this Court, being earnestly desirous of a renewed closure of his hart and affections to his wife, and that his future conversation with her might bee better then his former, were willing to extend what lenitie might bee, and in reference thervnto, with exhortation of him to amend his wayes respecting the p̃mises, hee was released att the p̃sent.

Notwithstanding, the wife of the said Williams, in reference vnto diuers scandulous reports cast abroad conserning her, desired that open proclamation might bee made in the Court tending to the clearing of her name, which accordingly was done as followeth :—

Wheras Elizabeth, the wife of John Williams, hath bine openly traduced and scandulised in her name, and by false reports and reproaches rendered as if shee were a dishonest woman, and that the child shee brought forth into the world was not legitimate, these are to declare openly before the countrey, that the Court, haueing had sundry occations to heare and examine p̃ticulars sun-

1665.

3 October.
PRENCE,
Govʳ.

[*110.]

1665.
3 October.
Prence,
Gov^R.

dry times relateing to the p̃mises, can find noe cause of blame in her in such respects, but that shee hath behaued herselfe as one that hath faithfully obserued the bond of wedlocke, and that shee and her frinds hath bine much wronged by such reports.

Mr Anthony Thacher is authorised by the Court to make contracts of marriage in the townshipe of Yarmouth, and likewise to adminnester an oath to any witnesses for the tryall of a case as occation may require within the said townshipe, and likewise to adminnester an oath to giue euidence to the grand enquest as there shalbee occation within the said township.

John Williams, Juni^r, is alowed & appointed by the Court to bee guardian vnto John Barker, and is required by the Court to bringe him vp in a way of education and learning, soe as may bee to his advantage and healp when hee comes to bee of age, by puting him forth to a trad, &ċ.

[*111.] *Orders and Conclusions, with seuerall Graunts of Lands, made, ordered, graunted, and concluded att the second Session of the Generall Court begun the seauenth Day of June last, adjourned vnto this p̃sent Day, being the eleuenth of October, Anno Dom̃ 1665.

Wheras, in regard of the remote distance of our honored Goũ his former habitation, and being the countrey saw reason to desire and request his remouall vnto the towne of Plymouth for the more conuenient adminnestration of justice, and that, by Gods prouidence hee is now remoued to his great inconvenience and detriment, —

This Court haue ordered, and doe vnanimously agree to alow vnto him the sum̃e of fifty pounds a yeare soe longe as hee shall remaine in the place of Goũ.

And wheras hee is resedent in a place purchased by the countrey for that end, this Court haue likewise ordered, that incase hee shall decease att any time whiles hee is in the place of Goũ and inhabiting the said seat or being, that then his family shall and may without molestation continew in the said place or seate for the full tearme of one yeare after his decease att the least; and likewise, that incase there should bee any alteration that any other should bee chosen to the place of Goũ whiles hee liueth, that hee shall and may, notwithstanding, remaine in the said place without molestation for the full tearme of one yeare after such alteration att the least.

In regard of the many occations that Captaine Soutworth hath bine imployed about in the behalfe of the countrey, wherby hee hath bine much hindered in his owne occations, to his great lose and detriment, the Court haue alowed him the sum̃e of ten pounds.

This Court hath ordered, in reference to the building of the Eelriuer bridge, that thirty pounds bee by the countrey alowed towards the same, the eight pounds alreddy payed being a p̃te; and if when the worke is done it doe appeer by a faire account that it hath bine much more chargeable, the Court doe engage to doe what further may be judged meet.

1665.

3 October. PRENCE, Gouᴿ.

Wheras formerly Richard Bourne and William Bassett were appointed by the Court to purchase a p̃cell of land desired by Thomas Butler, and that it doth appeer vpon tryall that the Indians will not p̃te with it, a further libertie and order is graunted to the said Richard Bourne and William Bassett, in the behalfe of the said Thomas Butler, to purchase other land desired by him, and that they make reporte therof to the Court, that they may doe therin as they shall see meet.

John Smith and John Russell, of the towne of Dartmouth, are appointed by the Court to make enquiry concerning some damage done to some Indians without the bounds of Acushenah by the horses of the English on the east syde of Acushenah, and to settle the said controuersy by takeing course for the satisfying of such damage as shall appeer vnto them.

Cornett Studson and William Paybody are appointed and requested by the Court to haue the ouersight of the worke in the rebuilding of the bridge att Jonses Riuer, intended and ordered to bee done by the countrey.

*The Treasurer, John Cooke, and Nathaniel Warren were appointed by the Court to treat with Phillip the sagamore about the sale of such lands as are to bee sold by him, and to purchase them in the behalfe of the countrey.

[*112.]

The major, the Tresurer, Cornett Studson, and Nathaniell Warren, or any three of them, are deputed by the Court to make sale of such lands as belonge to the countrey, not exceeding aboue eight hundred acrees.

Libertie is graunted vnto Mʳ John Alden, that if hee can find a portion of land fitt for accom̃odation, ether that hee may purchase it or that two of the other majestrates shall purchase it for him.

Wheras the Court haue formerly impowered Capᵗ Thomas Willett to purchase of the Indians certaine tracts of land on the north of Rehoboth towards the Bay line; the which hee hath done, and is out of purse some considerable sum̃e of money for the same; this Court haue appointed the honored Goũ, the Major Winslow, Capᵗ Southworth, and Mʳ Constant Southworth to treat with Capᵗ Willett concerning the said purchase, and haue impowered the abouenamed com̃ittee to take notice of what hath bine purchased by him, and what deeds hee hath, and what his disbursments haue bine for the same, and haue alsoe impowered them to settle vpon him such a proportion of the said lands as may appeer to bee equall vpon any graunt to him, and to accom̃odate the towne of Rehoboth respecting an enlarḡment of

1665.
3 October.
PRENCE,
Gouʳ.

theire towne, as the Court haue promised, and to take such course conserning the remainder as that hee may bee reimbursed of his just due, and those lands may bee settled by the Court.

In reference vnto the request of the Kinges comissioners, in the behalfe of Leiftenant Peregrine White, desireing that the Court would accomodate him with a portion of land, in respect that hee was the first of the English that was borne in these ptes, and in answare vnto his owne petition prefered to this Court respecting the pmises, —

Of this graunt see more in the great booke, folio 87, named Euidence of Lands enrowled.

The Court haue graunted vnto him two hundred acrees of land lying and being att the path that goes from Bridgwater to the Bay, adjoyning to the Bay line.

Threescore acrees of land, with four acrees of meddow, and a certaine smale iland att a place called Patonumatucke, is graunted by the Court vnto Josias Cooke.

One hundred and fifty acrees of land are graunted by the Court vnto the three sisters, the daughters of Roger Chandeler, deceased, viz§, to each of them fifty acrees, lying between the Bay line and the bounds of Taunton, according to the desire of John Bundey.

[*113.]

*Two hundred acrees of land is graunted vnto the four younger sonnes of Leiftenant James Torrey, lying aboue Waymouth, neare vnto the line of the Massachusetts, to bee att the disposing of Captaine Wiłłam Torrey for the good of the said children, according to a petition prefered to the Court to that purpose.

In answare vnto the petition of Thomas Little and Josias Keane, the Court haue graunted vnto them libertie to looke out for a portion of land for theire accomodation; and incase they can find it, the Court haue graunted vnto each of them one hundred acrees of land, viz§ : vnto Thomas Little one hundred acrees in reference vnto land surrendered vp by him att Manomett Ponds, and vnto Josias Kean one hundred in respect vnto his great nessesitie.

The Court haue graunted vnto Ensigne Eames and vnto Isacke Chettenden, to each of them, a hundred acrees of land lying and being neare vnto Accord Pond, viz§, that which some of Hingham formerly refused.

Mʳ Thacher, Mʳ Howes, and Robert Dennis appointed by the Court to looke after the order about the excise in the towne of Yarmouth.

Letters of adminnestration are graunted vnto Ann, the relect of Leiftenant James Torrey, late of Scittuate, deceased, to adminnester on the estate left by him, the said estate being left in her hand to be improued for the bringing vp of theire children, both whiles shee remaines a widdow and afterwards, if it please God to alter her condition, and for that end haue impowered Mʳ Joseph Tilden and Walter Hatch to bee ouerseers therof.

COURT ORDERS.

*Att the Court of Assistants held att Plymouth the 2^{cond} of December, 1665.

1665.

2 December.
PRENCE, GOU^R.

[*114.]

BEFORE Thomas Prence, Gou^r,
Wiłłam Collyare,
John Alden,

Thomas Southworth, and
Wiłłam Bradford,

Assistants.

IN reference vnto a complaint against Abraham Jackson for corrupting of seueral barrells of tarr by puting of dirt into the same, the Court, takeing notice of diuers testimonies to euince the truth therof, doe judge that noe other could doe it, and therfore doe centance him to pay a fine of fiue pounds to the vse of the collonie.

And in reference vnto the complaint of Gyles Ricard, Juni^r, that hee hath lost foure barrells of tarr, and supposing that hee hath found them amoñst the tarr of Abraham Jackson, the said tarr being attached and bound oner vnto this Court, the Court, hauing heard both p̃ties conserning the same, and suspecting that the said tarr is the said Ricards, doe require securitie of the said Jackson to make further answare thervnto att the Generall Court of his mat^{tie} to bee holden for this goũment the first Tusday in March next, vnless the said p̃ties agree the case before that time ; which incase they doe, then theire said agreement to bee a finall end therof in reference to the Courts takeing any further notice therof.

Abraham Jackson acknowlidgth to owe vnto our soũ lord the Kinge the sume of fiue pounds.

The condition, that if the said Abraham Jackson shall and doe appeer att the Generall Court of his mat^{tie} to bee holden att Plymouth the first Tusday in March next, to make further answare conserning foure barrells of tarr challenged amongst his tarr by Gyles Rickard, Juni^r, and not depart the said Court without lycence ; that then, &c̃.

Since this date Gyles Rickard, Juni^r, hath receiued of Abraham Jackson four barrells of tarr in reference vnto these bonds, according to order of Court.

In reference vnto the complaint of Wiłłam Hoskins against Robert Ransom, for calling him rogue and other abusiue tearmes, and alsoe for violent assaulting of him when hee was att his house and in his honest laboure, and for many threatening speches spoken by him against the said Hoskins, the said Ransome being by the Court admonished, and promising reformation, the said Hoskins rested satisfyed, and soe the matter was ended.

In reference vnto the complaint of Hester, the wife of John Rickard, against Ann, the wife of Wiłłam Hoskins, for slaundering her in saying the said Hester was as drunke as a bitch, and found in private companie in an ordinary with John Ellis, of Sandwich, the said Ann Hoskins acknowlidging

112   PLYMOUTH COLONY RECORDS.

1665. her fault in open Court in reporting such thinges, haueing noe sufficient
2 December. ground soe to doe, the said Hester Rickard therin rested satisfyed, and soe the
PRENCE, matter was ended.
Gou^r.
Att this Court, Nathaniel Bacon, John Chipman, John Tompson, and Trusterum Hull were approued by the Court to bee the select men of the towne of Barnstable.

Att this Court, an Indian, called John, haueing bin comitted to prison for stealing of a gun and an axe from William Harvey, of Taunton, forasmuch as neither the said Harvey nor any other appeered att the Court to procecute against him, hee haueing bine longe in durance and vndergon much hardship, hee was ordered by the Court to repaire to the said Harvey, and either by worke or otherwise to satisfy the wrongs done him by takeing away his said goods; and soe the said John, with warning to doe soe noe more, was sett att libertie.

1665-6. *Att the Court of Assistants held att Plymouth for the Jurisdiction
6 February. of New Plymouth, the sixt of February, 1665.
[*115.]

BEFORE Thomas Prence, Gouernor, &   Thomas Southworth, and
Josias Winslow,   William Bradford,
                        Assistants.

IN reference vnto the complaint of Mr Samuell Arnold against Mr William Thomas, for that hee charged him that in his catichisme hee had deliuered and taught horible blasphemy in teaching that Christ as God is equall with the Father, but as mediator the Father is greater than hee, although the testimonies doe not make out the extent of the charge, yett the Court doe adjudge, that it was great arogancy in Mr Thomas to expresse himselfe as hee did in tearmes as of horible blasphemy vpon his meer apprehensions, and can not but owne that which Mr Arnold hath asserted to bee an orthodox truth conseirning the controuersy, and therfore doe aduise the said Mr Thomas for the future to carry more soberly, and to bee willing to receiue the truth in the loue of it.

A judgment of 01 : 10 : 11 was graunted vnto James Cole, Seni^r, against John Sutten, in reference to an apparent debt owing by the said Sutten to the said Cole; the charges of the complaint is encluded in the abouesaid sume.

In reference vnto the complaint of Nathanell Warren against James

COURT ORDERS.   113

Barnabey, vpon suspison that the said Barnabey either burned a p̄cell of pyne   1665-6.
knotes appertaining to the said Warren or that the said Barnabey concealed
the burning of them, the Court haue awarded the said James Barnabey to pay   6 February.
or cause to bee payed vnto the said Nathaniel Warren the sum̄e of forty   Prence,
shillings.   Gou^r.

Leift Perigrine White, Ensigne Marke Eames, Anthony Snow, John Bourne, and Wiłłam Foard, Seni^r, are approued by the Court to bee the select men of the towne of Marshfeild.

Mr Josias Winslow and Anthony Snow are approued by the Court to bee gaurdians to two of the sonnes of Robert Waterman, deceased, viz$, Josepth Waterman and Robert Waterman; and supposing that Robert Waterman is vnder age, the Court appoints the said Mr Winslow and Anthony Snow to bee gaurdian to him, as aboue said.

Memorandum: that Mistris Rachell Dauenport, with her arbetrator, refuseth to refer the controuersy now depending betwixt Thomas Little and her vnto an arbetration, but rather refers the case to the determination of the Court.

In reference vnto the neglect of a Court order in the towne of Sandwich, conserning bounding of each mans p̄ticulare lands, the Court orders, that the said acte of Court bee obserued with all convenient speed, and for that end three or four men bee deputed by the towne to see that the said order bee put in execution; and incase it soe bee, that the forfeiture of theire former neglect bee remited.

Łers of adminnestration are graunted vnto Wiłłam Hoskins; and hee is heerby authorised to adminnester on the estate of Nicholas Hodgis, allies Miller, deceased.

---

*.All the Generall Court holden att Plymouth, for the Jurisdiction of   6 March.
    New Plymouth, the sixt of March, 1665.*   [*116.]

BEFORE Thomas Prence, Goū,   Thomas Southworth,
       John Alden,   Wiłłam Bradford, and
       Josias Winslow,   Thomas Hinckley,
                    Assistants, &c̄.

IN reference vnto an order of Court bearing date the third day of October, 1665, wherin our honored Goū, Major Winslow, Capt Southworth, and Mr Constant Southworth were appointed to bee a com̄ittee in reference vnto a

VOL. IV.   15

1665-6.

6 March.
Prence,
Govr.

certaine tract of land purchased by Captaine Willett on the north side of Rehoboth, which said order impowereth the said comittee to dispose and settle a proportion of the said lands on the said Capt Willett as they shall thinke meet, and doe therfore settle and confeirme vnto him foure or fiue hundred acrees of the said land, to bee layed out for him on the easterly side or end of the said land, to him and his heires for euer.

Wheras Josepth Whiston, the eldest son of John Whiston, of Scittuate, deceased, hath freely and absolutly made ouer and allianated his whole p̄te and share of land in Conihassett land, bee it more or lesse, vnto the rest of his brothers and sisters, the children of the said John Whiston; and wheras the said land, as it is in its p̄sent condition, is not like to conduce to the good and benifitt of the said children, these may certify, that with the free and full consent of the p̄ties on each side interested, the Court hath giuen libertie vnto the said Josepth Whiston, with the healp of his father in law, William Brookes, and his vnkell, Edward Jenkens, to make sale therof for the vse and benifit of the aforsaid children, and to bee disposed of vnto them by order from the Court in equall proportions, according as they or any of them are or shalbee of age to receiue theire p̄te therof.

In reference vnto a purchase of land made by John Cooke, in the behalfe of some others, of a p̄te of the iland called Nakatay, the Court haue ordered, that incase those for whom hee purchased the said land doe not satisfy him for the purchase therof and other nessesary charges about it betwixt this date and the next June Court to bee holden att Plymouth, that the said land bee then made ouer to him for satisfaction of the said purchase and charges.

In reference vnto a way desired by Mr Howland to his house and land att Rockey Nooke, the Court haue ordered, that in due and convenient time a jury bee impanneled to lay out the said way.

This bond is cancelled in open Court held att Plymouth March the 7th, 1667-1668.

These p̄sents witnesseth, that Capt James Cudworth and Mr Josepth Tilden doe by these p̄sents stand bound vnto the Court of Plymouth, in New England, in the sume of ten pounds, joyntly and seuerally, in reference vnto a p̄sell of coopers stuffe and bolts attached on Conahassett land, that they haueing libertie from the said Court to dispose of the said stuffe and bolts, that incase any other shall or doe appeer betwixt this date & the Court of his ma^{tie} to bee holden att Plymouth the first Tusday in June next, and can make proffe that they are belonging to them, if then the said Captaine Cudworth and Mr Tilden bee in a reddynes and doe make satisfaction for the said stuffe and bolts to such as shall soe cleare vp theire right thervnto, that then this engagement to bee void, or otherwise the said sume of ten pounds to bee payable to the Court vpon theire demaund.

COURT ORDERS. 115

Att this Court, Quachattasett, the Indian sachem, of Mannomett, came 1665-6.
into the Court, and owned that Nanumett and Nocroft, two other Indians,
haue a p̃te in Mannomett old feild; and hee doth heerby engage not to make 6 March.
sale therof from the said Indians, and that they shall haue libertie of wood PRENCE, Govr.
and timber for fiering and other vses out of the bordering woods to the said
feild; and it was mutually desired by the said Quachattasett and the said
Indians, that the p̃mises should bee heer recorded for theire securitie.

*In reference vnto the complaint of Mistris Howes against Edward Stur- [*117.]
gis concerning a p̃cell of sturgion could by some Indians vnto her, the Court,
finding vpon examination that the said sturgeon was not deliuered vnto her
according to agreement, doe order, that the said Indians bee required by order
of Court to make satisfaction vnto her for the same.

Att this Court, Josepth Howes, the constable of Yarmouth, complained
against Thomas Starr for opposing him and vseing threatening speeches to
him in the execution of his office; the said Starr desiring to haue the case
tryed by jury, a jury was impannelled, whose names are as followeth: —

sworne, { Mr Josias Winslow, Senir,
 Cornett Robert Studson,
 Christopher Wadsworth,
 Willam Harlow,
 Samuell Dunham,
 Josepth Warren, } sworne, { Edward Jenkens,
 John Turner,
 Willam Sabin,
 Leift Hunt,
 Gyles Rickard, Junir,
 Benajah Pratt.

These found the said Thomas Starr guilty of the said fact; and therfore
hee was centansed by the Court to pay a fine of fiue pounds to the vse of the
countrey.

Att this Court, Mr Anthony Thacher complained against Thomas Starr,
Jonathan Barnes, and Abraham Hedge for abusiue carriages towards him in
his house; in reference whervnto the said Starr, Barnes, and Hedge were sentanced to pay vnto the said Mr Thacher the sum̃e of fiue pounds, viz͠t : the said
Thomas Starr the sum̃e of forty shillings, Jonathan Barnes the sum̃e of forty
shillings, and Abraham Hedge the sum̃e of twenty shillings; and in reference vnto theire rietus carriages att the same time in breakeing the Kings
peace, for the which bonds was taken of each of them vntill this Court, the
Court sentanced them to bee com̃itted to prison, and theire to remaine during
the pleasure of the Court; which accordingly was pformed, and the next day
after their com̃ittment were sett att libertie, and theire bonds deliuered to
them.

And in reference vnto the said Thomas Starr and Jonathan Barnes theire

1 6 6 5-6.
6 March.
Prence,
Govr.

abusiue carriage to Francis Baker att the same time, they, the said Starr and Barnes, were sentanced by the Court to pay vnto the said Baker, each of them, the summe of twenty shillinges.

And in reference vnto the said Francis Baker and John Casley theire breach of the peace att the same time, they were fined by the Court, each of them, the summe of three shillinges and four pence to the vse of the collonie.

And wheras Elisha Hedge hath giuen testimony that the said Baker and Casley were drunke att the same time, incase any concurrant testimony shall appeer to cleare vp the truth therof, they shalbee lyable to suffer the penaltie of the law for the same.

William Honywell, haueing bine comited to jayle on suspision of buggery with a beast, att this Court was examined concerning the same, and stifly deneyed it; and wheras noe sufficient euidence appeered to convict him of the said fact, hee was sett att libertie.

John Barrow, for refusing to giue euidence before a majestrate in reference to the grand enquest, was fined ten shillings.

Benjamine Eaton, for the same default agreuated by cercomstances, find the summe of forty shillinges to the vse of the collonie.

[*118.]

*Wheras John Robinson, of Saconesett, hath bine convicted of some laciuious speches and actions manifested towards Francis, the wife of Thomas Crippen, the Court saw reason to require bonds of him for his good behauior, as followeth : —

John Robinson acknowlidgeth to owe vnto our soft lord the Kinge the summe of . . . . } 20 : 00 : 00

Isacke Robinson the summe of . . . . 10 : 00 : 00

Robert Dennis the summe of . . . . 10 : 00 : 00

Released.

The condition, that if the said John Robinson bee of good behauior towards our soft lord the Kinge and all his leich people, and especially towards Francis, the wife of Thomas Crippin, and appeer att the Court of his ma^{tie} to bee holden att Plymouth the first Tusday in June next, and not depart the said Court without lycence ; that then, &c.

Wheras Thomas Crippin hath bine convicted before the Court of laciuious speeches tending to the vpholding of and being as a pandor of his wife in lightnes and laciuiousnes, the Court saw reason to require bonds of him for his good behauior ; and wheras the said Crippin could not procure surties, hee hath and doth by these p̄sents bind ouer vnto the Court, in the behalfe of his ma^{tie}, the vallue of forty pounds out of his estate, as followeth, vizt, two mares, one cow, two yearling heiffers, two tweumonthing steers, and soe much of his other estate as will make vp the said summe.

COURT ORDERS.

The condition, that if the said Thomas Crippen bee of good behauior towards our soū lord the Kinge and all his leich people, and appeer att the Court of his ma^{tie} to bee holden att Plymouth the first Tusday in June next, and not depart the said Court without lycence; that then, &c.

1665-6.
6 March.
Prence,
Gou^r.
Released.

Wheras Jonathan Hatch hath bine convicted of vnnessesarie frequenting the house of Thomas Crippin, and therby hath giuen occation of suspision of dishonest behauior towards Francis, the wife of the said Crippin, the Court hath admonished him and warned him for the future not to giue such occation of suspision as aforsaid by his soe frequently resorting to the said house or by coming in the companie of the said woman, as hee will answare it att his p̄rill.

William Sabin, being p̄sented for pound breach, fined   02 : 10 : 00
Gorge Barlow, for being drunke the 2^{cond} time, fined .   10 : 00
John Crow, the son of Yeluerton Crow, for breach of the peace in striking John Tayler, fined . . . .   03 : 04

The Court aloweth vnto Gyles Rickard, Juni^r, from Abraham Jackson, ten shillings for charges in reference to a p̄sell of tarr of late in controuersye betwixt them.

Isacke Chettenden is alowed by the Court to draw and sell wine and liquors and to keep an ordinary in the towne of Scittuate.

The select men of the towne of Yarmouth approued by the Court are Mr Anthony Thacher, Mr Edmond Hawes, James Mathewes, John Miller, Josepth Howes.

Letters of adminnestration are graunted vnto Gorge Watson to adminnester on the estate of Mistris Margarett Hickes, deceased.

Łres of adminnestration are graunted vnto Mistris Mary Howes to adminnester on the estate of Mr Thomas Howes, deceased.

Att this Court, John Williams was discharged from being ensigne bearer of the milletary companie of Scittuate.

*These may certify to whom it doth conserne, that by mutuall consent and agreement between Richard Chadwell and Gorge Allin, the way is made that was in controuersy between them, that is, from the comon neare the said Richard Chadwells now dwelling house to the said Gorḡ Allins now dwelling house, and soe to Musett, and by theire agreement to continew for euer, prouided, that wheras Richard Chadwell hath bine willing for peace sake, and that loue might bee amongst them, they being soe neare dwellers, to make the way att the entery att the vper p̄te ouer a peece or p̄cell of dunge ground, being a choise place, where the said Richard Chadwell had yarded his cattle ;

[*119.]

1665-6.

6 March.
Prence,
Govr.

know this, that hee hath reserued to himselfe or his assignes, to take and carry away att his pleasure, by cart or otherwise, soe much of the ground in that said way as shalbee good for the manuring of his said land; alsoe, the desire is, that this theire acte and deed about the said way may bee enrowled in our Court booke att New Plymouth.

        Witnes,   EDMOND FREEMAN, Senr.

Sandwich, dated the 4th of July, 1665.

See June Court, 1665.

The rates for the countrey charges of this yeare, as they were leuied on the seuerall townes of this jurisdiction, are as followeth, vizt, as to the sume of one hundred and ten pounds, being a p̄te of one hundred and fifty pounds ordered by the Court, June 7th, 1665, to bee leuied as aforsaid, the sume of forty pounds therof bee leuied and payed in money soone after the said order was concluded, —

Plymouth,	10 : 03 : 06
Duxborrow,	09 : 05 : 02
Scittuate,	16 : 12 : 09
Sandwich,	09 : 05 : 02
Taunton,	09 : 05 : 02
Yarmouth,	07 : 17 : 11
Rehoboth,	13 : 17 : 09
Eastham,	07 : 08 : 06
Sowams,	04 : 02 : 06
Dartmouth,	05 : 10 : 00
	111 : 09 : 10

The Rate for the Officers Wages.

Plymouth,	03 : 14 : 00
Duxburrow,	03 : 07 : 04
Scittuate,	06 : 01 : 00
Sandwich,	03 : 07 : 04
Taunton,	03 : 07 : 04
Yarmouth,	02 : 17 : 04
Barnstable,	03 : 14 : 00
Marshfeild,	02 : 17 : 04
Rehoboth,	05 : 01 : 00
Eastham,	02 : 14 : 00
Dartmouth,	02 : 00 : 00
Sowams,	01 : 10 : 00

*_Att the Court of Assistants holden att Plymouth the first of May,_ 1666.

BEFORE Thomas Prence, Goū,   Thomas Southworth,
John Alden,   Wiłłam Bradford, and
Josias Winslow,   Thomas Hinckley,
Assistants, &c.

1 May.
PRENCE,
GOUᴿ.
[*120.]

Mᴿ CONSTANT SOUTHWORTH and Richard Bourne are requested and appointed by the Court, in due and convenient time, to repaire to a certaine place neare vnto Mannomett, called Penquine Hole, for to view and purchase a certaine p̄sell of land in reference vnto the accom̄odation of Wiłłam Paybody, in liew of a p̄sell of land relinquished by him vnto the countrey, lying att Taunton Riuer, incase hee can bee acom̄odated in a valluable way in the former place.

In reference vnto a deed surrendered vp vnto our Court by Leiftenant Holbrooke, of Weymouth, made and giuen by Josias Wampatucke and Webcowett vnto Serjeant Thomas Streame, for the lease of a certaine tract of land, for the gratifycation of the said Leift Holbrooke, and in reference to his free acknowlidging therof, the Court hath graunted vnto him one hundred and twenty acrees of land.

And wheras the Court haue graunted vnto the children of Leift Torrey, of Scittuate, deceased, two hundred acrees of land, att the request of Captaine Torrey, the Court hath appointed John Jacob, of Hingham, and John Whitmarsh, of Weymouth, to lay out the said lands within the bounds of the tract of land the said deed of lease expressed, and alsoe to lay out the said graunt of land vnto Leift Holbrooke att or neare the said place likewise.

This was graunted vnto the foure youngest sonnes of the said Leiftenant James Torrey. See the actes of October Court in this booke, anno 1665.

Wheras Mistris Rachell Dauenport and Thomas Little haue refered vnto the determination of this Court a controuersy or difference between them respecting rents due since the said Little entered vpon those lands that were som̄times the lands of Major Wiłłam Holmes, and haue agreed that this Courts determination shalbee a finall issue between them respecting the p̄mises, —

Wee, haueing seriously weighed and considered the matter, doe judge, that although rent was indeed sued for and buildinges, yett the jury that had it before them did not greatly consider of any thinge but the title of the land, and soe did neither prouide to secure Goodman Little respecting his building and improuement on that land nor determine conserning rents by her claimed, and are satisfyed that the p̄tyes themselues did soe vnderstand, as appeers

1666.
1 May.
PRENCE,
GOU^R.

by theire since puting it to arbetration and vpon other grounds; and, vpon the other side, considering the lands as they were wast in respect of buildinges and fences, and the meddowes som̃thing damnifyed, the rent must needs bee much the lesse, and takeing notice, alsoe, that the one halfe of her claime is satisfyed by her agreement with Josias Keine, wee doe award, that Thomas Little pay vnto Mistris Dauenport abouesaid or her order, as full satisfaction for all claimes and demaunds of rent of the said lands, fifteen pounds in good and current pay, the one halfe att present att or before the first of June next, and the other halfe att or before the 20th day of May, in the yeare 1667.

Wheras, by an order of Court bearing date the first of August, 1665, Major Winslow, Anthony Snow, John Bourne, and Wiłłam Paybody were appointed and impowered to issue a difference between Moses Simons and Samuell Chandeler in reference to the bounds of theire lands where they now dwell; in order thervnto, wee, the aboue named, mett vpon the place on the 28th of March, 1666, and haueing seen both theire records, viewed the bounds on the out sides of both theire lotts, and heard what could bee said on both sides, wee judge there is a mistake in ranging Edmond Chandelers land north and by east between Moses Simons and him, when as the other ranges on both sides are north and by west; wee settled the range between from an old root in the corner of Moses Simons his orchyard, north and by west to a little walnutt aboue the orchyard, and thence to a stake and heap of stones, and soe vp to a great blacke oake marked on four sides north and by east and south and by west throughout.

In witnes wherof wee haue heervnto sett our hands.

JOSIAS WINSLOW,
ANTHONY SNOW,
JOHN BOURNE,
WIŁŁAM PAYBODY.

In reference vnto the complaint of Abraham Jackson against Nathaniell Warren, for detaining and not owning a barrell of tarr deliuered in by the said Jackson for the townes vse, after many passages about it, the said Nathaniel Warren engaged, that incase Richard Willis did prosecute an attachment against Peter Steuens for a debt due to him from the said Steuens and proue his debt, that then the said Warren would answare the said barrell of tarr.

Richard Willis stands bound vnto the Court in the sum̃e of seauen pounds sterling to prosecute an attachment of seauen barrell of tarr against Peter Steuens att the Court of his ma^{tie} to bee holden att Plymouth the first

Tusday in October next, in reference vnto a debt due to him, the said Willis, from the said Steuens.

1666.
1 May. PRENCE, Gou^R.
[*121.]

*Wheras the Court haue ordered that Joneses Riuer bridge should bee repaired, and that, according to the Courts order, some lands haue bine sold for the defraying of the countreyes charges, these are to declare and order, that such sumes as are due and payable to the countrey for the said lands soe sould bee heerby made ouer and assured by these p̃sents vnto Mr Constant Southworth, Treasurer, for the accomplishing of the worke in repaireing or building of the said bridge, or soe much of them as shalbee requisite for that end.

Att this Court, John Williams appeered to make answare for his continued abusing of his wife, by vnaturall carriages towards her both in words and actions, by rendering her to bee a whore, and for p̃sisting on in his refusing to p̃forme marriage duty towards her according to the law of God and man; and forasmuch as the said Williams desired to bee tryed in reference to the p̃mises by a jury, the Court gaue him libertie soe to doe, either att this Court or att the Court to bee holden att Plymouth in June next; the said Williams desired it might bee att the last named, and heerby engageth to supply his wife in the mean time with money and other nessesaries which shee shall stand in need of, and hath expressed himselfe to bee willing that shee shall or may repaire to her frinds vntill then, and then and att that time to attend the issue of the case on the fift day of the said Court weeke.

In reference vnto the complaint of Marshall Nash against the constables of Marshfeild, for not paying p̃te of his sallary, the Court haue ordered him to buy soe much corne as comes to ten shillings, and it to bee required of John Bourne, forasmuch as the cause of the said neglect of payment was caused originally by him.

This is since payed.

It being a mistake in the warrant respecting John Bourne, it is cleared since the abouesaid entery.

1666.

5 June.

PRENCE, GOUᴿ.

[*122.]

*Att the Generall Court of Election holden att Plymouth the fift Day of June, 1666.

BEFORE Thomas Prence, Gouʳ,   Thomas Southworth,
Wiłłam Collyare,   Wiłłam Bradford, and
John Aldin,   Thomas Hinckley,
Josias Winslow,

Assistants, &c.

Mᴿ THOMAS PRENCE was chosen Gouʳ, and sworne.

Mʳ John Alden,
Major Josias Winslow,
Captaine Thomas Southworth,   } were chosen Assistants, and sworne.
Captaine Wiłłam Bradford, and
Mʳ Thomas Hinckley,

Likewise, Mʳ James Browne and Leiftenant John Freeman were chosen Assistants, but not sworne.

Major Josias Winslow and Captaine Thomas Southworth were chosen comissioners.

And Mʳ Thomas Prence was the next in nomination.

Mʳ Constant Southworth was chosen Treasurer, and sworne.

The names of the deputies chosen by the countrye out of the seuerall townshipes of this goūment to serue att this Court and the seuerall adjournments therof are as followeth : —

Mʳ John Howland,	‡Nathaniell Bacon,‡
Leifᵗ Ephraim Morton,	‡John Chipman,‡
Mʳ Constant Southworth,	‡Joseph Laythorp,‡
Christopher Wadsworth,	Ensigne Eames,
Cornett Robert Studson,	John Bourne,
Isacke Chettenden,	‡Mʳ James Broune,‡
Richard Bourne,	‡Mʳ Stephen Paine,‡
‡James Skiffe,‡	‡Leiftenant John Freeman,‡
James Walker,	‡Josias Cooke,‡
Wiłłam Haruey,	‡Daniel Cole,‡
Edward Sturgis,	John Willis,
Elverton Crow,	John Cooke.

COURT ORDERS. 123

The constables of the seuerall townes of this jurisdiction are as fol- 1666.
loweth : —
5 June.
PRENCE,
Gou^r.

Plymouth, ...	Edward Gray.
Duxburrow, ...	John Rogers.
^	Richard Dwelley.
^	William Peakes.
Sandwich, ...	Henery Dillingham.
Taunton, ...	John Hall.
Yarmouth, ...	John Miller.
Barnstable, ...	Thomas Huckens.
Marshfeild, ...	{ William Foard, Juni^r, Jonathan Winslow.
Rehoboth, ...	{ Samuell Carpenter, John Perram.
Eastham, ...	Robert Vixon.
Bridgwater, ...	Daniell Bacon.
Dartmouth, ...	William Palmer.

*The grand enquest are as followeth : — [*123.]

sworne, {
Anthony Snow,
Thomas Doged,
Mr Allexander Standish,
Experience Michell,
Josepth Aldin,
Samuell Sturtivant,
Samuell Fuller,
Gilbert Brookes,
Samuell Pecke,
John Cushen,
Hugh Cole,
}

sworne, {
James Lewis,
Jonathan Sparrow,
Thomas Leanard,
Henery Andrewes,
Henery Vincent,
Charles Stockbridge,
William Spooner,
John Thacher,
Josepth Burgis,
Job Bourne.
}

The surveyors of the highwayes are as followeth : —

Plymouth, ...	{ Jakob Cooke, Robert Finney, Thomas Lettice.
Duxburrow, ...	{ Josepth Wadsworth, Samull Chandeler.
Scittuate, ...	{ John Williams, Juni^r, William Barstow, Thomas Pincen.

1666.
5 June.
PRENCE,
GOUR.

Sandwich, ... { Stephen Winge,
                          Thomas Butler.

Taunton, ... { John Cobb,
                         Samuell Williams.

Yarmouth, ... { Samuell Rider, Seni^r,
                          Thomas Gadge.

Marshfeild, ... { John Dingley,
                          Josias Keine.

Rehoboth, ... { Gorge Kenericke,
                          Richard Bowin.

Eastham, ...   ^
Bridgwater, ...   ^
Dartmouth, ...   ^

The Names of the Celect Men in each Towne approued by the Court.

Plymouth :
 Mr John Howland,
 Gorg Watson,
 Leiftenant Morton,
 Robert Finney.
Duxburrow :
 Christopher Wadsworth,
 Mr Josias Standish,
 Benjamine Bartlett.
Scittuate :
 Mr Thomas Kinge,
 Cornett Robert Studson,
 Isacke Chettenden.
Sandwich :
 ^
Taunton :
 Gorg Hall,
 Richard Williams,
 Walter Dean,
 James Walker,
 Willam Harvey.
Yarmouth :
 Mr Anthony Thacher,
 Mr Edmond Hawes,
 James Mathewes,

 John Miller,
 Josepth Howes.
Barnstable :
 Nathaniel Bacon,
 John Chipman,
 John Tompson,
 Trusturm Hull.
Marshfeild :
 Leiftenant White,
 Ensigne Eames,
 Anthony Snow,
 John Bourne,
 Willam Foard, Seni^r.
Rehoboth :
 ^
Eastham :
 Leiftenant Freeman,
 Josias Cooke,
 Richard Higgens.
Bridgwater :
 Nicholas Byram,
 Leiftenant Howard,
 John Willis.
Dartmouth :
 ^

*Att this Court, Elizabeth, the wife of John Williams, appeered with complaint against her husband, the said John Williams, for his great abusiue and vnaturall carryages towards her, both in word and deed, in defaming her in rendering her to bee a whore, and by psisting in his refusing to pforme marriage duty vnto her according to what both the law of God and man requireth, which more att large appeereth by a writing vnder her hand.

1 6 6 6.
5 June.
PREXCE,
Gov^R.
[*124.]

And wheras the said John Williams obtained liberty of the Court to haue the case tryed by a jury, accordingly a jury was impanneled for the tryall of the said case, whose names are as followeth : —

John Tompson,	Ephraim Tinkham,
John Dingley,	Gilbert Brookes,
John Smalley,	Robert Vixon,
Trustrum Hull,	John Done,
John Joyce,	John Washburne,
John Pecke,	John Howland.

These all sworne.

These found the abouesaid complaint to bee true or just.

And accordingly the Court proseeded to pase centance against him as followeth : —

Wheras Elizabeth, the wife of John Williams, exhibited a complaint against her said husband vnto the Court of Assistants held att Plymouth the first day of May last past before the date heerof, for many abusiue carriages towards her both in word and deed, by defaming her in rendering her to bee a whore, and psisting in his refusing to pforme marriage duty vnto her, as alsoe that hee hath not onely withheld nessesary comforts and conveniencyes suitable to her estate from her, but hath carryed bitterly towards her in many respects; and wheras hee should haue bine a shelter and a protection vnto her, hath endeauored to reproach, insnare, and betray her, &c̄, as by that her declaration aboue mentioned is more att large expressed; & that att the said John Williams his request the abouesaid complaint was att this Court put vpon tryall by a jury of his equalls, and a verdict brought in against him, and that they found her complaint to bee true or just, which did alsoe appeer to our satisfaction by euidence, himselfe alsoe declaring his insufficiency for converse with weomen, —

The first day of May.

The Court, haueing seriously considered of the matter, doe judge, that it is not safe or convenient for her to liue with her husband, but doe giue her liberty att psent to depart from him vnto her frinds vntill the Court shall

1666.

5 June.
Prence,
Govr.

otherwise order or hee shall apply himselfe vnto her in such a way as shee may be better satisfyed to returne to him againe, and doe order him to apparrell her suitably att the present, and furnish her with a bed and beding and such like nessesaryes, and to alow her ten pounds yearly to maintaine her while shee shalbee thuse absent from him, and for pformance heerof doe require that hee put in cecuritie, or that one third p̄te of theire estate bee cecured for her liuelihood and comfort.

Att the earnest request of his wife, this p̄te of the centance was remited and not executed.

2^{condly}. For that hee hath greatly defamed and otherwise abused his said wife as in the p̄mises, wee adjudge him to stand in the street or markett place by the post with an inscription ouer him that may declare to the world his vnworthy carriages towards his wife.

3dly. Inasmuch as these his wicked carryages haue bine contrary to the lawes of God and man, and alsoe very disturbing and expensiue to this goū-ment, wee doe amerce him to pay a fine of twenty pound to the vse of the collonie.

In reference to the Courts centance of John Williams his fine, and the cecuring of one third of his estate towards his wifes maintainance, the Court orders the cheife marshall to make distresse on the goods of the said Williams for his fine to the countrey according as in such case by law is prouided; and as to the cecuring of one third of his estate for his wifes maintainance or liuelyhood, the Court orders, that incase hee refuse to sett out one third to his wifes order which is desired, or to giue her cecuritie for the payment of the ten pounds annually according to order, then the cheife marshall to see an equall deuision of the said estate, vizt, lands, goods, and chattles, into three p̄tes, which shalbee brought to his view or cognizance by Elizabeth, the wife of the said Williams, with the healp of Captaine Cudworth, Isacke Chettenden, or any other of her naighbours; and being soe deuided, to deliuer one of the three p̄tes vnto the said Elizabeth or her order, to bee desposed by her for the ends aforsaid; the said marshall being to take care, in pformance of this his order, that it bee done in such a way as may bee least prejudiciall to the said estate.

[*125.] *An Order sent to the Milletary Company of Scittuate, as followeth.

Gentlmen: Wee haue taken notice of youer voate and nomination of the psons for p̄sent management of youer milletary exercises and affected with youer condition, and must signify vnto you that wee judge that youer voate was very vnaduised, and with respect to Captaine Cudworth, directly against our aduise and such reasons as wee did expect might haue bine satisfactory; and wee vnderstand that youer voate, although it did soe pas as it did, was att that instant protested against by many sober and discreet psons amongst you, and theire reasons layed downe; and alsoe conserning Mr Peirse, wee haue not to object concerning him but that hee is a stranger to vs, and doe therfore att p̄sent order Serjeant John Damman to take that charge, whoe was next in nomination by youer owne voate, and will manage it to the best of his abillities, and wee conceiue to a generall satisfaction as any that can bee proposed. Wee doe therfore expect that you doe peacably and reddily attend the same vntill wee may otherwise prouide for you; and forasmuch as times doe threaten more then ordinary danger and trouble to the countrey, wee shall take the best care that in vs lyes for you, as for other townes of this goūment, in that respect, & rest carefull of youer peace and welfare, &c̄.

1666.
5 June.
Prence,
Gou^r.

Serjeant John Damman: These are to signify vnto you, that the Court haue and doe heerby order and appoint you to take the charge and comand of the milletary companie of Scittuate vntill further order, requiring you to call them into armes and to drill and exercise them according to order to the best of youer abillities, and incase of any reall seruice that Gods prouidence may any way put vs vpon; for which nessesary defence or otherwise you are to attend to such orders as by the Court or councell of warr shalbee directed vnto you.

In p̄suance of an order of the Court for the jurisdiction of New Plymouth, giuen out for the laying out of two hundred acrees of land graunted by the Generall Court of the said jurisdiction vnto the children of Leift James Torrey, deceased, vizt, vnto his four youngest sonnes, wee, whose names are subscribed, haue, according to theire speciall order, measured, buted, and bounded the said two hundred acrees of land, joyning on the easterly side to the land formerly layed out to Clement Briggs; that is to say, two hundred rodds in length easterly, and eight score rodds in breadth, sett out by marked trees. This wee say wee haue finished and done, the 30th of May, 1666.

JOHN JACOB,
JOHN WHITMARSH.

Libertie is graunted by the Court vnto Francis Combe, as by right of his father, whoe was an ancient freeman, to looke out land for his accomodation, and to make report therof to the Court, that soe a competencye therof may bee alowed vnto him answarable vnto other ancient freemen.

The major and the Treasurer are appointed by the Court to lay out two hundred acrees of land graunted vnto Cornett Studson. It is alsoe ordered

1666.
5 June.
Prence,
Govr.

by the Court, that when they come vpon the place, that they are to alow him such a proportion therof as they shall thinke meet considering the badnes of the land there.

Liberty is graunted vnto John Morton to looke out for an accomodation of land; and incase hee can find any fitt for his accomodation, to haue fifty acrees.

Liberty is likewise graunted vnto Yeluerton Crow to looke out for land for his accomodation.

Nathaniel Warren and William Clarke are appointed by the Court to settle the bounds of the land of Robert Finney where hee now liueth.

[*126.]

*Two hundred acrees of land is graunted vnto Mr Thomas Prence, to bee layed forth for him either att or about Rootey Brooke or att the head of the pond.

It is graunted by the Court, that Ensigne Barnard Lumbard, John Finney, and Isacke Robinson bee suplyed with fifty acrees apeece or more of vpland att Pausatuke Necke or theraboutes, with six acrees of meddow left to the descretion of Mr Hinckley and Mr Bacon to view, purchase, and lay out vnto them; Mr Bourne alsoe being aded to them, to bee healpfull therin.

See June Court, anno 1662, in this booke, and there you shall find a list of theire names.

The Court haue graunted vnto the ancient servants, that they shall either bee accomodated att Saconett, according to a former graunt, or on the southside of Weymouth, between the land of Clement Briggs and Waymouth bounds; and incase they haue it att the latter place, that they shall haue fifty acrees apeece; and that Richard Beare bee accomodated with them; and that the Treasurer and Cornett Studson shall lay it forth to them, prouided that it bee done betwixt this date and Nouember next.

The hundred and fifty acrees of land formerly graunted to Mr Edmond Freeman, Juni^r, is fully confeirmed vnto him by the Court, viz: one hundred and fifty acrees of land, with the meddow adjoyning to the bounds of Saconeesett and vnto a place called Tassacust, being purchased by Richard Bourne and William Bassett, appointed thervnto by the Court; that is to say, all the meddow within the said purchase made of Quachattasett and Sepitt, his son, bearing date the seauenth of August, 1665.

The major, the Treasurer, and Cornett Studson are appointed by the Court to take course and agree with some workmen for the building of Joneses Riuer bridge.

In reference vnto the land formerly graunted vnto Zachary Eedey, the Court haue ordered, that Serjeant Tinkham and Henery Wood shall lay out the said land; and conserning the way that hee is to make in liew therof, that they are alsoe to see that it bee made soe and in such place as may bee most convenient for the countrey and least prejudiciall to him.

1666.

5 June. PRENCE, GOV^R.

Fifty acrees of land is graunted by the Court vnto Josepth Whiston, the heire of John Whiston, deceased, lying att the southermost side of the land graunted to Walter Woodward vpon the path goeing from Bridgwater to Waymouth, bounding att the east end vpon a little brooke, and the west end to the comon land, and the southermost side likewise to the comon.

It was ordered and agreed by this Court, that a rate of two hundred and thirty pounds should bee leuyed on the countrey for publike charges for this p̃sent yeare, besides the sume of seuen pounds to pay for sume law bookes appertaineing to the countrey.

Wheras there is a great neglect in both William Barstow and Robert Barker in not keeping of an ordinary fitt for the entertaining of strangers, the Court haue ordered, that William Barstow shall make competent prouision for strangers for theire entertainment and refreshment for this yeare, and that the other bee required to forbeare ; and that incase the said Barstow shall neglect soe to doe, that then the Court will take some other course about the same.

This Court hath called in the lycence that was giuen to Francis Sprague to keep an ordinary att Duxburrow.

The Court doth alow a fine of fiue pounds due from fiue Indians att Dartmouth, or soe much of it as can bee had, towards the building of a bridge there.

*In reference vnto the presentment of William Sutton, for takeing away a Bible out of the meeting house att Barnstable, and keeping it, and saying hee bought it and would haue sould it, hee is centanced by the Court to pay vnto Mr Hinckley, or vnto the Treasurer or his order, the sume of twenty shillinges, and for telling of a lye about it the sume of ten shillinges.

[*127.]

A fine of fiue pounds due from William Paybody was by this Court remited.

The Court haue graunted vnto Gyles Hopkins, the widdow Mayo, of Eastham, and Jonathan Sparrow a certaine p̃sell of land neare Eastham, being a smale necke of land called Sampsons Necke, and the wast land lying between the head of the fresh water pond and the westerly bounds of the widdowe Mayoes land, and soe downe to the coue.

Wheras a way hath formerly bine layed out by a jury which goeth through the land of Isacke Barker att Namassakesett, being greatly prejudiciall vnto him, the Court haue ordered, that this yeare the naighbours shalbee contented with such barrs as hee shall sett vp to keep his pasture through which the said way goeth ; and that it bee proposed to them, that they either

1666.
5 June.
Prence,
Govr.

make the fence alonge the way through the said pasture, or to bee contented with gates which the said Isacke Barker is to sett vp, and in the mean time not to through downe his barrs to his damage.

The Verdict of the Corroners Enquest concerning the sudden Death of Mary, the Wife of Thomas Totman, of Scittuate.

Wee, whose names are vnder subscribed, being impanelled on a jury by the constable of Scittuate, the 10th day of Aprill, 1666, to enquire after the death of Mary, the wife of Thomas Totman, and haueing viewed the corpes and heard what euidence can speake, doe giue in this following as our verdict : —

That Mary, the wife of Thomas Totman, gathered, dressed, and did eate a root, which wee judge, shee mistakeing it, thinking it to bee the same which shee had formerly often eaten of; but the root being of a poisonous nature, eateing of it, wee judge, was the sole cause and occation of her death; and that wee all agree heervnto, witnes our hands this 24th of Aprill, 1666.

P me,   JAMES CUDWORTH,
WILLAM WITHERELL,
HUMPHERY TURNER,
JOHN TURNER,
JOHN BRYANT,
JOHN ROGERS,
ELISHA BESBEY,
the marke of EZEKIELL MAYNE,
JOB Γ JUDKIN, his marke.
EDWARD E WRIGHT, his marke.
EDWARD E W WANTON, his marke.
HENERY H E EWELL, his marke.

Josepth Deuell, of Dartmouth, tooke the oath of fidelitie this Court.

The Court haue graunted vnto Serjeant Ephraim Tinkham twelue acrees of vpland on the east side of Whetstones Vinyard Brooke, and on the south east of the old Indian path, bounded att the westward end with a rid oake tree next the path and brooke, and a rid oake standing on a hill neare the Stony Brooke; and att the east end its bounded with a rid oake next the path and a white oake tree on the southward side therof; on the north side the land butts home to the path.

Measured for him by William Crow.

COURT ORDERS.

*In reference vnto Willam Paybody his exchange of his land, the Court haue ordered Mr Constant Southworth and Mr Bourne, of Sandwich, to proportion out vnto him how much hee shall haue of that hee desireth, in liew of that hee exchangeth for it.

1666.
5 June.
PRENCE,
Govr.

[*128.]

The Court haue graunted vnto Mr John Done one hundred acrees of vpland att Pottamumaquate Necke, and six acrees of meddow theraboutes; and Leiftenant Freeman and Josias Cooke are to view it and purchase it of the Indians for him.

The Court haue graunted vnto Leifft Ellis a portion of land not exceeding one hundred acrees att Maconsett Necke, and a smale quantitie of meddow therabouts; and Richard Bourne is ordered by the Court to lay it out for him.

The Court haue graunted vnto Esra Perry a smale quantity of land of about thirty acrees in the necke of land where Mr Edmond Freeman, Juni^r, hath his land that was last graunted vnto him by the Court.

The Court haue graunted vnto James Skiffe a smale quantitie of land, being about forty acrees, lying on the easterly side of the herring brooke att Monnomett, lying next to Mr Josias Standishes land there, a highway lying through it; and the Court haue ordered Richard Bourne to purchase it and to laye it out for him.

The Court haue graunted, that Willam Shirtliffe shalbee accomodated with land amongst the servants neare vnto the Bay line.

The Court haue graunted vnto Mr John Howland one hundred acrees of land in that land which Captaine Willett made purchase of att Tetiquott.

Likewise, the Court haue graunted vnto John Chipman and Jonathan Sparrow, to each of them, fifty acrees of land att the same place where Mr Howland is to bee accomodated next aboue mensioned.

Likewise, the Court haue graunted vnto the said Mr Howland, John Chipman, and Jonathan Sparrow to bee accomodated with meddow land answarable to theire proportions of vpland in the purchase made by Captaine Willett as aforsaid, if itt bee there to bee had; if not, that they shalbee accomodated elswhere with meet proportions, if it can bee found and purchased. The Court haue sence aded to Jonathan Sparrow and Mr Chipman fifty acrees of land apeece.

If the land will beare it : this was aded July, 1673.

The Court haue graunted vnto John Hanmore the three acrees of meddow desired by him lying neare the Indian Head Riuer.

Forty acrees of land is graunted by the Court vnto Rebecka, the wife of Hezekiah Hoare, of Taunton, in some convenient place neare Taunton bounds.

1666.

5 June.
PRENCE,
Gov^R.

Experience Michell hath libertie to looke out land for his accomodation.

Likewise, Mr Thomas Dexter, Juni^r, hath libertie to looke out for land for his accomodation.

Likewise, John Rogers, of Duxburrow, hath libertie to looke out for land for his accomodation.

Likewise, Benajah Pratt hath the like libertie to looke out land for his accomodation.

Likewise, Wiłłam Holmes hath libertie to looke out land for the accomodation of his children.

5 July.
[*129.]

*Att the Court of his Matie held att Plymouth the fift Day of July, 1666.

BEFORE Thomas Prence, Goũ,   Thomas Southworth,
John Aldin,   William Bradford, and
Josias Winslow,   Thomas Hinckley,
Assistants, &ð.

ATT this Court, a certaine Indian named Daniell, allies Tumpasscom, was presented before the Court and examined conserning his strikeing of Samuell Hickes, of Acushena, soe as the said Samuell Hickes languisheth and is in danger of death ; hee, the said Indian, confesseth that hee strucke or punched the said Hickes with an axe or the helue of it, but saith that the said Hickes first strucke him ; the said Indian was returned to prison, there to remaine in close durance vntill the last Tuesday in October, 1666.

‡This Court giueth liberty vnto John Copp, of Scittuate, to still strong waters there from the tearme of six monthes from the date heerof, prouided that what liquors hee stilleth bee sent or con ⌢   ⌢ ‡

Wheras John Copp, of Scittuate, hath sett vp a still for the stilling of liquors before the order of Court prohibiting the same without lycence was extant, and that the not improueing of it might proue prejudiciall vnto him, the Court haue giuen him liberty to still liquors att Scittuate for the space of six monthes from the date heerof, prouided that hee retaile nor sell any in this jurisdiction lesse then the quantitie of ten gallons, on the penaltie in that case ordered ; and if within the time prefixed noe complainte bee exhibited by the said towne to the Court against him, that att the period therof the Court will doe as to enlargment of his libertie or otherwise as they shall see cause.

COURT ORDERS.　　　　　　　　　　　133

These may certify vnto all whom it may concerne, that wheras Peter Steuens somtimes bought an horse of Nathaniel Warren, of Plymouth, that the said Peter Steuens hath surrendered vp the said horse vnto the said Nathaniel Warren againe; and that the said Nathaniell Warren haueing, neare vnto the time of the buying of the said horse, receiued of the said Steuens a p̱sell of tarr for the said horse, these are alsoe to giue notice and to certify all whom it may conserne, that the said Nathaniell Warren hath relinquished the said tarr, soe as since it hath bin attached att the suite of other creditors, and is disposed of according to law soe farr as it will extend for theire satisfaction.

1666.
5 July.
PRENCE,
Gov^R.

In reference vnto Thomas Barnes, servant vnto Mr John Barnes, of Plymouth, vpon complaint vnto the Court of the nott agreement between the said m^r and servant, the case being refered by such as were interested therin, viz₸, the said Mr Barnes, and Mr Rocke, of Boston, in the behalfe of the said Thom̄ Barnes, for a full and finall determination, vnto our honored Go⊔, hee hath ordered, with the consent of the Court aforsaid, that the said Thomas Barnes shalbee surrendered vp vnto the said Mr Rocke, to bee att his dispose, and that hee is released from his master, John Barnes, prouided that the said Mr Rocke pay or cause to bee payed vnto the said John Barnes the sum̄e of

*In reference vnto the request of Mr Thomas Dexter, Seni^r, concerning the amesurement of his land att Barnstable, hee consciueing that wanteth of his full due in that behalfe, the Court haue ordered, that the surveyors or measurers of land att Barnstable, viz₸, Ensigne Barnard Lumbard and Thomas Laythorp, bee authorised to measure or lay out the said land, with the healp and assistance therin of Mr Hinckley, John Chipman, and Wilłam Crocker.

[*129^b.]

Att this Court, Edward Land, and John Cooper, and John Simons, for prophane and abusiue carriages each towards other, on the Lords day, att the meeting house att Duxburrow, were centanced to pay, each of them, a fine of ten shillinges to the vse of the countrey; the said John Cooper, being most faulty, was ajudged worthy of corporall punishment; but forasmuch as in some sort hee tooke to the euill with some manifestation of sorrow, the aforsaid fine of ten shillinges was excepted for satisfaction for this time.

1666.
31 October.
PRENCE,
GOU^R.
[*130.]

*Att the Generall Court of his Matie held att Plymouth, for the Jurisdiction of New Plymouth, the 31st of October, 1666.

BEFORE Thomas Prence, Gou̅,   Thomas Southworth,
John Alden,   Wil̃am Bradford, and
Josias Winslow,   Thomas Hinckley,
Assistants, &c̃.

IT was ordered by the Court, that wheras Wil̃am Nicarson, of Manna-moiett, hath very scandulously reproached this his. ma^{ties} Court of New Plymouth and the freemen of this jurisdiction to the Hono^{ble} Collonell Richard Nicolls, Gou̅ of his ma^{ties} collonie of New Yorke, as appeers in a writing to the said hono^{ble} collonell bearing date Aprill the second, 1666, vnder the hand of the said Nicarson, a coppy of which writing being read in this p̃sent Court vnto Wil̃am Nicarson, not deneying the same, answared, hee should bee reddy in time and place to make out euery p̃ticular in his said writing to Collonell Nicholls ; his sonnes in law, Robert Eldred and Nathaniel Couell, hearing the said writing read, did acknowlidg̃ theire priuity and consent vnto it ; and Trustrum Hedges, another son in law of the said Nicarsons, deneyed not his priuitie and consent vnto the same ; the Court therfore judge themselues bound to vindecate the great scandall of his ma^{ties} Court, as alsoe the freemen of this jurisdiction, and doe require the said Wil̃am Nicarson, Robert Eldred, & Nathaniel Couell to giue sufficient securitie for theire appeerance att the next Generall Court of his ma^{tie}, to be holden for this jurisdiction att New Plymouth the first Tusday in June next insueing the date heerof, viz͡t : the said Wil̃am Nicarson fiue hundred pounds, and for each of his sons aboue mensioned an hundred pounds apeece.

An Acknowlidgment appointed to bee recorded, as followeth.

These p̃sents witnes, that wheras I, Wil̃am Nicarson, Seni^r, of Manna-moiett, haue through my mistake vttered or expressed in a letter to Barnstabl̃, and another to the Court of Plymouth, sundry expressions of a scandulous nature, tending to the great defamation of Thomas Hinckley, of Barnstable, Assistant, as that hee deneyed him justice notwithstanding his oath to God and the Kinge, and that hee was in combination with them that had a hand in royett and route, as is more att large expressed in the said letters ; for which I ame hartily sorry, and doe heerby acquit the said Thomas Hinckly from the imputation of the said crimes, or what else may in either of the said letters reflect vpon him to his defamation, desireing the said Thomas to forgiue mee the wrong donn him therby; and alsoe, I, the said Wiłłam Nicarson, doe by these p̃sents graunt to the said Thomas Hinckley that it shall and may bee lawfull for the said Thomas to read these p̃sents, or cause them to be read, in open Court, or where else hee shall thinke meet, for his vindecation from all and euery the said expressions tending to the defamation of the said Hinckley. In witnes wherof I haue heervnto sett my hand, this 18th of June, 1666.

1666.

31 October. PRENCE, GOUR.

By me, WILŁAM NICARSON.

In p̃sence of
Wiłłam Hedge,
Trusturm Hull,
John Miller.

*A Coppy of a Com̃ission, as followeth. [*131.]

New Plymouth. To Samuell Nash, Cheif Marshall of the Jurisdiction of New Plymouth, with Barnard Lumbert and Josepth Howes, greet̃.

These are in his maties name to will and com̃aund you, vpon receipt heerof, with all convenient speed, to repaire to Mannamoiett, and, according to an order of Court bearing date the seauenth day of June, 1665, to lay out to Wiłłam Nicarson, Mr Thom̃ Hinckley, all such portions of land att Mannamoiett, both vpland and meddow, according to youer best descretion for quantity and manor of laying it out as is expressed in the said order of Court, and in the name and behalfe of the said his maties Court of New Plymouth to giue each of the said psons posession of the whole by twigg and turffe, or of sume p̃te of it in stead of the whole; and if you find any cregular psons felling or squaring of timber, or preparing to sett vp any cottages in any of the said lands, that you warn them in his maties name to desist and be gon, as they will answere the contrary att theire p̃ill, and make returne of youer proceedings att the next Court of Assistants; and see you faile not in the p̃mises att youer p̃rills.

THOMAS PRENCE, Gou.
WILŁAM COLLYARE,
JOHN ALDEN,
JOSIAS WINSLOW.

Dated att Plymouth the 30th of June, 1665.

*Wheras complaint is made vnto the Court, in the behalfe of the towne [*132.] of Scittuate, of the neglect of the gathering in of a rate agreed vpon by the

1666.
31 October.
PRENCE,
Gouʳ.

towne for the maintainance of theire minnesters, for which a warrant was directed vnto Walter Briggs, late constable of Scittuate aforsaid, this Court hath ordered, that the said Briggs shall with all convenient speed gather in what is not gathered of the said rate, soe as it may bee payed to the minnester vnto whom it belongeth; and incase hee doe neglect soe to doe, that hee shall pay it himselfe.

And for his not obeying the warrant directed vnto him as aforsaid, it being such an ill p̃sedent, hee is centanced by the Court to pay a fine of fiue pounds to the vse of the collonie.

Att this Court, John Phillips, of Marshfeild, tendered to make payment of the sum of ten pounds vnto Grace Halloway, the daughter of Wiłłam Halloway, deceased, the said Grace Halloway being now of age to receiue the said sum̃e as her portion, and shee haueing requested Major Winslow to aduise her in reference vnto the future way of her liulyhood; the Court, alsoe, approueing therof, haue alsoe ordered, that the said sum̃e of ten pounds bee deliuered vnto him for to be improued by him for her vse.

Liberty is graunted vnto Ensigne Wiłłam Merricke and Richard Biship, that incase they be not accom̃odated with land amongst them with whom they are listed neare the Bay line, that they may looke out for accom̃odation elswher; or incase that Saconett can be purchased of the Indians, that then the said p̃ties may haue there portions of land there, if they please.

Att this Court, Gyles Ricard, Seniʳ, his lycence for keeping an ordinary and selling wine and liquors by retaile was called in; onely wheras hee saith hee hath some liquor that would bee lost if not sold, hee hath liberty to sell it vntill it is spent, both vnto strangers and others alsoe of the towne of Plymouth, prouided that what hee seleth to any of the towne of Plymouth, it be for the releife of the weake or sicke, and that alsoe with the consent and approbation of Captaine Southworth.

In reference vnto the complaint of Elizabeth, the wife of Gorḡ Vaughan, and alsoe the complaint of the wife of Samuell Eaton, against an Indian called Sampson, allias Bump, for most insolent and intollorable carriages towards them, whoe coming into the house of the said Vaughan, hee not being att home, and held vp his knife att the said Elizabeth Vaughan seuerall times in a threatening way and manor as if hee would haue wounded her, with other insolent carriages that much affrighted her, and alsoe carrying to the wife of Samuell Eaton att the same time very wickedly by twisting of her necke to the indangering of her life, and alsoe other insolent carriages to Francis Billington att the same time, whoe was sent for to rescue the said weomen from his violence and wickednes; for which said facts, agrauated by diuers other

COURT ORDERS.

p̃ticulars, hee was centanced by the Court to be seuerly whipt att this p̃sent Court, and to bee branded in the shoulder with a Roman P, which accordingly was inflicted.

1666.
31 October.
Prence, Gouʳ.

In reference vnto the complaint of Edward Gray against Joseph Billington, for hunting his oxe with a dog, and for the wrong don to his swine and fence, the said Billington is awarded by the Court to pay vnto the said Gray the sũme of twenty shillings; and as for his syth, vsed by the said Billington without the said Gray his leaue, hee is ordered to returne it to him agaîne.

In reference vnto John Bates and Wilłam Burden, theire breaking the Kinges peace by striking each other, they were sentanced by the Court to pay, each of them, three shillings and four pence; and the said Burden, for being drunke att the same time, is fined fiue shillings; and wheras the said Bates abused the said Burden att the same time, by lying vpon him and striking of him, wherby hee was disabled for a certaine time to attend on his calling, hee, the said Bates, is ordered by the Court to pay vnto the said Burden the sũme of twenty shillings.

John Siluester, for his affronting of the constable of Marshfeild in the execution of his office, is fined ten shillings to the vse of the collonie.

In reference vnto a hogg in controuersy lying vnder an attachment, which in the costody of an Indian called Sampson, the Court finds the said hogg to appertaine to Mʳ Thomas Prence; and if the said Indian find himselfe agreiued, that then Josepth Billington is to giue him satisfaction.

*Jabez Howland acknowlidgeth to owe vnto our soũ lord the Kinge the sũme of . . . . } 20 : 00 : 00

[*133.]

The condition, that if the said Jabez Howland shall and doe appeer att the Court of his maᵗⁱᵉ to be holden att Plymouth the first Tusday in March next, to make further answare for misdemenior towards Josepth Billington by striking and otherwise abusing of him, and in the mean time carry peacably towards all manor of p̃sons, and not depart the said Court without lycence; that then, &c̃.

Released.

Joseph Billington acknowlidgeth to owe vnto our soũ lord the Kinge the sũme of . . . . } 20 : 00 : 00

The condition, that if the said Joseph Billington shall and doe appeer att the Court of his maᵗⁱᵉ to be holden att Plymouth the first Tusday in March next, to make further answare for his misdemeaning himselfe on the 30ᵗʰ day of October att the house of Gyles Rickard, and not depart the said Court without lycence; that then, &c̃.

Released.

In reference vnto the complaint of Mʳ Josepth Tilden and Wilłam Barstow against John Palmer, Juniʳ, for ployning and pilfering of a p̃sell of

1666.

31 October.
Prence,
Govr.

boards from the saw mill, the Court haue ordered, that what boards of the said p̃sell soe ployned can be made appeer by those that attend the said mill to belong to the said Joseph Tilden and William Barstow, that they are to haue them; and such as are mixed with and amongst the said boards soe stollen, which shall appeer to belong to the said Palmer, hee to haue them; and if any others shall lay any just claime to any of the said p̃sell soe ployned, they to haue them; and that what charge the said p̃ties haue bin att in bringing the case to hearing, that they be fully satisfyed for the same by the said Palmer; and for his fact in soe pilfering and ployning the said boards, hee is centanced by the Court to pay a fine of twenty shillings to the vse of the collonie.

In reference vnto an Indian called Daniell, allies Pumpanaho, for his dangerously striking of Samuell Hickes, wherof hee hath languished and hath bine in danger of death, and although recouered, yett much hindered in his time and occations, wherfore the said Indian is centanced by the Court to pay vnto the said Samuell Hickes the sum̃e of four pounds and four shillings in reference vnto his bill of charges, and forty shillinges for the losse of his time, and ten shillings vnto John Haward for his coming to Plymouth with him by the constables order.

Wheras Mr Timothy Hatherley, by his last will and testament, hath made, ordained, and appointed Mr Joseph Tilden to be his sole exequitor; and the said Joseph Tilden doth refuse to accept of the said exequitorship according to the said will; wherfore the Court haue appointed him to be adminnestrator on the estate of the said Mr Hatherley, to pay all debts and legacies due and owing from the said estate soe farr and by equall proportions as it will amount vnto.

The Court haue ordered Myles Blacke, of Sandwich, in the behalfe of the countrey, to see the line run eight miles into the woods westerly vpon the south bounds of Plymouth.

[*134.]

*In answare to a petition prefered to the Court by Captaine James Cudworth, bearing date the 30th of October, 1666, in which hee soliseteth the Court for the deuision of a certaine p̃sell of marsh meddow between the said Capt̃ Cudworth and John Williams, Juni^{r}, which said p̃sell of marsh lyeth att Conihassett, being the 23 share or lott of marsh there on the west end of the Great Necke, and is bounded towards the north east to Capt̃ Cudworths marsh att a stone stucke vp in the marsh close by a great rocke att the point of the necke, and from thence ranging towards the northwest and by north to the mouth of a creeke att a stone stucke in the marsh, and from thence takeing in all the marsh between the Great Necke and Gulfe Iland and about Gulfe

COURT ORDERS. 139

Iland, and soe along southward and the Great Necke and the Great Creeke 1666.
vntill it comes to the southerly side of Castle Rocke att a stone stucke in
the marsh att the westerly point of a ledge of broken rockes, and from   31 October.
thence ranging towards the west northwest to the creeke and stone stucke PRENCE,
in the marsh; which said p̃sell of marsh soe bounded was soñitimes the   Gou^r.
marsh of John Whiston, deceased, and by him sold, the one halfe therof vnto
the said Capt Cudworth, and the other halfe vnto Samuell House, deceased,
and by him sold vnto John Williams, Juni^r, afforsaid, the said Williams being
averse to a deuision, notwithstanding the said captaine hath proposed it to him
seuerall times, and hath suffered great damage by the neglect therof, which
nessesitateth him to make suite to the Court for a deuision as aforsaid.

This Court haue therfore ordered, that twelue men bee warned to giue meeting vnto Major Josias Winslow on the thirteenth of this instant Nouember, att the house of Mr Thomas King, att Scittuate, to be by him, the said major, impannelled to serue on a jury to make deuision of the said p̃sell of marsh according to this order.

Theire names are as followeth : —

    John Hollett,   William Peakes,
    Walter Briggs,   Mathew Ganett,
    Jeremiah Hatch,   John Both,
    Henery Luce,   Rodulphus Elmes,
    Richard Standlake,   John Daman,
    John Ensigne,   Joseph White.

John Andrew, att this Court, for teling of a lye, fined ten shillings. And the said John Andrew, for breakeing the Kinges peace by striking Josepth Bartlett, was fined three shillinges and fourpence.

And the said Josepth Bartlett, for breakeing the Kinges peace in striking the said Andrew, fined three shillings and fourpence.

*A Writing appointed to be recorded by the Goũ, as followeth.   [*134^a.]

John Whiston, aged eighteen yeares or therabouts, being the next eldest brother to Josepth Whiston, late deceased att Boston, whoe hath giuen him an estate, as wee are enformed, and hee, the said John Whiston, hath made choise of his vnkle, Edward Jenkens, of Scittuate, for to be his gaurdian, to cecure what estate soeuer is his vntill hee comes of age.

    January 4th, 1666.   The marke 〄 of JOHN WHISTON.
    Witnes, William Brookes, ⟨mark⟩ his marke.
        Timothy Foster.

1666-7.
5 March.
PRENCE,
Govr.
[*135.]

*Att the Court of his Matie held att Plymouth the fift Day of March, 1666.

BEFORE Thomas Prence, Goũ,   Thomas Southworth,
John Alden,   Wiłłam Bradford, and
Josias Winslow,   Thomas Hinckley,
Assistants, &c̃.

WIŁŁAM NICARSON, for sundry scandulouse charges against Mr Thomas Hinckley, Assistant of this goũment, highly tending to the defaming of his ma^{ties} authoritie in this his Court, to the stiring vp of faction and sedition, as appeers vnder his hand, is centanced to pay a fine of fifty pounds vnto the countreyes vse; but incase hee shall acknowlidge in open Court this his miscarriage, that then thirty pounds of this fifty shalbe remited, or otherwise the whole to be exacted.

Wiłłam Nicarson did acknowlidg in open Court, that in these scandulouse and reproachfull charges, which hee sofĩtimes layed vpon Mr Thomas Hinckley, as hee was a minnester of justice and an Assistant in this goũment, hee did scandulize his ma^{ties} authoritie and this his Court of which hee is a member, and is very sorry for his miscarriage therin, and hopes it shalbe a warning to him for the future.

This acknowlidgment in Court was accepted soe as to abate thirty pounds of the fifty pounds abouesaid.

Wiłłam Lumpkin and Peter Worden, for causing disturbance att the meeting house att Yarmouth on the Lords day, were fined, each of them, ten shillings to the vse of the collonie.

Jabez Howland, for breakeing the Kinges peace by striking of Joseph Billington, is fined three shillings four pence to the vse of the collonie.

Joseph Billington, for the like default toward Jabez Howland att the house of Gyles Rickard, on the 30th day of October, 1666, is fined three shillings and four pence to the vse of the collonie.

Arther Howland, Juni^r, for inveigling of Mistris Elizabeth Prence and makeing motion of marriage to her, and procecuting the same contrary to her parrents likeing, and without theire consent, and directly contrary to theire mind and will, was centanced to pay a fine of fiue pounds and to find surties for his good behauior, and in speciall that hee desist from the vse of any meanes to obtaine or retaine her affections as aforsaid.

Mr Samuell Saberry, being sumoned to this Court, appeered to make answare for that by writing vnder his hand and otherwise hee hath busied

COURT ORDERS.   141

himselfe to scandulise and defame the minnestry of Duxburry; but not takeing 1 6 6 6-7.
notice therof to acknowlidgment, and not giueing satisfaction in that behalfe, 5 March.
but rather the contrary, hee was exhorted and admonished by the Court vnto   PRENCE,
his duty in that behalfe, and likewise warned to desist from such disturbing Gov^R.
practices, the which if the Court shall receiue further information therof, hee
must expect to be againe questioned about it, and be reddy to giue better
cecurity for his better walking, and soe for the p̄sent was released.

*Letters of adminnestration was graunted by the Court vnto Joseph [*136.]
Holley and Marke Redley to adminnester on the estate of Mr Trustrum Hull,
of Barnstable, deceased.

In reference vnto a box attached by John Rickard for a debt of fifteen
shillings due from Elizabeth More, the Court haue awarded vnto the said
Rickard a petticoate of the said Mores, which is to answare the said debt and
the charges of the suite.

In reference vnto the desire of Robert Barker, that a p̄sell of meddow Memorandum:
might be recorded vnto him lying att the North Riuer att Robinsons Creeke,   that a coppy
and that hee hath produced seuerall euidences to satisfy the Court about it, heerof be sea-
the Court haue ordered, that if the towne of Duxburrow, or any of that towne, Duxburrow.
doe not produce any thing to the contrary betwixt this Court and the shuting
vp of June Court next, that then hee, vpon such euidence as hee shall then
produce, may haue the said meddow recorded vnto him.

Joseph Hollett and Elizabeth, his wife, for com̄itting carnall coppulation
each with other before marriage or contract, fined ten pounds.

Letters of adminnestration was graunted vnto Hosea Joyce to adminnester on the estate of Mr John Joyce, deceased.

Memorand̄: that Samuell Edson be sum̄oned to the next Court to
answare for his neglect to appeer to serue on a jury, being sum̄oned for that
purpose.

Memorandum: that Dinah Siluester, Sarah Smith, and the daughter of
Edward Jenkens, bee sum̄oned to the next Court.

Arther Howland, Juni^r, acknowlidgeth to owe vnto⎫
  our sou lord the King the sum̄e of . . . . . .⎬ 50 : 00 : 00
John Daman the sum̄e of . . . .   25 : 00 : 00
Timothy Williamson the sum̄e of . . . . . .   25 : 00 : 00

The condition, that wheras the said Arther Howland hath disorderly and Release 1 July
vnrighteously indeauored to obtaine the affections of Mistris Elizabeth Prence 3, 1667.
against the mind and will of her parents, if, therfore, the said Arther Howland
shall for the future refraine and desist from the vse of any meanes to obtaine
or retaine her affections as aforesaid, and appeer att the Court of his ma^{tie} to

142   PLYMOUTH COLONY RECORDS.

1666-7. be holden att Plymouth the first Tusday in July next, and in the mean time
5 March. be of good behauior towards our soū lord the King and all his leich people,
PRENCE, and not depart the said Court without lycence; that then, &c̄.
Gouʳ.

[*138.]   *According to the Courts appointment, wee layed out vnto Cornett Robert Studson a certaine tract of land bounded as followeth, viz͠: on the north side by those lands that were graunted att Accord Pond; on the east by the line of the towne of Scittuate vntill it crosse a deepe, still brooke; and on the southwest and westerly side by the said brooke; and soe againe from the townes line as Mʳ Hatherleyes land runs westerly vntill it crosse the said brooke there againe, with all the spotts and holes of meddow that are within the abouesaid bounds.

Witnesse our hands,
JOSIAS WINSLOW,
CONSTANT SOUTHWORTH.

1667.   *THE councell of warr, being assembled att Plymouth the 2cond day of
2 April. Aprill, namily, Mʳ Thomas Prence, president, Mʳ John Alden, Major
[*139.] Josias Winslow, Captaine Thomas Southworth, Captaine William Bradford, Mʳ Thomas Hinckley, Mʳ Anthony Thacher, Mʳ Constant Southworth, and Mʳ Nath Bacon, did then order and conclude as followeth : —

Viz͠: that euery com̄ission officer in the seuerall milletary companies of this jurisdiction shall haue a com̄ission deliuered vnto them vnder the seale of the goūment, and signed with the president of the said councell.

The forme of the said com̄issions are as followeth : —

First, of a captaine : —

You, A B, haueing bine orderly chosen and accepted to the office of a captaine of the foot companie of the towne of P., you are heerby authorised and required to take the com̄aund and charge of that companie, to exercise and traine them vp in the vse of theire armes according to such orders as are or may bee setled by the Court or councell of warr in that respect, and alsoe impowered to com̄and or lead any or all that are vnder youer com̄and vpou reall duty and seruice for ofence and defence as occation may require; and you are therin required carefully to attend such orders and instructions as you haue or shall from time to time receiue from the councell of warr; and in defect therof, shall acte according to such advice as you shall haue respecting any sud̄daine exegent from such in youer towne as are appointed to be a councell with you in such cases; and soe acting, you may expect full and reddy obeidience from all vnder you in theire respectiue places, and be warranted and accepted in youer good endeauors.

1 6 6 7.
2 April.
PRENCE,
Gouʀ.

Giuen by the councell of warr for the jurisdiction of New Plymouth this 2cond of Aprill, 1667.   T. P., Presedent.

For the Leiftenant.

You, A B, haueing bine orderly chosen and accepted to the office of leiftenant of the foot companie of the towne of P., are heerby authorised and required to bee assistant to the captaine of that place in the exercising and training vp of the souldiers of that towne in the vse of theire armes according to such orders as are or may be settled by the Court or councell of warr, or by order from youer capt in that respect, and alsoe impowered to comaund and lead that companie, either in peace or warr, in the absence of youer captaine, with as absolute comand as youer said captaine hath when p̃sent; and you are required carefully to attend such order and instructions as you haue or shall from time to time receiue from the councell of warr, and in defect therof to acte according to such advise as you shall haue respecting any suddaine exegent from such in youer towne, or the major p̃te of them, as are appointed to be a councell in such cases;* and soe acting, you may expect full and reddy obeidience from all vnder you, and be warranted and accepted in youer good endeavors.

Giuen, &c.

*Except the vrgentcy of the occation, to youer best vnderstanding, calls for such speedy action as not safe to delay for theire advice, in which case you are authorised to acte as you see the matter may require.

For the Ensigne.

You, haueing bine orderly chosen and accepted to the office of ensigne of the foot companie of the towne of P., you are heerby authorised and required to be assistant to the captaine and leiftenant of that place in exercising and training of the souldery of that towne in the vse of theire armes according to such orders as are or may be settled by the Court or councell of warr & said officer in that respect, and alsoe impowered to comand, vnder youer said officers, in such a capasitie as occation may require for ofence and defence; and in the absence of youer said capt and leiftenant, to comand and lead that companie, either in peace or warr, with as absolute comaund as either of them haue when p̃sent; and you are required discreetly and valliantly to defend and maintaine that badge of youer honor and youer countreyes, and carefully to attend such orders and instructions as you haue or shall from time to time receiue from the councell of warr, and in defect therof to acte according to such advise as you shall haue, respecting any suddaine exigent, from such in youer towne, or the major p̃te of them, as are appointed to be a councell in such cases,* and soe acting, you may expect full and reddy

1667.
2 April.
Prence,
Gouᴿ.

[*140.]

obeidience from all vnder you, and be warranted and accepted in youer good endeauors.

Giuen, &c.

*1. The councell of warr haue determined, that during any appeerance of danger a milletary watch be kept in each towne, in the most convenient place or places for takeing and pasing an alarum, according to the descretion of the comanders and councell in each towne, and according to the danger that p̃sents; and alsoe some in each sea towne bee appointed to looke out to sea in the day time to discouer any shipps that may be on the coast, and to obserue theire motion.

2. That the fiering of three musketts shall make an alarum in the night, and that fiers be alsoe made in the night att the place where the alarum did rise.

3. That the troop in each towne be ordered by theire owne officers, or where such are not, by such as are of the grand councell in that towne, to be redy att all times to goe forth as scouts vpon discouery to carry intelligence from place to place as there may be occation, and to doe such seruice further as need may require, vntill by speciall order of theire cheife comaunders they are called off.

4. That there be serch made how horse and foot are prouided with armes and amunition, and defects to be returned.

5. That the souldiery of euery towne shalbe att the free dispose of theire respectiue comaunders in any seruice that they shall require att theire hands according to theire comission and instructions giuen them.

6. It is determined, that Duch and French be looked vpon as our comon enimie whiles soe to our nation, and shalbe resisted, opposed, and expelled by the forces of this jurisdiction to theire vtmost power, and that all advantages shalbe vsed to that end.

7. It is ordered, that if any towne or plantation be destressed by an enimie, vpon intelligence the next towne shall forthwith send them such assistance as theire need may require, be it to a third or halfe theire men.

8. That the Indian sachems heerabouts be sent for, and advised to imploy theire men in looking out to sea for shiping, and giue speedy intelligence to the English of any vessell and theire motions, and that they be warned by theire p̃sent losse not to adventure on board of any strange vessels, but to theire power doe joyne with vs for defence of theire and our comon interest against a comon enimie, and that they be forbiden the fiering of any guns in the night or making any false alarums.

COURT ORDERS.

9. That there be noe shooting att pigions or any other game by day or night whiles dangers psents, but onely att an enimie.

*10. That euery towne prouide som place of retire for theire weomen and children in case of an alarum, as the descretion of each place may giude them, that soe the men may with lesse destraction face an enimie.

11. That in time of danger the troopers of Plymouth repaire to the Goū as his gaurd, vntill further order.

12. That all psons in any township, although aboue sixty yeares of age, or otherwise vncapable of bearing armes, but are of competent estates, and shalbe soe judged by theire comaunders and councell of that towne, they shalbe lyable to find a man to watch and ward as occation be, and it be required of them.

13. That whosoeuer shall refuse or neglect to doe his duty in watching and warding when required shalbe lyable to pay a fine of fiue shillinges for euery such defect, vnlesse they can giue a satisfying answare to theire comaunders and theire councell in theire owne towne, and this to be forthwith leuied by the constable; but incase they hold themselues agreiued, they may haue libertie, after the fine payed, to appeale to the councell of warr.

14. That it shalbe in the power of such as are appointed a councell, in euery towne, in any exigent or suddaine occation, to dispose of the generall stocke of armes and amunition in that towne or any pte of it as occation may require.

1667.
2 April.
PRENCE,
GOUR.
[*141.]

The Names of those that are appointed to bee of Councell with the Comission Officers in each Towne.

Plymouth :
   The Goū,
   Capt Bradford.
Duxburrow :
   Mr John Aldin,
   Mr Constant Southworth,
   Leift Josias Standish.
Scittuate :
   Cornett Studson,
   John Daman,
   Iscake Chettenden,
   Edward Jenkens,
   Isacke Bucke.

Marshfeild :
   Mr Josias Winslow, Senir.
Sandwich :
   Mr Richard Bourne,
   William Bassett,
   James Skiffe, Senir.
Taunton :
   James Walker,
   Willam Harvey,
   Richard Williams.
Rehoboth :
   Capt Willett,
   Mr Paine, Senir,

1667.

2 April.
Prence,
Govr.

Mr Thomas Cooper,
Gilbert Brookes.
For Yarmouth :
Mr Anthony Thacher,
Mr Edmond Howes,
Thomas Howes.
For Barnstable :
Mr Thomas Hinckley,
Mr Nath Bacon,
John Chipman.

For Eastham :
Leiftenant Freeman,
Josias Cooke,
Richard Higgens.
For Bridwater :
Samuell Edson,
Nicholas Byram,
John Willis.

For Dartmouth, Sarjeant James Shaw to exercise the inhabitants in armes till the next June Court, and that then the towne are to p̃sent some to the Court to be settled in office according to order; and that the said Serjeant Shaw to advise with John Cooke, Samuell Hickes, and John Russell, incase of any danger p̃senting for the best defence of the place in such respect, and to see how men are prouided with armes and am̃unition, and to returne the defects to the said Court.

[*142.]   *Seuerall Orders appointed by the Councell of Warr to be obserued by the seuerall Courts of Gaurd in this Jurisdiction.

Gentlemen Souldiers : You are required carefully to attend youer duty in watching, warding, and such other seruice as shalbe required of you by youer com̃aunders and councell, wherin p̃ticularly obserue these following orders : —

Imp^r. That noe outrage be com̃itted by any p̃son vpon duty by prophane swearing, cursing, drinkeing, quarrelling, or fighting one with another.

2^{ly}. Noe man shall hold correspondencye with the enimie, or confer with any trumpett, drum, or messenger of the enimie, but by appointment.

3. None shall neglect his watch or other service com̃itted to him, sleep on his sentenelship, or depart thence vntill releiued.

4. None shall make the word knowne to the enimie, or change the word, but by order.

5. None shall make any needles alarum by day or night.

6. Att the soundage of an alarum, euery one shall repaire to theire coullers or place appointed them.

7. None shall fly in battle vntill a retreat be com̃aunded, nor quite any place com̃itted to theire trust whiles defencable.

COURT ORDERS.   147

8. Euery private souldier is required to keep his armes fixt and cleane, and not to paune, sell, or play away his armes.

9. None, vpon prill of theire liues, shall attempt to abuse any sentenell that is out vpon duty, but shall reddily make themselues knowne and obey him.

10. That all centenells, vpon the like penaltie, shall carefully attend theire charge giuen them for the discouering of an enimie and prevension of danger and mischeife to any of our owne people.

1667.
2 April.
PRENCE,
GOU^R.

The councell of warr haue alowed fourteen dayes from this date for the townes to send in theire accomts of armes and amunition vnto the major; and that if within the said time any that haue bine att this meeting of the said councell returned defectiue shall be supplyed before the said time be expired, they shall not be fineable for breach of order in that behalfe.

Att the Generall Court of Election holden att Plymouth, in New England, the fift Day of June, 1667.

5 June.
[*143.]

BEFORE Thomas Prence, Gou, and   Wilłam Bradford, and
John Aldin,   Thomas Hinckley,
        Thomas Southworth,
                Assistants, &c.

MR THOMAS PRENCE was chosen Gou, and sworne. And

Mr John Alden,
Major Josias Winslow,
Captaine Thomas Southworth,
M^r Wiłłam Bradford,   } were chosen Assistants, and sworne.
Mr Thomas Hinckley,
Leiftenant John Freeman, and
Mr Nathaniel Bacon,

The Comissioners chosen were Major Winslow, Captaine Southworth. And the next in nomination was Mr Thomas Hinckley.

The Treasurer chosen was Mr Constant Southworth, and sworne.

148   PLYMOUTH COLONY RECORDS.

1667.

5 June.
PRENCE,
Gou^r.

The deputies of the seuerall townes were,—

Mr John Howland,	Edward Sturgis,
Leift Ephraim Morton,	Yelverton Crow,
Mr Constant Southworth,	Joseph Laythorp,
Christopher Wadsworth,	Ensigne Marke Eames,
Cornett Robert Studson,	John Bourne,
Isacke Chettenden,	Leiftenant Peter Hunt,
Richard Bourne,	Ensigne Henery Smith,
Thomas Tupper, Seni^r,	Daniell Cole,
William Harvey,	John Willis,
James Walker,	John Cooke.

The Grand Enquest.

Mr Joseph Tilden,		Joseph Warren,	
Mr Josias Standish,		Andrew Hallott,	
Phillip Delanoy,		Jacob Cooke,	
John Bryant,		William Foard, Seni^r,	
William Crocker,		Daniel Smith,	
John Dingley,	sworne,	Samuell Newman,	sworne.
Thomas Linkorne,		Marke Snow,	
Thomas Gibbs,		Samuell Tompkins,	
Miacaell Blackwell,		Richard Sisson,	
Joseph Wilbore,		James Cobb,	
John Winge,			

[*144.]

*The Constables of the seuerall Townes.

Plymouth, ...	Francis Comb, sworne.
Duxburrow, ...	Samuell Hunt, sworne.
Scittuate, ...	{ Micaell Peirse, William Brooks, } sworne.
Taunton, ...	Richart Burt, sworne.
Yarmouth, ...	Thomas Howes, sworne.
Barnstable, ...	Abraham Blush.
Sandwich, ...	Emond Freeman, Juni^r.
Marshfeild, ...	{ Nathaniell Winslow, Josias Keine, } sworne.
Rehoboth, ...	{ Nicholas Pecke, John Titus, } sworne.

COURT ORDERS.

Eastham, ...	John Banges, sworne.	1667.
Bridgwater, ...	John Willis, Junir.	2 June.
Dartmouth, ...	Peleg Tripp, sworne.	PRENCE, Gour.

Surveyors of the Highwayes.

Plymouth:
  Mr John Barnes,
  Ensigne Bradford,
  Hugh Cole.
Duxburrow:
  ^
Scittuate:
  William Barstow,
  John Ensigne.
Sandwich:
  ^
Taunton:
  ^

Yarmouth:
  Thomas Gage,
  Judah Thacher.
Barnstable:
  ^
Marshfeild:
  ^
Rehoboth:
  ^
Eastham:
  ^
Bridgwater:
  ^
Dartmouth:
  ^

*The Celect Men in each Township. [*145.]

Plymouth:
  Leiftenant Morton deputed to adminester an oath respecting theire place as occation may require.
  { Leiftenant Morton, Nath Warren, William Harlow, William Clarke, William Crow, } sworne.

Duxburrow:
  Christopher Wadsworth deputed to giue oath as abouesaid.
  { Christopher Wadsworth, Mr Josias Standish, Benjamine Bartlett, } sworne.

Scittuate:
  Isacke Chettenden to adminnester an oath as aforsaid.
  { Cornett Studson, Mr Thomas Kinge, Isacke Chettenden, } sworne.

Sandwich:
  Thomas Tupper to giue the said oath.
  { Thomas Tupper, Senir, James Skiffe, Senir, Thomas Burgis, } sworne.

1667.

5 June.
PRENCE,
Govr.

Taunton:

James Walker to ad-
minnester the said
oath.
{ Gorge Hall,
Walter Deane,
James Walker,
Richard Williams,
Wiłłam Harvey, } sworne.

Yarmouth:
{ Mr Edmond Howes,
Edward Sturgis,
James Mathewes,
Yelverton Crow,
Samuell Sturgis, } sworne.

Barnstable:
{ Wiłłam Crocker,
John Chipman,
John Tompson,
Josepth Laythorp, } sworne.

[*146.]
*Marshfeild:
And John Bourne
appointed to ad-
minnester an oath.
{ Anthony Snow,
Ensigne Eames,
John Bourne, } sworne.

Rehoboth:
Mr Stephen Paine,
John Allin,
Mr James Browne.

Eastham:

Bridḡwater:
{ John Willis,
Nicholas Byram,
John Carey, } sworne.

Dartmouth:
Arther Hathewey to
giue the aforsaid
oath.
{ John Russell,
Samuell Hickes,
Arther Hathewey.

Receiuers of the Excise in each Towne.

Plymouth, ... Benajah Pratt.
Duxburrow, ... Henery Sampson.

COURT ORDERS.

Scittuate, ...	{ Edward Jenkens, John Cushen.		1667.
Sandwich, ...	{ Tupper, Juni^r, Thomas Tobey.		5 June. PRENCE, Gou^R.
Taunton, ...	Richard Burt.		
Yarmouth, ...	{ Mr Anthony Thacher, John Miller.		
Barnstable, ...	{ Thomas Huckens, Joseph Laythorp.		
Marshfeild, ...	William Maycomber, Seni^r.		
Rehoboth, ...	Daniel Smith.		
Eastham, ...	Will Walker.		
Bridgwater, ...	Arther Haris.		
Dartmouth, ...	Samuell Hickes.		

*In reference vnto the complaint made against Phillip, the sachem of Pacanacutt, by an Indian, that hee was in complyance with the French against the English in New England, the Court, haueing heard his answare, and therin certifyed that the ground of such reports arose from a certaine sachem of the Narragansetts, doe order Lieftenant Hunt and Ensigne Smith to repaire to Warwicke in some convenient time for the Court to be holden att Plymouth in July next, and that the said Phillip doe there giue them meeting before one of the majestrates there, that soe the said sachem may make out what hee hath spoken in that behalfe, and that Ninnegrett haue notice therof, that soe hee may vnderstand what is charged against him. [*147.]

Att this Court, proclamation was made that if any can lay any just claime vnto any due debt from the estate of William Hacke, John Turner, and Thomas Ewer, they may come in within a twelumonth and a day of this date, and they shalbe satisfyed soe farr as the estate will amount vnto.

This Court alowed vnto the major, in reference to his journey to the sachem Phillip, in the behalfe of the countrey, the sume of fiue pounds.

To Captaine Southworth, for his paines and time, forty shillings.

To the Treasurer, respecting his longe time and paines, three pounds.

To Cornett Robert Studson, his horse, time, and paines, forty shillings.

Two shillings and sixpence a day is alowed vnto the troopers, to each of them that went on the abouesaid expedition, viz$\int$, to each of them, for him and his horse,

Ten shillings is alowed vnto Nicholas Hyde for bringing of a letter to the Gou^R, and his other time and paines about it in reference to the abouesaid busines.

1667.

5 June.
PRENCE,
Gov⁺.

This Court haue graunted vnto Andrew Ringe a smale ꝑsell of land lying att the end of his land att Namassakett, viz$, all the land lying att the end of his lott between the path and a smale brooke and the valley the full breadth of his lott.

The Court haue graunted vnto Thomas Butler a necke of land called Tassacausett, lying neare to Edmond Freemans land, being deuided by a creeke or brooke on the southerly side, which said land is bought by the said Butler of an Indian called Charles, allies Pampmumitt, for a yoake of oxen, prouided the said Indian returne the sume of three pounds to the said Butler.

In reference vnto the graunt of land graunted vnto Gyles Hopkins, Jonathan Sparrow, and the widdow Mayo, the Court haue ordered Leiftenant Freeman either to purchase it or hier it for them as occation shall require, as hee shall see meet.

Liberty is graunted vnto Thomas Paine to looke out some land for his accomodation.

[*148.] *The Accomt of the Liquors brought into Yarmouth the Year last past, giuen in by M⁺ Thacher.

The 15 of the first month, Elisha Hedge, one barrell of rum.

M⁺ Hedge, 9 gallons of sacke.

September 14, (66,) by John Barnes, for Elisha Hedge, fifty gallons of rum.

For M⁺ Sprague, 10 gallons of rum.

For Samuell Sturgis, 30 gallons of rum.

For Edward Sturgis, Juni⁺, 25 gallons.

For John Mokeney, six gallons.

Jonathan Barnes brought sundry barrells of liquors to the towne, since which hee did not invoyce with vs, but did after some distance of time invoyce it with the Treasurer.

The first weeke in Aprill, (67,) Edward Sturgis, Seni⁺, 22 gallons of sacke, which was invoyced, thõ not in due time according to order.

Att that time, there were fiue or six barrells of rum bought of the marchant att Satuckett, which was not invoyced, but concealed one barrell; Jonathan Barnes had another barrell; Joseph Ryder three more, hee seized for the countrey, which haue bine since condemned, viz$: Samuell Sturgis, one barrell of rum ; Edward Sturgis, Juni⁺, one barrell of rum ; and Abraham Hedge, one barrell of rum, which lyes responsable for his father to cleare betwixt this and the Court in July next.

Boardman, halfe a barrell, or somwhat more, which hee invoced.

COURT ORDERS. 153

The first weeke in June, 67, Jonathan Barnes invoyced one barrell of rum for John Mokaney. Abraham Hedge had about three barrells last sum̃er, which it is vncertaine whether invoced or noe.

1667.
5 June.
PRENCE,
Gou^R.

The cellect men of the towne of Yarmouth, this Court, returned the names of Teage Jones, for not coming to meeting, and Nicholas Nicarson, for refusing to appeer att the sum̃ons of the said cellect men, and for neglecting to come to the publicke worship of God.

This Court haue ordered and appointed Capt James Cudworth and Mr Joseph Tilden, in the behalfe of Elizabeth Williams, the wife of John Williams, to demaund and receiue what is due to her from her said husband for her annuall allowance according to order of Court, and that incase there shalbe occation therof, that one of them bee an apriser of that which shalbe payed vnto her in that behalfe, and incase either of them shalbe by Prouidence hindered from pforming what is required of them in that case, that then John Hallett is to supply his rome by the Courts appointment.

In reference to the complaint of Willam Randall against John Bryant,

*John Cooke was appointed by the Court to solemnize marriage in the towne of Dartmouth, and to giue oath to witnesse for the grand enquest and for the tryall of causes.

[*149.]

Sarjeant James Shaw and Arther Hathewey are appointed by the Court to exercise the men in armes in the towne of Dartmouth.

In reference vnto the estate of Thomas Ewer, the Court haue appointed Thomas Laythorp and Shuball Linnitt to take his estate and adminnester theron, and to be gaurdians alsoe to the children.

Thomas Huckens is authorised by the Court to adminnester on the estate of John Turner, deceased, and, with the advice of Mr Hinckley and Mr Bacon, to pay some smale debts due from the same.

A Writing appointed to be recorded.

To our honored Gou, Mr Prence, and the rest of the honored Court, our humble petition, which wee, whose names are vnderwritten, doe present vnto youer fauorable consideration, that forasmuch as it hath pleased God by his ordering hand of Prouidence to dispose of things soe that our father in law, Willam Nicarson, hath purchased a portion of land att Manamoiett or therabouts to accom̃odate his children and posteritie withall for our comfortable subsisting, and that through the blessing of God vpon our labors wee might liue and not be chargable, hee hath gīen it vnto his children to accom̃odate vs

1667.

5 June.
Prence,
Gou^r.

and our posteritie withall; and wee doe not desire to liue alone, but are willing to receiue soe many inhabitants as theire is land to accomodate them with, soe that wee may goe on in a way of peace and loue, for the glory of God and the good and welfare of the goûment, and the inlargment therof and the good one of another; for the greatest p̃te of vs haue bine brought vp vnder this goûment, and our desires are to continew vnder this goûment; still, if the Lord shalbe pleased to graunt vs to find fauor with the Court to graunt our request, and our request to the honored Court is, that they would be pleased to graunt vs libertie to settle a township att Manamoiett or therabouts with as many inhabitants as wee shall see the land will comfortably accomodate, soe that they be townsmen that wee can close with, wee shall willingly receiue them, vpon the condition that they shall pay theire p̃tes of the purchase according as wee shall agree, and not otherwaies; and if the Court shalbe pleased to graunt our petition, wee shall count it a great fauor from God and fauor from *and fauor from* the Court; thuse hoping to find fauorable answare from the honored Court, wee rest,

          WIŁŁAM NICARSON, Seni^r,
          NICHOLAS NICARSON,
          ROBERT NICARSON,
          SAMUELL NICARSON,
          JOHN NICARSON,
          WIŁŁAM NICARSON, Juni^r,
          JOSEPH NICARSON,
          ROBERT ELDRED,
          TRUSTRUM HEDGES,
The 4th of July, 1663.   NATHANIEL COUELL.

[*150.]

*Att this Court, Benjamine Bartlett complained against his servant, named John Cooper, for refusing to serue him vnlesse his indenture could be produced, which was supposed by him to bee ployned and made away; the Court, vnderstanding by sufficient euidence that hee is yett to serue him three yeares, ordered him either to accept of such conditions as were agreed on betwixt his said master and him since this controversy arose, or to be forthwith publickly whipt and forced to returne to his said master; after this they renewed the conditions, and soe the mater for p̃sent is ended.

Att this Court, Robert Pinion was taken vp as a vagarant and publickly whipt, and ordered with a passe forthwith to depart the goûment.

Att this Court, a jury was named and ordered to bee impaneled to lay out all waies requisett in the township of Bridgwater.

COURT ORDERS.

Theire names are as followeth : —

		1667.
Nicholas Byram,	Arther Harris,	5 June.
Samuel Edson,	John Carrey,	PRENCE, Govr.
Thomas Haward, Senr,	Ensigne John Haward,	Captaine Bradford ordered by the Court to impanell this jury.
Packer,	Marke Laythorp,	
Mr Nathaniel Willis,	Robert Latham,	
Leiftenant Thomas Haward,	Joseph Aldin.	

And if by Prouidence any of these be hindered, that then Samuell Allin and John Aimes doe supply.

Lres of adminnestration were graunted vnto Willam Bassett, Juni^r, to adminnester on the estate of Willam Bassett, Seni^r, deceased.

Lres of adminnestration were graunted vnto Henery Dillingham and John Dillingham to adminnester on the estate of Mr Edward Dillingham, deceased.

Lres of adminnestration were likewise graunted vnto Mary Hacke to adminnester on the estate of Willam Hacke.

Letters of adminnestration were likewise graunted vnto Mr Joseph Tildin to adminnester vpon the estate of Mr Timothy Hatherley, deceased; and the said Mr Tilden is heerby ordered and impowered to receiue and dispose of the said estate in reference vnto payment of debts and legacies due from the estate soe farr as there is estate to discharge, and in all points to acte and doe what euer may be requisite for preseruing and disposing of that estate as an adminnestrator according to the will of the deceased. _{These were graunted October 30, 1666. See more, Wills and Inventoryes recorded.}

*Richard Bourne and Willam Paybody are appointed by the Court to view a certaine peece of land purchased of the Indians by Thomas Dexter, Juni^r; and incase they shall judge, that for quantity and quallitie it will nott accomodate more then one, that it be then settled vpon the said Thomas Dexter. [*151.]

Joseph Burge, of Sandwich, for disorderly healping away of horses out of the collonie, is fined twenty shilling to the vse of the collonie.

Samuell Jackson, for breaking the Kings peace, is fined three shillings and four pence.

Att this Court, Willam Nicarson, Robert Eldred, and Nathaniell Couell appeared, according to theire bond, but gaue noe satisfaction to the Court for theire offence, and att last themselues and some frinds desired further time to consider, as alsoe a coppy of his writing to Collonell Nicolls to puse and take notice of the pticulars, promising to apply themselues speedily to giue satis-

1667.

5 June.
PRENCE,
Gov.

faction, wherevpon the Court, willing yett to extend lenitie, desireing reformation rather than scuerity and sharpnes, gaue them vntill the next Court of his ma^tie, to be holden att Plymouth the first Tusday in July next, to giue theire answare, alsoe takeing theire owne engagement for theire appeerance theratt.

Forasmuch as the inhabitants of Plymouth haue graunted vnto Nathaniel Warren and Joseph Warren, to each of them, fourteen acrees of meddow att or about Agawaam, out of that which was formerly purchased, they being in great nessesitie therof, and the said towne not in a capasitie otherwise to supply them, the Court, not willing to alow of any p̃ticular proprietie there, yett for the reasons forenamed doe approue therof, and doe prohibite any further graunt in that kind vntill they shall otherwise order.

Att this Court, Mary Hacke, of Taunton, sollisited the Court to haue libertie to bestow herselfe in marriage, and produced diuers testimonies to make it manifest to the Court that Wiłłam Hacke, her husband, is dead, hee haueing left her about three yeares since, and went for England, and that shee neuer receiued any letter from him since, nor any other intilligence from or concerning him, saue the said testimonies, which serued to euidence that hee is deceased. The Court not being satisfyed in the testimonies soe fully as to graunt her libertie of marriage att the p̃sent, they refered the case for further clearing vntill the next October Court.

This Court was adjourned vntill the third day of July next in reference vnto the Court of Majestrates and Deputies.

[*152.] *Instructions for the Com̃issioners for the Jurisdiction of New Plymouth.

1. That incase the confederation hold, that it be better obserued then it formerly hath bine.

2. That whatsoeuer the com̃issioners doe agree vpon, either relateing to desolueing and breakeing vp of the confederation between the collonies or theire revniting, shalbe proposed to the seuerall Generall Courts of the respectiue goũments, and assented vnto by them before it shalbe binding vnto them.

3. That you indeauor to vindicate the collonie from the false aspersions that are cast vpon vs conscerning the breach of the former confederation.

4. That if there be a revniting, some speedy course may be taken to settle the propositions both of men and charges more equally then it is att p̃sent, by reason that since the first settlement therof some of the collonies are more increased then others.

5. That inquiry be made about the wampam in Conecticutts hands.

6. That if there be a revniting, (which wee rather desire, may it be

vpon equall tearmes,) wee desire it may be taken notice off and expressed that
wee reserue our alligience to the crowne of England.

1667.

5 June.
PRENCE,
GOUR.

Memorand : that you signify vnto the Massachusetts comissioners, that wee take it ill that wee can not for our moneyes be supplyed with amunition, although they haue good quantities in theire hands.

And signed by order of the Court for the jurisdiction of N. Plymouth,

P me, NATH: MORTON, Secret.

N. Plymouth, June the fift, 1667.

Att this Court, warrant were issued out from the Court to leuy by rate the sume of two hundred eighty six pound eighteen shillinges and eight pence, for the publicke charges of the countrey.

*Att the Court held att Plymouth the 2cond of July, 1667.

2 July.
[*153.]

BEFORE Thomas Prence, Gou,   William Bradford,
John Aldin,   Thomas Hinckley,
Josias Winslow,   Nath Bacon, and
Thomas Southworth,   John Freeman,
Assistants, &c.

WHERAS William Nicarson, Robert Eldred, and Nath Couell, of Mannamoiett, were bound to appeere att the Court holden heer for his matie the first Tusday in June last, to make answare to a writing exhibited to the Honnoble Collonell Richard Nicolls, bearing date Aprill the second, 1666, wherin are contained many pticulars greatly scandulous to his maties Court of this jurisdiction of New Plymouth, in which Court the grand enquest were detained in order to the issueing of the case vntill the said Nicarson seemed to fall in the case, and seemed willing to apply himselfe to take notice of his abuses therin offered, and to giue satisfaction for the same ; which that hee might the better doe, the Court graunted him a coppy of his aforsaid declaration in writing, vpon his engagement to giue timely knowlidge vnto Mr Hinckley or some of the majestrates there what hee would doe therin, and soe this Court might be in a reddines to proceed to an issue of the case ; but hee failing to make timly returne about the pmises, and not applying himself to giue any reasonable satisfaction to answare vnto this complaint, and foras-

1667.

2 July.
Prence,
Govr.

much alsoe as wee haue in this interem of time receiued another letter of his to Collonell Nicolls, dated February, 66, wherby it appeereth hee still goes on to abuse them as formerly, vpon the considerations aboue mensioned, this Court haue seen cause to bind ouer the abouesaid Nicarson, Eldred, and Couell vnto the next Court, to bee holden heer on the last Tusday in October next, to answare for the abouesaid scanduloue papers.

Mr Hinckly and Mr Bacon were ordered by the Court to make dilligent enquiry concerning the liquors brought into the towne of Sandwich.

Daniell Smith is alowed by the Court to keep an ordinary in the towne of Rehoboth for the entertainment of strangers, incase Goodwife Abell lay it downe; and hee is likewise authorised to looke after the excise in that towne, and to draw and sell liquors there.

It is ordered by the Court, that the first p̃te of the rates to be directed to the Treasurer be brought in by the first of October next.

[By a mistake of Secretary Morton, no pages were numbered *154–*157.]

[*158.]

*Att this Court, Nicholas Nicarson was detected before the Court by two witnesses for speakeing of some approbrious speeches against Mr Thomas Thornton, in saying that the said Mr Thornton said, that if a man haue not of his owne to pay towards the minnesters maintainance, hee must borrow it of his naighbour; the said Nicarson alsoe affeirmed, that a certaine sermon the said Mr Thornton taught was halfe of it lyes; hee, the said Nicarson, acknowlidging before the Court that hee hath done him wronge in soe saying, and engaging that hee would publickly acknowlidge his fault therin, likewise att a convenient time att the meeting house att Yarmouth, and promising reformation in that behalfe, was released, and this fault passed by.

In reference vnto the complaint of John Barnes against Thomas Dotey, for detaining of fourscore and ten pounds of marchantable tobacco, and a debt of seauen shillinges due for goods, as the said Barnes saith, the Court doe award the said Thomas Dotey to pay or cause to be payed vnto the said John Barnes or his order one hundred pounds of marchantable tobacco within one month after the date heerof; and in reference vnto the seuen shillinges nominated, that incase John Holmes should come in and testify vpon his oath that hee hath payed fiue shillinges vnto the said Barnes in the behalfe of the said Dotey, that then the said Barnes should rest satisfyed; which accordingly the said Holmes did before the Court broke vp, and soe the case was finally determined.

Arther Howland, Juni^r, did sollemly and seriously engage before this

Court, that hee will wholly desist and neuer apply himselfe for the future, as formerly hee hath done, to Mistris Elizabeth Prence in reference vnto marriage.

1667.
2 July.
PRENCE, Gov^R.

The Court haue alowed the sume of ten pounds towards the building of a bridge ouer Taunton Riuer.

The Court haue alowed the sume of twenty two pounds, with that which is alreddy expended, towards the building of a bridge ouer the Eelriuer, in the place wher it now is; and incase it be not accepted, that it be signifyed to the next October Court, that soe the Court may order a way and bridge elswhere.

The Court doth pmitt the towne of Sandwich, in regard of theire scarcitie of men fitt for publicke imployment, to send but one deputie to the Generall Courts.

*The Court haue graunted vnto Esra Perrey twenty acrees of land, to be aded to his thirty acrees formerly graunted, being in the purchase of Mr Edmond Freeman, Juni^r, and not suitable for any one besides, being ther is noe meddow belonging to it.

[*159.]

One hundred acrees of land is graunted vnto Henery Wood vpon Namassakett Riuer or elswhere, if it may be found, haueing a great posteritie to succeed him.

Thirty or forty acrees of land is graunted vnto Mr William Collyare, with some meddow to it, for his grand child, if it may be had, vizt, that grand child whoe is now seruicable vnto him.

The Court haue graunted vnto William Paybody the remainder of that land hee payed for, being a psell of poor, silly, barren land.

The Court doe admitt of Richard Church to come with the ancient seruants for a share of land att Saconett.

The Court haue graunted vnto Hugh Cole respecting his fathers graunt, being an ancient freeman, and his owne graunt, sixscore acrees of land betwixt Mattapoisett Riuer and the easter bound of Acushenah.

The Court haue graunted vnto Sarah, the wife of Thomas Haward, Juni^r, sixty acrees of land lying betwixt the line of the collonies and the bounds of Bridgwater.

The Court haue graunted vnto John Mecoy twenty six acrees of land and ten acrees of meddow, which was giuen him by the sachem of Sautuckett, lying vpon the south sea.

The Court haue graunted vnto Thomas Tupper, Seni^r, in reference vnto a former graunt giuen him, that if hee can find the land, that hee shall haue sixscore acrees.

1667.
2 July.
PRENCE,
GOUᴿ.

[*160.]

Liberty is graunted vnto Joseph and Barnabas Laythorp to looke out for land for theire supply.

The Court haue graunted vnto Ensigne Marke Eames and Isacke Chettenden that they may haue theire portions of land formerly graunted them in some other place, forasmuch as the place formerly graunted them was not sufficient to accomodate them.

Libertie is graunted vnto Daniell Cole to looke out a p̃sell of land to accomodate him and his children, and to purchase it by order from the Court.

*The Court haue graunted vnto William Barstow, that hee shall haue a p̃sell of land ordered and layed out vnto him lying to the westwards of Cornett Studsons graunt, in reference to satisfaction for his paines, &c̃, in the countrey busines, to be soe ordered and layed forth by the major and the Treasurer; and if that they shall judg̃ it more then his said paines deserues, that hee shall pay for the rest.

The Court haue graunted vnto some ancient freemen liueing in Taunton, viz𝔰, Richard Williams, Walter Dean, Gorge Hall, Allis Dean, the wife of John Deane, deceased, Mʳ John Poole, Peter Pitts, James Walker, and Henery Andrewes, that they shall haue some supplyes of land vpon the west syde of Taunton Riuer, if not alreddy graunted to any other; or some other place, if it may be obtained.

The Court haue ordered, that Captaine Bradford and the Treasurer shall view the land desired by Bridg̃water in reference to theire inlargment, according to theire petition prefered to the Court July the fift, 1667, and to make report therof to the Court, that soe the Court may determine therin as they shall see cause.

The Court haue graunted vnto Robert Finney one hundred acrees of land where Mʳ Alden and Captaine Southworth hath land att Namassakett Riuer, if it may be had there; if not, then to haue such a portion with Hugh Cole, neare Acushenett.

Libertie is graunted vnto Henery Sampson to looke out land to accomodate his children.

Likewise, libertie is graunted vnto William Clarke, Joseph Burge, of Sandwich, Thomas Huckens, John Tompson, Edward Dotey, and his brother John Dotey, and James Cole, Juniʳ, to looke out for some supplyes of land, if it may ᷍ had for theire accomodation.

Wheras Mʳ Thomas Hinckley and Mʳ Nathaniel Bacon hath had a former graunte of meddow, which att the p̃sent can not be purchased, and that forasmuch as that there is land and meddow in that tract purchased by William Bassett betwixt Wakoiett and Saconeesett bounds, the Court haue graunted a

COURT ORDERS. 161

portion of vpland and meddow within the aforsaid purchase, if the land may be had, the which quantitie is to be forty acrees to a pson with meddow, according to theire former graunt.

1667.
2 July.
PRENCE,
Gouᴿ.

*In reference vnto two neckes of land purchased by Mʳ Thomas Dexter, Juniʳ, —

[*161.]

The Court haue graunted vnto the said Thomas Dexter one hundred acrees of the vpland therof, and haue ordered, that the remainder therof shalbe settled, and doe graunt that it shall appertaine to the minnesters house att Sandwich.

This is otherwise ordered: see att the foot of this page.

The Court haue graunted vnto Richard Bourne, of Sandwich, a smale skirt of sedge, with some smale tract of vpland to it, to be viewed by William Paybody; and incase it be not found prejudiciall to Mʳ Standishes land, that it be settled and confeirmed to him.

The Court haue graunted vnto John Rogers, Seniʳ, of Duxburrow, one hundred acrees of land lying vpon Coteticutt Riuer, being alreddy purchased, if it may be had; if not, that hee hath libertie to looke out elswhere.

The Court haue graunted libertie vnto William Browne, of Sandwich, that Richard Bourne may purchase a smale p̄sell of land for him of Nonquitnumacke, if it may be had; if not, that then hee may haue libertie to looke out elswhere for the quantitie of about forty acrees of vpland and six acrees of meddow.

The Court haue ordered, that the land graunted before mensioned shalbe purchased betwixt this date and the next Election Court, or otherwise to be suspended and rest vnpurchased for the tearme of seauen yeares after.

Libertie is graunted vnto Joseph Burge, of Sandwich, William Clarke, Thomas Huckens, John Tompson, Edward Dotey, and his brother John Dotey, and James Cole, Juniʳ, to looke out for some supplyes of land, if it be to be had.

Joseph Bartlett is alowed the sume of seauen pounds towards the repaireing of his damage in the losse of his horse in the countreyes service.

The generall training is appointed to be this yeare att Taunton on Wedensday in the second weeke of October next.

The Court haue graunted vnto Mʳ Thomas Dexter, Juniʳ, one hundred acrees of vpland, where hee shall make choise of it vpon either of those neckes of land by him purchased; and incase the necke that hee shall pitch vpon doe nott containe soe much, hee shall take the remainder att the end of the other necke that is next adjoyning and all the meddowes by him purchased.

And they haue alsoe graunted the resedew of those lands by him there

1667.
2 July.
PRENCE,
GOVR.
[*162.]

purchased vnto the towne of Sandwich, for the vse of the minnestry of that place, they paying theire proportion toward the purchase of the said land.

*Samuell Fuller, the son of Samuell Fuller, Senr, of Barnstable, for selling liquors to the Indians, is fined twenty shillinges.   This to be payed to Mr Hinckley.

Richard Dwelley, being convicted of drunkenes the second time, is fined ten shillinges.

In reference vnto Sarah, the daughter of John Smith, of Barnstable, her comitting of fornication, although the sume of ten pounds fine might be required for her said default, yett on some considerations the Court haue remited the one halfe therof, and doe require the sume of fiue pounds.

Elizabeth Soule, for comitting fornication the second time, was centanced to suffer corporall punishment by being whipt att the post, which accordingly was executed and pformed.

Dinah Siluester, for comitting fornication, fined ten pounds.

Joseph Hallott & his wife, for comitting carnall copulation before marriage and before contract, fined 10^{li} : 00 : 00.

[*163.]

*Mr Myles and Mr Browne, for theire breach of order in seting vp of a publicke meeting without the knowlidge and approbation of the Court, to the disturbance of the peace of the place, are fined, each of them, the sume of fiue pounds, and Mr Tanner the sume of twenty shillings.

And wee judge, that theire continuance att Rehoboth, being very prejudiciall to the peace of that church and that towne, may not be alowed, and doe therfore order all psons concerned therin wholly to desist from the said meeting in that place or township within this month; yett incase they shall remoue theire meeting vnto some other place, where they may not prejudice any other church, and shall giue vs any reasonable satisfaction respecting theire principles, wee know not but they may be pmitted by this goũment soe to doe.

Memorandum. Wheras there hath bine a controuersy of many yeares standing in this Court concerning a psell of land about Mannamoiett, pretended to be purchased by Wiłłam Nicarson, Senr, of Mattaquason, and John Quason, Indians, which said Nicarson was somtimes of Yarmouth, —

This is to be minded as a reall truth, that in all this time the said Wiłłam Nicarson was neuer able to produce any deed or legall euidence of any such purchase, although hee hath bine seuerall times vrged thervnto in open Court, that soe the truth and certainty of his claime might appeer, whether for yeares, or tearme of life, or for inheritance.

All that hath appeered in Court is, that there hath bine diuers goods giuen by the said Nicarson, and reconed by the Indians by way of bargaine for some land, but neuer agreed how much or vpon what tearmes; Nicarson

boldly afeirming, and the Indians as peremtorily deneying, and soe it remaines
att this present; therfore it doth easely appeer how much the countrey was
abased by him that hath noe legall right to any lands there.

1667.
2 July.
PRENCE,
GOUᴿ.

And it is further ordered by this Court, that since soe much trouble and
contest hath arisen heerabouts, and complaints from the Indians alsoe, that
from henceforth the Indians be required not to make any further bargaine or
contract with the said Nicarson about the said lands, except in the hearing or
presence of such as the Court shall appoint for such an end.

John Cooke, of Dartmouth, is authorised by the Court to make contracts
of marriage in the towne of Dartmouth, and likewise to adminncster an oath
to giue euidence to the grand enquest, and likewise to adminnester an oath to
any witnesses for the tryall of a case as occation may require; and incase any
pson or psons resideing in this jurisdiction shall haue occation to comence a
suite against any stranger or forraigner, it shalbe lawfull for the said John
Cooke to issue out warrants in his maᵗⁱᵉˢ name to bind ouer any pson or psons
to answare the said suite att his maᵗⁱᵉˢ Court to be holden att Plymouth att
any time by attachment or summons as occation may require, and that hee
shall giue forth suppenaes to warne wittnes.

*Vpon a motion of marriage betwixt John Phillips, of Marshfeild, and
Faith Dotey, of Plymouth, in the jurisdiction of Plymouth, in New England,
in America, these p̃ticulars were joyntly concluded of by the abouesaid p̃ties,
as followeth: —

[*164.]

Imprimis. That the children of both the said p̃ties shall remaine att the
free and proper and onely dispose of theire owne naturall parents, as they
shall see good to dispose of them.

Secondly. That the said Faith Dotey is to enjoy all her house and land,
goods and cattles, that shee is now posessed of, to her owne proper vse, to
dispose of them att her owne free will from time to time, and att any time, as
shee shall see cause.

Thirdly. That incase by death God should remoue the said John Phillips before her, that shee come to be left a widdow, that then shee shall haue
and enjoy one third p̃te, or one p̃te of three, of all his estate that hee dieth
posessed of for her liuelyhood during her life, — that is to say, one third of
all his estate, either house, lands, or any other his reall estate, — and att the
end of her life, then it shall returne to the heires of the said John Phillips,
excepting her wearing apparrell and her bed and beding, and such furniture
as belonges thervnto, which shee shall and may giue att her death to whom
shee pleaseth, all the rest of the thirds to returne to the heires of the said

1667.
2 July.
PRENCE,
Gouʳ.

John Phillips. In witnes wherof the said John Phillips and Faith Dotey haue mutually and joyntly sett heervnto theire hands, this twenty third of February, anno 1666.

      The marke of   JOHN PHILLIPES.
      The marke of FAITH DOTEY.

In the p̱sence of
 Thomas Southworth,
 Desire Dotey.

[*165.]   *May the 20ᵗʰ, 1667.

Then receiued of John Allin, John Pecke, and John Woodcocke the full and whole sume of twenty pounds, which was of the goods of Richard Ormsbey, deceased, which the Court graunted vnto John Godfrey, which is to be in full satisfaction vnto the said Godfrey for all former debts, dues, and demaunds from the said estate by the said Godfrey or any vnder him from the begiñing of the world to this day ; I, the said Godfrey, doe heerby discharge and acquitt Richard Ormsbey, his heires, exequitors, adminnestrators, or either of them ; alsoe, I, John Godfrey, doe discharge and acquitt John Allin, John Pecke, and John Woodcocke, which was appointed by the Court to adminnester vpon the estate of Richard Ormsbey ; and I doe heerby engage, that I, neither any vnder mee, shall neuer trouble nor molest the said Allin, Pecke, or Woodcocke, or any of them ; whervnto I haue sett my hand and seale, the 20ᵗʰ day of May, 1667.

    The marke of JOHN GODFREY, and a (Seale.)

Signed, sealed, and deliuered in the p̱sence of vs,
 John Cobleigh,
 Thomas Wood,
 Gedion Allin.

[*166.]   *July the 2ᶜᵒⁿᵈ, 1667.

The first session of this Court, June the 4ᵗʰ, 1667, Phillip, the sachem of Pocanakett, being ordered thervnto by Major Winslow and Captaine Southworth, made his psonall appeerance.

The cause was this : the Goū being informed by post letters from Rehoboth that the said Phillip, though in confeederation with vs, had expresed himselfe in the p̱sence of seuerall of his men, importing his reddines to comply with French or Duch against the English, and soe not onely to recouer theire lands sold to the English, but inrich themselues with theire goods ; vpon which intelligence Major Winslow, Captaine Southworth, the Treasurer

Southworth, and others, with a p̃ty of horse, were speedily dispatched to Rehoboth to enquire of the truth of that report; who, coming thither, found the Indian, the first reporter of it, to be one of Phillip the said sachems men, whoe freely and boldly did avouch it to his face, and soe to p̃ticularise time, place, and seuerall psons, which, with diuers other cercomstances from other Indians and English, made the matter appeer very probably true, att least, as to some agitation; but the said sachem, Phillip, stifly deneyed it, and said that Ninnegrett, a Narragansett sachem, had hyered this Indian to accuse him to vs, and doubted not but in time soe to make it to appeer, yett withall confessed the English had just cause to doe as they did vpon such a report, and for his fidelitie to the English was willing to surrender vp his armes to costody of the English, which was accepted, and hee ordered to appeer att June Court, if happily hee might cleare himselfe of this charge.

1667.
2 July.
PRENCE, Govr.

Att this Court, therfore, appeering as formerly, professing his loue and faithfulnes to the English, and that it was a meer plott of Ninnegrett, the Narragansett sachem aforsaid, his professed enimie, that had hiered this Indian to raise such a report of him, to breake that longe continewed loue and amitie between the English of N. Plymouth and him, by whom hee and his brother and father had bine vpheld, and to that end p̃sented a letter from another Indian sachem of Narragansett speaking much to the same purpose; but the Court, suspecting that it might bee but some faigned, as indeed it did appeer afterwards, resolued to send Leiftenant Hunt and Ensigne Smith, of Rehoboth, vnto Warwicke, with some of Phillips men, and to haue the said Narragansett sachem examined before a majestrate of that jurisdiction, to heare what the said sachem could testify in the case, whoe vtterly disclaimed that hee had or could say any such thinge concerning Ninnegrett, as was signifyed to the Court vnder the hand of Mr Smith, a majestrate att Warwicke, and the same affeirmed by Leiftenant Hunt and Ensigne Smith, soe that Phillip was left to find other proffe; as alsoe a letter att the same time from Mr Roger Williams asserted to the like purpose, onely that hee rendered the Indian that accused Phillip to haue bine a very vile fellow formerly. The said sachem, Phillip, still protested his inosency and faithfulnes to the English, by whom himselfe and progenitors had bine preserued from being rewined by the Narragansetts, those potent enimies, pleading how erationall a thing it was that hee should desert his long experienced frinds, the English, and comply with the French or Duch, whoe had the last yeare kiled and carryed eighteen psons, both men and weomen, of his from Martins Viniyard, affirming still that it was a plott of Ninnegreets, thõ hee was not att p̃sent able to make it out, expressing his *great confidence that hee had in that ancient league

[*167.]

1667.

2 July.
[PRENCE,
GOVERNOR.]

with the English, which hee hoped they would still continew, professing that theire withdrawing of theire wonted fauor was little lesse then a death to him, glading his enimies, greiueing and weakening his frinds, and soe left himselfe and case to the Court; who takeing it into serious consideration, not willing to desert him and lett him sincke, though there was great probabillitie that his tongue had bine runing out, yett not haueing such due proffe as was meet, judged it better to keep a watchfull eye ouer him, and still to continew tearmes of loue and amitie with him, vnlesse somthing further did manifestly appeer, and hee to beare pte of the charge, and soe haueing twenty dayes giuen him to appeer att Plymouth to make a finall issue; att which day appointed hee and his principall men appeered, where, after much debate with the Gou, Major Winslow, Captaine Southworth, and the Tresurer, came to this issue:—

1. That if noe further matter did appeer against him, wee should looke att him and carry towards him as formerly.

2. And that hee should beare forty pound of the charge of the expedition, and the countrey the rest.

3. And that incase any such occation should be for the future, except apparently dangerous, wee would send to him by letter or messenger; vpon notice by either, hee engaged speedily to come.

4. That incase hee can yett make it out that this late report is indeed a meer plott betwen Ninnegrett and the Indian, wee will giue him the best aduise wee can that hee may haue som due reparation.

5. Haueing giuen bills for the payment of the forty pounds aforsaid, his armes both att Plymouth and Rehoboth were all ordered to be deliuered againe vnto him and to his men; which was thankefully accepted, and soe the case att psent issued.

*Att the Court held att Plymouth, for the Jurisdiction of N. Plymouth, the thirtieth of October, 1667.

1667.
30 October.
[PRENCE, GOVERNOR.]
[*168.]

BEFORE Thomas Prence, Gou^r, William Bradford,
John Alden, Thomas Hinckley,
Josias Winslow, John Freeman, and
Thomas Southworth, Nathaneell Bacon,
Assistants, &c.

WHERAS the Court haue formerly determined, that John Williams, Junr, of Scittuate, shall alow vnto Elizabeth, his wife, the sume of ten pounds p yeare for her maintainance vntill, by theire mutuall agreement or the Courts appointment, they shall come to liue together againe, this Court doth further order, that the said Williams shall yearly renew bonds for the current discharge and payment therof.

Att this Court, three Indians, namely, Simon, Monchase, and Assoot, for goeing on board the boate of Simon Steuens att Cape Cod and takeing away a caske of liquor, and haueing a hand in the imbezeling and spending therof, were centanced by the Court to be whipt att the post att Plymouth, which accordingly was pformed; likewise, other six Indians, vizt, Lawrance, Quequequancett, James, Moses, and Wamant, and Monchasacke, for theire being ptenors with the other in the imbezeling away of the said liquor, were centanced and stand bound vnto the Court to pay the sume of ten pounds, to be deliuered to Leiftenant Freeman att his house att Eastham in Indian corne, or porke, or feathers, for the collonies vse, betwixt the date heerof and the first day of May next ensuing.

Att the request of the towne of Yarmouth, the Court haue appointed Andrew Hallett, Thomas Howes, and John Thacher to be aded vnto the comittees of Yarmouth for the desposing of lands in that township, and to acte in all such like cases as formerly the said comittee hath done.

The Court doe approue of and appoint John Miller to keep an ordinary att Yarmouth.

The Court doe appoint Captaine Southworth to purchase the land of the Indians which is desired by Henery Wood, according to a former graunt.

Wheras the Court is informed that there is a mare, and a coult, and a gun, and a little linnine cloth, and a sow, and three piggs in the costody of John Allin, John Woodcocke, and John Pecke, adminnestrators of the estate of Richard Ormsbey, deceased, the Court haue ordered the said pticulars to be deliuered to the two youngest sonns of the said Ormsbey.

1667.

30 October.
PRENCE,
GOV^R.

James Doughtey, for his eregular carriage in indeauoring to release Thomas Sumers, a prisoner orderly comitted, is fined the sume of forty shillings to the collonies vse.

Abraham Sutliffe, for expressing of vngodly and atheisticall speeches in his drunkenes, is fined the sume of four pounds, and for his being drunke is fined fiue shillings, to the collonies vse.

Wiłłam Nicarson appeered att this Court to answare for his exhibiting of a writing to the Hono^{ble} Collonell Richard Nicolls, bearing date Aprill the 2^{cond}, 1666, and alsoe another writing bearing date the 23 of February, 1666, the former wherof consented vnto by Robert Eldred and Nathaniel Couell, sons in law to the said William Nicarson, in which said writings are contained many p̄ticulars greatly scandulous to his ma^{ties} Court of this jurisdiction of New Plymouth and the body of the freemen therof, in which respect they might justly haue bin amerced in a great sume to haue payed by way of fine; notwithstanding, the Court, obseruing that they did in som sort take to and acknowlidg theire fault therin, and alsoe in reference vnto the request of the said Collonell Nicolls in theire behalfe, haue fined the said Nicarson the sume of ten pounds, and the said Eldred and Couell, each of them, fiue pounds.

The sume of fifty shillings is ordered by the Court to be payed vnto Samuell Jackson by Hugh Cole, for the takeing vp of his boate, which went on drift.

Łres of adminnestration was graunted by the Court vnto John Thacher to adminnester on the estate of Mr Anthony Thacher, deceased.

Likewise, letters of adminnestration were graunted vnto Sarah, the wife of Nathaniel Warren, deceased, to adminnester on his estate.

[*169.] *Att this Court, John Arther, of Road Iland, appeered to make complaint of seuerall Indians for abusing of him by dispossesing him of his house and otherwise att Pocasseeset, neare Road Iland ferry; vnto which the Court answared, that incase hee would nominate the said Indians, and be reddy to make out against them the said charges, they would warne them in to make answare theruunto.

Thomas Delanoy, for haueing carnall coppulation with his now wife before marriage, fined the sume of ten pounds.

In reference vnto a controuersy between the English and the Indians about runing the line of the bounds of Dartmouth, the Court haue ordered, that incase Robert Hazard, of Rhode Iland, may be procured, that hee run the line, with the inspection of such as shalbe approued both by the English of the said towne and the Indians; but incase hee can not be procured, that John Cobb, of Taunton, shall run the said line; and that this shalbe a finall

COURT ORDERS. 169

end of this controuersy, and that the charge of the busines shalbe bourne by the said towne.

1667.

30 October.
Prence,
Gouʳ.

[*170.]

*Wheras libertie hath bine formerly graunted by the Court for the jurisdiction of N. Plymouth vnto Captaine Thomas Willett and his naighbours att Wannamoisett, to become a township there if they should see good; and that lately the said Capt Willett and Mʳ Myles, and others theire naighbours, haue requested of the Court that they may become a township there or neare thervnto, and likewise to haue graunted vnto them such p̃sells of land as might be accom̃odate thervnto not desposed of to other townships, this Court haue graunted vnto them all such lands that lyeth between the saltwater bay and coming vp Taunton Riuer, vizₜ: all the land between the said salt water and riuer and the bounds of Taunton and Rehoboth, not prejudiceing any mans p̃ticular interest; and forasmuch as Rehoboth hath meddow lands within the line of Wannamoisett, and Wannamoisett hath lands within the line of Rehoboth lying neare the south line of Rehoboth, if the two townshipps cannot agree about them amongst themselues, the Court reserues it within theire power to determine any such controuersy.

The Court haue ordered and authorised Mʳ Thomas Kinge, of Scittuate, to adminnester an oath to such witnesses as shalbe disabled through weaknes to appeer att the Court to giue euidence or testimony to any case, and likewise to graunt subpenaes for the warning of witnesses to giue testimony to any case or tryall, and likewise to swear witnesses to giue euidence to the grand jurymen within the towne of Scittuate as occation may require.

Septem̃ 20, 1667.

Wee, whose names are vnderwritten, being warned to bee vpon a corroners enquest vpon the death of a child of Daniell Dones, whoe was drownded in a well, wee doe all of vs judge that the child was accedentally drownded.

JOSEPH ROGERS,
EDWARD BANGES,
DANIEL COLE,
WILLAM MERRICKE,
RICHARD KNOWLES,
ROBERT VIXON,
THOMAS WILLIAMS,
BENAJAH DUNHAN,
BENJAMINE HIGGENS,
JONATHAN SPARROW,
JOHN MAYO,
JOHN ROGERS.

1667. The verdict abouesaid was attested by the psons next aboue written before mee.

30 October.
PRENCE,
GOUR.

JOHN FREEMAN, Assistant.

[*171.]

*Yarmouth.

In the yeare 67, vpon the 14th day of October, wee, whose names are heervnder written, being warned by authoritie to view the corpes lately deceased, viz§, the child of Nicholas Nicarson, haue found in the windpipe of the child a pece of a pumpian shell; the which wee, being all and euery one of vs agreed, doe judge that it was the cause of its death.

                      WILŁAM LUMPKIN,
                      JOHN HALL,
                      WILŁAM ALDREDGE,
                      THOMAS GAGE,
                      JOHN BURGE,
                      JOHN CROW,
                      PAULE SAERS,
                      JOHN HALL,
                      ZACARIAH PADUCKE,
                      JOSEPH HALL,
                      NATHANIELL HALL,
                      JOHN ELDREDGE.

18 November.

Nouember the 18th, 1667.

Timothy Poole, son of Captaine Wiłłam Poole, being about twenty fiue yeares old, on the 15th day of Nouember, 1667, in the morning, went from the house of James Bell, pretending to goe to kill some fowle, to a smale pond about halfe a mile from the house of James Bell; Hester, the wife of James Bell, reported that Timothy Poole told her that hee had killed some fowle, and that hee had some expectation to kill some more; but returning not that day, James Bell, comeing home to his house that day, made some serch in the woods for him, but not finding him, came to the towne to haue some others to goe to seeke him, with whom there were Henery Andrewes, John Hall, Jehud Talbut, Samuell Hall, Nathaniel Williams, Joseph Williams, and some others, which after some serch made by these by the syde of a smale pond, thē found on the snow his tract, and by that came where they found his gun and most of his clothes, and from thence saw where the yice had bine formerly broken into the pond; and after that, when they had feched a cannoe, and after some time of dilligent serch, Henery Andrewes discouered him att the bottome of the pond, about twelue foot deep in the water; which when they had gotten vp, they brought to the shore, and finding noe hurt on him any otherwise but that hee perished in and by the water and the extremity of cold; and this the verdict of the jury which was warned by the constable, which are these vnderwritten by vs.

1667.
30 October
PRENCE,
GOUR.

GORG: HALL,
GORG: MACEY,
NICHOLAS WHITE,
JOHN COBB,
JOSEPH WILBORE,
PETER PITTS,
WILLIAM HAILSTONE,
THOMAS CASWELL,
JOHN DEANE,
RICHARD BRIGGS,
JONAH AUSTIN, Junir,
WILLAM HARVEY.

February 3th, 1667.

1667-8.
3 February.

The majestrates, being mett together on speciall occasions, did then order, that Major Winslow and Cornett Studson, or either of them, in the behalfe of the countrey, to purchase a certaine tract of land, in the which the cornetts purchase is encluded.

In reference vnto a graunt of land graunted vnto Josias Keine, the Court haue ordered Cornett Studson to laye it forth for him according to the graunt, on the southerly syde of the land graunted to the children of Leiftenant Torrey.

The majestrates haue agreed, that in respect vnto a graunt of land made vnto Francis Combe, that all the land that lyeth betwixt that little brooke that is next to the majors land att Namassakett, vpon the riuer, containeing the feild comonly called the Blacke Sachems Feild, and soe vnto a springey swamp about fifty or sixty rod on the southerly syde, and soe from the said swamp to a swamp where there is a little hole of meddow, it being alsoe encluded; and from thence as shalbe judged meet by the Gou shalbe settled vpon him, the said Francis Combe.

*These are to declare vnto all whom it may concerne, that Mr John Winge, master of the ship called the Hopewell, and John Irons, and Herculus Toute, seamen appertaining to the said shipp, ariueing att the harbor of Plymouth, in New England, on Thursday, the sixt of this instant February,

6 February.
[*172.]

1 6 6 7-8.

6 February.
PRENCE,
GOUʀ.

1667, repaired vnto mee, Nathaniel Morton, Secretary to the Court for the jurisdiction of Plymouth aforsaid, on the seauenth of the said month of February, and protested against the said shipp as insufficient for the sea, forasmuch as that they, seting sayle in her from Boston, in New England, on the fift of the month of February fornamed, being in companie with other shipps, by that time they had sayled about six or seauen leagues from Nantaskett, they found, that in a moderate gale of wind, and carrying but little sayle, they were in danger seuerall times to haue bine ouersett, and tooke in diuers tuns of water vpon her decke, and that shee had a leake sprunge vpon her, whervpon they were constrained to make to the first harbour they could, and by Gods prouidence came in att Plymouth aforsaid on the seauenth of this instant forenamed; and desired that theire said protest against the said shipp might be entered on the recordes of this Court; which accordingly by these p̃sents is done, and a transcript heerof deliuered the same day vnto the said mʳ and seamen abouenamed, vnder the hand of the Secretary aboue mensioned.

28 February.

The bounds of Francis Combe his land, layed out by the Goũ : his westerly bounds vpon Namassakett Riuer, his southsyde from the riuer bounded by a great beach tree in two p̃tes on one roote, from thence to a little red oake marked, and from thence vp into the woods a direct line to the southermost syde of a little spott of meddow to a marked white oake tree; on the easterly syde of the said spott of meddow, all that meddow spott to be included within his line, and from the said oake to a marked pyne tree, and from thence through a swamp to a marked white oake standing on the north syde of the path that bounds that land called the Majors Purchase; and that southermost path that comes from Namassakett to Lakenham is his syde bounds till it comes to a ridgg of hills that runs downe to Namassakett Riuer, which is the bounds betwẽn that land giuen to the major and the new lands of Francis Combe, his lands vpon the riuer being about sixty rodd breadth, be it more or lesse, that p̃te being called the Black Sachems feild, buting vpon the riuer against the stone ware; and all the rest of the land expressed within the bounds aboue mensioned, be it more or lesse, layed out to him on the 24th of February, 1667.

As attesteth   THOMAS SOUTHWORTH, Assistant.

Plymouth, the 28th of February, 1667.

*Att the Court of his Matie held att Plymouth for the Jurisdiction of New Plymouth, the fift Day of March, Anno Dom 1667.

1667-8.
5 March.
PRENCE, GOU^R.

BEFORE Thomas Prence, Gou,
John Alden,
Josias Winslow,
Thomas Southworth,

William Bradford,
Thomas Hinckley,
John Freeman, and
Nathaniel Bacon,
Assistants, &c.

[*173.]

THE Court haue ordered, that Mr Alden, Captaine Southworth, and the Treasurer shall, on the second day of May next ensueing the date heerof, repaire to Marshfeild, and take notice of the bounds of some land in controuersye, and the differences therabout between Captaine Thomas and the towne of Marshfeild, and to make report therof to the next Court.

Leiftenant Morton and Gorge Bonum are appointed by the Court to range the land of Edward Gray att Rockey Nooke, and alsoe to lay out a highway by it, which land is to be ranged and to run on the same point of the compas as Mr Howlands att Rockey Nooke next vnto John Cookes doth, that is to say, on a west southwest line.

Leiftenant Morton and seuerall others of the naighbours liueing towards the Eelriuer gaue in att this Court an account of a late amesurment and ranging of theire lands, viz(), theire twenty acree lotts, with theire additions or enlargments; that is to say, of theire said twenty acree lots, from the widdow Churchills bounds on the northeren syde to William Clarkes southerly bounds or line, and respecting the said aditions from Nathaniel Mortons northerly syde or line to William Clarkes southerly line of his addition, or the southermost bound of the vper end of his land att the Eelriuer; and the Court ordered, that the said ranges and bounds should be recorded, and are extant elswher in the records of the Court, and to be feirme and settled for the future, and not to be altered.

See Booke of Euidences of Land recorded, folio 133.
‡The great booke of orders and passages of the court, folio 133.‡

It is ordered by the Court, that wheras a certaine Indian appertaining to our jurisdiction is now in hold att Boston for matter of fact, and that there is probabillitie of a tender of some land for his ransome from being sent to the Barbadoes, that incase the said land be tendered to acceptance, that it shalbe improued and expended for the defraying of the charge of the printing of the booke intitled New Englands Memoriall.

In reference vnto a claime made by Benjamine Bartlett vnto some land giuen by Mr Jonathan Brewster, deceased, vnto his wife, which is said to lye in Alkarmus Feild, the Court haue ordered, that incase hee can produce any

1667-8.

5 March.
Prence,
Govr.

testimony to manifest wher Mr William Brewsters land lyeth within the said feild, that then hee shall haue four acrees layed out vnto him by William Crow; and incase that afterwards hee can produce any other euidence that more is due vnto him there, that hee shall haue it layed out to him.

Wheras there hath bine a controuersye between the towne of Duxburrow and Robert Barker about a p̃sell of meddow lying att Robinsons Creeke, in the township of Duxburrow, and that there was an order directed from the Court vnto the towne of Duxburrow, bearing date March the fift, 1666, in which said order is expressed, that incase the said towne of Duxburrow, or any of them, did not produce any thinge to the contrary betwixt that Court and the shuting up of the June Court following, that then, vpon such euidence as hee should produce, should haue the said meddow recorded vnto him; and that since that time, nothing hath appeered to the Court to be a sufficient reason to obstruct the same; this Court doth therfore heerby ratify, confeirme, and settle vnto the said Robert Barker the said p̃sell of meddow, being nine acrees and an halfe, be it more or lesse, being bounded on the northerly syde with the meddow of Robert Sprout, and with the meddow of Gorge Russell on the southerly syde, and with the meddow of William Tubbs on the westerly syde.

[*174.]

*Wheras, att the Court held att Plymouth the 2^{cond} of July, 1667, the said Court graunted vnto Richard Bourne, of Sandwich, a smale skirt of sedge or creeke stuffe, with some smale tract or p̃sell of vpland to it, lying neare Mr Josias Standishes land att Mannomet, which was to ^ viewed by William Paybody; and incase that it should not be found p̃judiciall to the aforsaid land of Mr Standishes, that it should be confeirmed to him, the said Richard Bourne.

Att this Court, the said William Paybody came into the Court, and certifyed the Court that hee hath viewed the said skirt of sedge or creeke stuffe, and findeth it not prejudiciall vnto the said land; and therfore the Court doth settle and confeirme vnto the said Richard Bourne the said smale p̃sell of vpland and creeke stuffe, and some smale inconsiderable p̃sells of meddow heer and ther amongst it, to him and his heires and assignes for euer, hee satisfying the right Indian propriators for the same.

In answere vnto a petition prefered to the Court by John Jacob, of Hingham, and others the p̃tenors in the land graunted to Mr Hatherly att Accord Pond, that forasmuch as some of the p̃tenors, whoe haue but smale portions in the said lands, are not willing to consent vnto such good orders as the generallitie of them doe agree vpon in reference to the said land, incase that such p̃sent decenting p̃tenors doe not concurr and come to an agreement

with the rest in reference vnto such orders betwixt this date and the next 1667-8.
June Court, that then it shalbe att the libertie of the generallitie of them to
make deuision of the said lands.

5 March.
PRENCE,
Gouᴿ.

Łres of adminnestration were graunted vnto Mistris Elizabeth Thacher
and vnto John Thacher to adminnester on the estate of Mʳ Anthony Thacher,
deceased.

Łres of adminnestration were graunted vnto Mary, the wife of Anthony
Dodson, to adminnester on the estate of John Williams, Seniʳ, of Scittuate,
deceased.

It being desired that a ferrey should be kept on our side to transport
p̃sons ouer to Road Iland, the Court hath appointed John Cooke and other
the naighbours of Dartmouth to take order with one to doe the same; and the
Court likewise giues libertie, that hee whom they shall order to be imployed
therin to erect some smale building and to improue some land there, with the
Indians p̃mission, for his more comfortable healp and carrying on whiles hee
is in the said imployment.

This Court doth alow and approue of Mʳ Nathaniell Bacon and Joseph
Laythorpe to be gaurdians vnto Joseph Hull, the son of Mʳ Trustrum Hull,
deceased.

Daniell Wilcockes tooke the oath of fidelitie this Court.

In reference vnto the complaint made against Ralph Smith, of Eastham,
concerning oppression and hard dealing with a carpenter named Crispen
Wadlen, whoe was one of Captaine Allins companie, which said Wadlen kept
about three weekes att the said Smithes house, the Court haue ordered, that a
certaine p̃scll of tooles which the said Smith had of the said carpenters shalbe
deliuered vnto Nicholas Snow, to be sent to the said Wadlen; and that the
said Snowes receipt of them shalbe the said Smithes discharge; and that a
certaine p̃scll of cotten woole, which the said Smith had of the said Crispin
Wadlen, shalbe by him, the said Smith, kept, if hee please, for full satisfaction for the time & charge hee was att when att his house as aforsaid.

And in reference vnto the complaint of Captaine Allen against the said
Ralph Smith for like oppression or hard dealing, forasmuch as none appeered
in the Court to be authorised to procequte against him in his behalfe, the
Court doe leaue it to the said Captaine Allin further to proceed therin as hee
shall see cause.

*The Court doe alow and approue that the township graunted vnto [*175.]
Captaine Willett and others, his naighbours, att Wannamoisett and places
adjacent, shall hensforth be called and knowne by the name of Swansey.

The Court haue appointed Captaine Willett, Mʳ Paine, Seniʳ, Mʳ Browne,

PLYMOUTH COLONY RECORDS.

1667-8.

5 March.
PRENCE,
Govr.

John Allin, and John Butterworth to haue the trust of admittance of towne inhabitants into the said towne, and to haue the disposall of lands therin, and ordering of other the affaires of the said towne.

The Court haue graunted liberty vnto Captaine Willett to purchase what lands hee can in the behalfe of the Court within the township of Swansey soe as hee doe not to much straiten the Indians.

The Court haue declared, that soe farr as in them lyeth they are willing that for such stronge liquors as are or shalbe brought into the said towne by forraigners in the way of trad, it shalbe costom free soe as it be not retailed; and this libertie to continew for the tearme of seauen yeares from the date heerof.

It is further ordered by the Court, that the towne of Swansey shall send downe one to serue in the office of a constable for that constablericke, and one for a deputie, and a grandjury man, vnto the next June Court, to take office to serue in theire respectiue places and offices for that towne.

Eastham, the 24th of the 10th month, 1667.

Fines.

Wee, whose names are vnderwritten, being impannelled vpon a jury to make dilligent and carefull serch and enquiry, according to that measure of wisdome and discretion that God hath giuen vs, concerning the death of Robert Chapell, James Nicolls, and William Pidell, that were of the companie of Captaine John Allen, which by Gods prouidence was put on shore vpon Cape Codd, wee find, according to our best wisdome and descretion, that the cause of Robert Chapells and James Nicolls was wett, extream cold, and some liquors which they dranke; these thinges working together vpon them wee judge to be the cause of theire death; and concerning William Pidell, wee apprehend that former sicknes which we vnderstand was vpon him, and wett, and extream cold wee judge to be the cause of his death; heerin wee all agree. Witnes our hands,

       MARKE SNOW,
       JOSEPH SNOW,
       BENJAMINE HIGGENS,
       DANIELL DONE,
       JOHN COLE,
       JOSHUA BANGES,
       RICHARD HIGGENS,
       THOMAS PAINE,
       BENAJAH DUNHAM,
       JOHN SMALLEY,
       JOHN MAYO,
       JONATHAN SPARROW.

COURT ORDERS. 177

*Wee, whose names are vnderwritten, being impanneled vpon a jury, this first day of January, 1667, to serch and inquire, according to that measure of wisdome and descretion God hath giuen vs, concerning a child about fiue or six yeares old, which was kept by John Smalley, Seniʳ, of Eastham, being found dead in the woods, about six or seauen miles from the house of John Smalley abouesaid, wee doe all judge, that it came by his death by straying away, lost its right path to gitt home againe, and was killed by the cold.

1667-8.

5 March.
Prence,
Govʳ.
[*176.]

    BENJAMINE HIGGENS,
    WILLIAM SUTTON,
    SAMUELL DOTEN,
    ELIAS WHITE,
    EDMOND FOARD,
    BENJAMINE SPILLER,
    ROBERT WIXAM,
    GYLES HOPKINS,
    GORGE CRISPE,
    WILLIAM TWINING,
    RICHARD KNOWLES,
    JOHN YOUNGE.

Samuel Smith tooke the oath of fidelitie the 25ᵗʰ of October, 1667.

In reference to the p̃sentment of Joseph Turner, for his breach of the peace in strikeing Thomas Perrey, is fined 00 : 03 : 04.

The said Joseph Turner, for makeing and publishing a scurrilous and infamous writing, wherin is contained many laciuious and filthy verses, hee is centanced by the Court to be publickly whipt, or to pay a fine of fiue pounds; and in reference to his frequency in speakeing falsely and scandulously of others as in that paper, and att other times, hee is centanced by the Court to find surties for his good behauior vntill the next June Court.

Joseph Turner acknowlidgeth to owe vnto our soū lord the Kinge the sume of . . . . } 20 : 00 : 00
Nathaniell Turner the sume of . . . . 10 : 00 : 00
Richard Dwelley the sume of . . . . 10 : 00 : 00

The condition, that if the said Joseph Turner be of good behauior towards our soū lord the Kinge and all his leich people, and in speciall that hee beware of speaking scandulously and falsly of others, and appeer att the Court of his maᵗⁱᵉ to be holden att Plymouth the first Tusday in June next, and not depart the said Court without lycence; that then, &c̃.

Released.

Joseph Bartlett, for breakeing the Kinges peace in strikcing of an Indian called Sampson, is centanced to pay a fine of 00 : 03 : 04.

VOL. IV.   23

1667-8.

5 March.
Prence,
Govr.

And for his abusing the said Indian therin, hee is ordered by the Court to pay to the said Indian a bushell of Indian corne.

In reference vnto a controuersy between Joseph Turner and Hester Wormall, concerning reports deuoulged by the said Turner against the said Hester Wormall, forasmuch as that notwithstanding such testimonies as haue bine produced on both sydes for the clearing of the case, it lyes dubiouse to the Court, it is for the p̄sent suspended vntill further complaint and euidence shalbe produced vnto the Court for the clearing vp therof.

[*177.]

The said Nathaniel Soule, requiring to be tryed by his peers according to law, was indited for the said fact, and vpon the reading of the inditment owned himselfe guilty therof.

*Att this Court, Nathaniel Soule, being sumoned, appeared to answare for his abusing of Mr John Holmes, teacher of the church of Christ att Duxburrow, by many false, scandulous, and opprobriouse speeches, as appeared to the Court by many testimonies, for which hee was centanced by the Court to make a publicke acknowlidgment therof att this p̄sent Court, and to find surties for his good behauior, and to be sett in the stockes duering the pleasure of the Court; att the earnest request of the said Mr Holmes, the latter p̄te of the centance was remitted; the two former p̄tes therof were pformed as followeth :—

These are to declare vnto all men, that wheras I, Nathaniel Soule, of Duxburrow, being p̄sented before this honored Court now in being att Plymouth, and alsoe indited for wickedly speaking, and with an high hand contumeliously villifying and scandulising Mr John Holmes, minnester of the gospell att Duxburrow, the which accordingly as I did owne myselfe to be guilty of the abouesaid p̄ticulares, wheras the said inditment was read in the Court, soe doe I now; and that this my wickednes in soe speaking of soe godly a man is greatly agrauated in that it hath a tendency to the hinderence of the efficacye of that great and honorable worke of the preaching of the gospell vnto which hee is called; and soe, as it is rightly said in the aforsaid inditment, I haue dishonored God, and what in mee lyeth in the aforsaid respects hindered the good of the soules of his ma^{ties} good subjects, and therby haue not onely incurred the wrath and great displeasure of God, but alsoe doe deserue seuere punishment from this honored Court to be inflicted on mee, and doe desire that noe other may be any way incurraged by my wicked example att any time to speake soe wickedly and abominably, and that this may be a warning to mee whiles I liue to take heed that I noe more soe falsely & wickedly speake as I haue done of the said reuerend man, nor of any other, being willing to submitt myselfe vnto the centance of the Court, as being justly inflicted on mee, and being farr lesse then my demeritts in reference to the p̄mises; and that this my publicke acknowlidgment may be

COURT ORDERS.   179

entered on the records of this honored Court, and for the truth of this my   1667-8.
acknowlidgment, I haue heervnto subscribed my hand in the p̃sence of this
honored Court.   5 March.
                          NATHANIEL SOULE.   PRENCE,
                                                                             GOUR.

Nathaniel Soule acknowlidgeth to owe vnto our soũ ⎫
    lord the Kinge the sum̃e of . . . . ⎬ 20 : 00 : 00
                                                   ⎭
Gorge Soule, Seni^r, the sum̃e of . . . . 10 : 00 : 00
John Soule the sume of . . . . 10 : 00 : 00

The condition, that if the said Nathaniel Soule be of good behauior Released of
towards our soũ lord the King and all his leich people, and be carefull not to these bonds.
speake contumeliously or scandulously either of Mr John Holmes or any other,
as hee hath done, and appeer att the Court of his ma^{tie} to be holden att
Plymouth the first Tuesday in June next, and not depart the said Court without
lycence; that then, &c̃.

Francis, the sachem of Nausett, for his vnciuill and inhumaine words and
carriages to Captaine Allin when hee was cast away on Cape Cod, was com̃it-
ted to ward for a certaine time, and fined 10 : 00 : 00.

---

*Att the Generall Court of Election held att Plymouth the third   1668.
               Day of June, Anno Dom̃ 1668.
                                                                   3 June.
                                                                   [*178.]
    BEFORE Thomas Prence, Goũ,   William Bradford,
           John Aldin,   Thomas Hinckley,
           Josias Winslow,   John Freeman, and
           Thomas Southworth,   Nathaniel Bacon,
                         Assistants, &c̃.

MR THOMAS PRENCE was chosen Gou^r, and sworne.

     Mr John Alden,   ⎫
     Major Josias Winslow,   ⎪
     Capt Thomas Southworth,   ⎪
     Capt William Bradford,   ⎬ were chosen Assistants, and sworne.
     Mr Thomas Hinckley,   ⎪
     Mr John Freeman, and   ⎪
     Mr Nathaniel Bacon,   ⎭

180   PLYMOUTH COLONY RECORDS.

1668.

3 June.
PRENCE,
GOUR.

Major Josias Winslow and Captaine Thomas Southworth were chosen Comissioners.

Mr Thomas Prence was the next in nomination.

Mr Constant Southworth was chosen Treasurer, and sworne.

The Names of the Deputies of the seuerall Townes.

Leiftenant Ephraim Morton,	John Chipman,
Samuell Dunham,	Anthony Snow,
Mr Constant Southworth,	Ensigne Eames,
Mr Josias Standish,	Leiftenant Peter Hunt,
Mr Thomas Kinge,	Ensigne Henery Smith,
Thomas Burgis,	Daniell Cole,
James Walker,	Jonathan Sparrow,
William Harvey,	John Willis,
Thomas Howes,	John Cooke,
John Thacher,	John Allin.
Leiftenant Laythorpe,	

[*179.]   *The Names of the Grand Enquest.

Mr Willam Clarke,	Ensigne John Haward,
Mr James Browne,	Jeremiah Howes,
Mr Samuell Saberey,	Benjamine Nye,
Henery Wood,	Paule Saers,
John Otis,	John Wadsworth,
John Turner, Seni^r,	Arther Hathewey,
John Damman,	John Done, Juni^r,
Phillip Walker,	John Hall,
Jonathan Blisse,	Edward Bobbitt,
Nathaniel Thomas,	Jabez Lumbert.
John Rogers,	

The Constables of the seuerall Townes in this Jurisdiction.

Plymouth, ...	John Wood.
Duxburrow, ...	Joseph Wadsworth.
Scittuate, ...	{ Mathew Gannett, { Benjamine Studson.
Sandwich, ...	William Swift.

COURT ORDERS.

1668.

3 June.
PRENCE,
Gouʳ.

Taunton,	Samuell Smith.
Yarmouth,	Richard Tayler.
Barnstable,	Henery Bourne.
Marshfeild,	{ Clement Kinge, Samuell Sprague.
Rehoboth,	{ Robert Fuller, Gorge Kendricke.
Eastham,	Samuell Freeman.
Bridgwater,	Nicholas Byram.
Dartmouth,	John Briggs.
Swansey,	Nathaniel Pecke.

Surveyors of the Highwaies.

Plymouth,	{ Gorḡ Bonum, Joseph Howland, Jonathan Morey.
Duxburrow,	{ Gorge Partrich, Henery Howland.
Scittuate,	{ Cornett Robert Studson, Serjeant William Tickner, William Peakes.
Sandwich,	{ Myls Blackwell, Edward Perrey.
Taunton,	{ Leiftenant Gorge Macye, Peter Pitts.
Bridgwater,	
Yarmouth,	{ Thomas Gage. Judah Thacher,
Barnstable,	{ John Crocker, Senʳ, John Finney, Senʳ.
Marshfeild,	{ Joseph Bedle, Resolued White.
Eastham,	{ Jonathan Banges, William Walker.
Rehoboth,	
Dartmouth,	
Swansey,	

1668.

3 June.
PRENCE,
GOVR.
[*180.]

*The Celect Men of each Towne of this Jurisdiction.

Plymouth, ... { Leiftenant Ephraim Morton,
Serjeant William Harlow,
William Crow.

Duxburrow, ... { William Paybody,
Christopher Wadsworth,
Benjamine Bartlett.

Scittuate, ... { Mr Thomas Kinge,
John Sutton,
Isacke Bucke.

Sandwich, ... { Thomas Tupper, Senir,
James Skiffe, Senir,
Edmond Freeman, Junir.

Taunton, ... { Gorge Hall,
Richard Williams,
Walter Deane,
William Harvey,
James Walker.

Yarmouth, ... { Mr Edmond Hawes,
James Mathewes,
Thomas Howes,
John Miller,
John Thacher.

Barnstabł, ... { Thomas Huckens,
William Crocker,
John Tompson,
John Chipman,
Leiftenant Laythorpe.

Marshfeild, ... { Leiftenant Peregrine White,
Ensigne Marke Eames,
Anthony Snow.

Eastham, ... { Richard Higgens,
Daniell Cole,
Nicholas Snow.

Bridḡwater, ... { John Willis,
Nicholas Byram,
John Carrey.

Jdedia Lumbert and his wife, for comitting carnall coppulation before marriag̃, after contract, fined 05 : 00 : 00.

COURT ORDERS.

*The Names of such as are appointed by the Court to reciue the Excise in each Towne of this Jurisdiction.

1668.
3 June.
PRENCE, Gov^R.
[*181.]

Plymouth,	Benajah Pratt.
Duxburrow,	Henery Sampson.
Scittuate,	Isacke Chettenden.
Sandwich,	{ Thomas Tobey, and { Thomas Tupper, Juni^r.
Taunton,	William Harvey.
Yarmouth,	{ John Miller, { John Hawes.
Barnstable,	{ Leiftenant Laythorpe, { Thõ Huckens.
Marshfeild,	Anthony Snow.
Rehoboth,	Daniel Smith.
Eastham,	Ensigne Merricke.
Bridgwater,	John Eames.
Dartmouth,	Serjeant Shaw.

Memorandum: that Samuell Sturgis, Edward Sturgis, Eliza Hedge, Thomas Starr, John Crow, Juni^r, Abraham Hedge, John Mocoy, and Marke Redly be sent for to the next Court, to giue a reason of theire bringing in such great quantities of liquor into the collonie.

In reference vnto the complaint of an Indian called Powas against Peter Pitts, of Taunton, for detaining of his gun from him on pretence of none pformance of a bargaine about breaking vp of ground, the Court haue ordered, that the said Indian shall breake vp twenty rodd of ground for the said Peter Pitts; and when that is don, hee shall haue his gun returned to him againe in good culture.

Mr Hinckly, Mr Bacon, and Mr Freeman, or any two of them, are appointed by the Court to settle a difference betwixt Gorḡ Allin and Richard Chadwell in reference to a highway, either as they returne home from this Court or as they come to July Court; the said way to be twenty foot in breadth, or more, if it may be convenient.

In reference to the complaint of Sacary Ryder against Richard Berrey, on suspision of the stealling of an axe from him, the Court haue ordered Mr Hinckley and Mr Bacon, forasmuch as matters cannot att present be cleared, it is refered to Mr Hinckley and Mr Bacon to end it att home.

In reference vnto the complaint of Thomas Howes, the late constable of Yarmouth, against William Nicarson, Seni^r, Nathaniell Couell, Samuell

1668.
3 June.
Prence,
Govr.

Nicarson, Joseph Nicarson, and William Nicarson, Juni^r, for affronting him in the execution of his office, and offering diuers abuses to him therin, the Court haue centanced them all to sitt in the stockes dureing the pleasure of the Court, which accordingly was pformed ; and pticularly, forasmuch as the said William Nicarson, Seni^r, hath binc principall and leader in the said affront, hee was centanced by the Court to find surties for his good behauior vntill the Court to be holden att Plymouth in October next, or to be comitted to prison vntill hee soe doe ; hee, refusing to prouide surties, stood comitted three daies, and after that gaue bonds as followeth : —

William Nicarson acknowlidgeth to owe vnto our soū lord the Kinge the sume of . . . . } 20 : 00 : 00

James Cole, Seni^r, the sume of . . . . 20 : 00 : 00

Released.

The condition, that if the said William Nicarson be of good behauior towards our soū lord the Kinge and all his leich people, and appeare att the Court of his ma^{tie} to be holden att Plymouth aforsaid the last Tusday in October next, and not depart the said Court without lycence ; that then, &c.

[*182.]

*In reference vnto a psell or tract of land formerly graunted vnto Mr Thomas Prence, lying att Namassakett, the Court haue appointed Major Winslow, Captaine Southworth, and Leiftenant Morton to lay out a proportion of the land hee hath lately purchased there vnto him, as they shall thinke meet, or to settle the whole of it to him, if on the sight and viewall therof they shall see cause.

In answare to a proposition made by Mr Thomas Prence, Goū, to purchase the seate hee now liueth on att Plaindealing, in the township of Plymouth, this Court did voate the sale therof vnto him, and accordingly ordered Mr Hinckley, Mr Bacon, Mr Constant Southworth, Treasurer, Daniell Cole, John Allin, John Chipman, and Leiftenant Morton, in the behalfe of the collonie, to make sale therof.

The tearmes and conditions wherof are as followeth : —

Viz^t : that the said house and land, with all and singulare the appurtenances and priuilidges belonging thervnto, vizt, the whole seat, with all the additions and enlargments appertaining thervnto, is bargained and sold vnto the said Mr Thomas Prence, to him and his heires and assignes for euer, for and in consideration of the sume of one hundred and fifty pound, in current countrey pay, to be payed one third therof this time three yeare, another third therof this time six yeare, and the other third this time nine yeare. It is likewise agreed by and between the said pties, that if it be to be sold att any time, the countrey shall haue the refusall therof, and to haue it on the same tearmes it is now sold, prouided that what it shalbe the better by any expence

COURT ORDERS.

on it in the interem, it be payed for ouer and aboue the sume aboue mensioned.

1668.

3 June.
PRENCE,
Gouʳ.

The Court haue likewise ordered, and doe by these p̃sents impower Mʳ Constant Southworth, Treasurer, for and in the behalfe of the collonie, to giue and seale deeds and euidences further requisite in law for the full ratifycation and ample confermation of the said p̃mises vnto the said Mʳ Thomas Prence, hee, his heires, and assignes for euer, allowing and approueing as authenticall whatsoeuer the said Constant Southworth shall doe therin as theire acte and deed.

A portion of land is graunted vnto Experience Michell lying next vnto Hugh Coles graunt, which is betwixt Mattapoisett Riuer and the easterly bounds of Acushena, on the westeren syde of the said riuer.

This Court, Josias Wampatucke came into the Court, and owned that the three mile square of land by Accord Pond, which was graunted by the Court to Mʳ Hatherley, that hee hath sold it to Mʳ Hatherley, and is by him fully satisfyed for it.

It is ordered by the Court, that Paomett and soe farr as the Cape Head be reputed within the constablericke of Eastham.

It is likewise ordered, that the lands att Mannamoite be att present reputed to be in the constablericke of Eastham, and liable to pay publicke charges there.

It was ordered by the Court, that the ferrey att Pochasett be ordered and to farme lett by John Cooke and Daniell Wilcockes in the behalfe of the countrey.

This Court, John Briggs, John Sherman, and Ralph Earle tooke the oath of fidelitie.

*The Court haue ordered, that a tract of land containing a mile and a halfe, lying on the north side of the towne of Rehoboth, is alowed to be the proper right of the said township, and for such lands as are lying betwixt the Bay line; and it is to be accompted within the constablericke of Rehoboth vntill the Court doe order it otherwise; and that such farmes as lyeth within the said liberties shalbe responsible in point of rateing att the collonies despose.

[*183.]

The Court, haueing taken into consideration the controuersy att Dartmouth, arising from a diuersitie of expressing the eastermost bounds of Dartmouth, and finding vpon serch of the first ancient record that the bounds was to take place from the riuer and two miles eastward, but this Court alowes of three miles eastward, and doth mind the riuer, and not the bay, to take the three miles from, and the tree that hath bine theire bounds soe longe, and hath bin proued, the Court sees noe reason but you ought to rest satisfyed in.

1 6 6 8.

3 June.
PRENCE,
Gov⹁.
A testimony
appointed to
be recorded.

The testimony of Richard Sisson, aged sixty or therabouts : John Archer, being att my house, did speake as followeth, and said, the deed of gift made by Namumpam to John Sanford and himselfe was a cheatt, and the intent therof was to deceiue Namumpam, squa sachem, of her land ; and they were to haue both corn and peague to cecure her land from Wamsutta or Peter Talmon, and was to resigne vp the deed att her demaund.

And I, Mary Sisson, doe testify, that I heard the same words att the same time ; and further, when my husband was gon out of the house, I heard them both say they were troubled in consience that they had concealled it soe longe, and did refuse to take p̃te of the grattification.

This was attested vpon oath before mee,

May 27, 1668. JOHN COOKE.

Richard Sisson was sworn to this testimony aboue written this 3 of the 4, 68.

Before mee, JOHN ALDEN, Assistant.

Att this Court, the sum̃e of twenty pound in countrey pay was ordered to be improued by the Treasurer for and towards the printing of the booke intitled New Englands Memoriall; and it was likewise recom̃ended to the seuerall townes of this jurisdiction by theire deputies to make a free and vouluntary contribution in mony for and towards the procuring of paper for the printing of the said booke.

This Court, Ensigne Henery Smith is authorised by the Court to make contracts of marriage in the towne of Rehoboth, and likewise to adminnester an oath to giue euidence to the grand enquest, and likewise to adminnester an oath to any witnesses for the tryall of a cause as occation may require ; and incase any p̃son within this goũment shall haue occation to com̃ence a suite against any stranger or forraigner, it shalbe lawfull for the said Ensigne Smith to issue out warrants in his ma[ties] name to bind ouer any such p̃son or p̃sons to answere the said suite att the Court of his ma[tie] to be holden att Plymouth by attachment or summons att any time as occation shall require, and likewise to graunt subpenaies as occation shall require for witnesses in the case.

[*184.]

*Nathaniell Soule, standing presented vntill this Court, and summoned thervnto to answare, for his telling of a p̃nisious lye, did put the case vpon trauerse, not owning the p̃sentment.

The names of the jury are as followeth : —

COURT ORDERS.

1668.
3 June.
PRENCE,
Govr.

Mr John Jacob,		Robert Barker,
William Barstow,		Nathaniell Thomas,
Thomas Paine,	sworne,	James Cole, Juni^r,
Serjeant Tinkham,		James Cobb,
Thomas Pope,		John Cole,
Phillip Walker,		John Smith,

These found the p̱sentment.

And the said Soule, for telling of a pnisious lye, was fined, according to law, the sume of 00 : 10 : 00.

Att this Court, Joseph Turner, for misdemeaning himselfe in speaking dishonorably and offenciuely by vttering seuerall words concerning the Goū, was centanced to sitt in the stockes during the pleasure of the Court; but att the earnest request of the Goū, and on the said Turner his promise of reformation, this centance was remitted.

Att this Court, Thomas Starr, for being distempered in drinke, was fined fiue shillings. . . . . 00 : 05 : 00

John Mathews, for excessiue drinking, was fined fiue shillings. . . . . 05 : 00

John Haddawey, of Barnstable, for abusing himselfe with drinking, was fined fiue shillings. . . . . 00 : 05 : 00

Walter Joyce, of Marshfeild, for abusing himselfe with drinke, fined . . . . 00 : 05 : 00

Joseph Trewant, for distempering himselfe by excessiue drinkeing, fined fiue shillings. . . . . . . 00 : 05 : 00

Mary Phillips and Jane Hallowey, for breaking the Kings peace by strikeing each other, were fined each . . . . 00 : 03 : 04

Att this Court, vpon the oftens and earnest suite of William Tubbs to be diuorsed from his wife, shee haueing for a longe time sequestered herselfe from him, and will not be p̱swaded to returne to him, the Court haue directed letters to Road Iland to the goūment there, in whose jurisdiction shee now is, to request them to take course that shee may be informed of the Courts pleasure and determination, that incase shee, the said Marcye Tubbs, the wife of William Tubbs, doe not returne vnto her said husband between this date and the Court of his ma^{tie} to be holden att Plymouth the first Tusday in July next, that then hee, the said William Tubbs, shalbe diuorced from her.

Edward Gray, for vseing reuiling speeches to John Bryant, the son in law to Steuen Bryant, of Plymouth, on the Lords day, as soone as they came out of the meeting, was fined . . . . 10 : 00

1668.
7 July.
PRENCE, GOUR.
[*186.]

*Att the Court of his Matie holden att Plymouth the 7th of July, 1668.

BEFORE Thomas Prence, Gour, William Bradford,
John Alden, Thomas Hinckley,
Josias Winslow, John Freeman, and
Thomas Southworth, Nathaniel Bacon,
Assistants.

THIS Court, takeing notice of much injury alreddy don and more like to insue to this collonie by haueing sundry of our swamps pillaged lying within our line, doe therfore order and impower Major Josias Winslow, Mr Constant Southworth, Treasurer, and Cornett Robert Studson, or any two of them, to sell all such swampes, or soe many as they shall see cause, to the best advantage of this collonie.

And wheras there was an order of Court to lay out a p̄sell of land to William Berstow for some service of his to the countrey in runing the line, and that the proportion is not mencioned, the Court haue ordered, that the psons aboue named lay him out forty acrees of arrable land, or att the vtmost but fifty, if they judge it conuenient, and that they make sale of the rest of the land in that purchas either to the said Barstow or any other to the best advantage for the collonie.

In reference vnto a former graunt, vpon a petition presented vnto the Court by Bridḡwater, desireing theire inlargment may extend the whole six mile that they purchased of the Indians by order from the Court, the Court haue graunted vnto the township of Bridḡwater that they shall haue six mile from the center on the northsyde where the line of the collonie hindereth not, and on the westsyde vp to Taunton bounds, and on the south and southeast syde vnto Teticutt Riuer as farr as the six mile extends; and soe likewise on the east syde, that is to say, the whole six mile from the center east, west, north, and south, alwaies prouided, that what graunts of land formerly made by the Court be not molested. It is alsoe ordered, that those lands that are between Bridḡwater and Namassakett alreddy graunted shalbe determined by the Court vnto what township they shalbelong; and that the Indians be not molested, notwithstanding this inlargment; and that all those graunts that are within this six mile shall belong to the township of Bridḡwater; and that the town of Bridḡwater be carefull to accom̄odate Mr Keith with a competency of land within the said graunt of the said six mile.

In reference vnto a motion made to the Court by Thomas Andrews, in the behalfe of Gorge Vicory and Gorḡ Partrich, to haue a supply of land settled vpon them in reference to a former graunt vnto them as ancient servants, the Court haue ordered the Treasurer and Cornett Studson to lay out to each of them sixty acrees of land between the line of the collonie and John Hanmores lott, principally to the westward of the old path leading from Bridḡwater to Waymouth; or if any other be found therabouts that the said psons deputed shall see meet to lay out vnto them, that they haue each of them a like proportion, both for quantity and quallitie, as farr as conveniently they can.

1668.
7 July.
PRENCE,
GOUR.

In reference vnto the printing of the booke intitled New Englands Memoriall, the Court haue ordered, that the Treasurer shall indent with the printer for the printing therof; and to improue that which is or shalbe contributed thervnto with the sume of twenty pounds, ordered by the Court to that end, and the sume of fiue pound more if hee shall see cause, the said twenty fiue pound to be out of the countreyes stocke; and to indent with Mr Green to print it, if hee will doe it as cheap as the other; and for the number of coppyes, to doe as hee shall see cause.

*The Court confeirmeth vnto Ensigne Barnard Lumbert, John Finney, Senir, and Isacke Robinson a certaine necke of land, with the meddow adjoyning thervnto, comonly called Passuntaquanuncke Necke, on the South Sea, heertofore graunted to them, and as is now layed out to them by Mr Thomas Hinckley, Mr Nathaniel Bacon, and Richard Bourne, appointed thervnto by the Court, being bounded westerly by a river which deuides between the said necke and Quenaumett, and by the next river easterly, together with a stripp of land coming vp from the said necke to the high way which leads from Barnstable to Saconeesett for theire comon and out lett, being p̄te of those lands purchased by the said Thomas Hinckley, and Nathaniel Bacon, and Richard Bourne, mencioned in a deed of sale bearing date the second of December, 1667, signed by Quachatasett, Sepitt, and Acomont, sachems; alsoe, this Court confeirmeth vnto Mr Thomas Hinckley and Mr Nathaniel Bacon all the resedue or remainder of the lands, both vpland and meddow, contained within the said deed of sale, from the aforsaid riuer easterly extending to Wequasett, according to the bounds mensioned in the abouesaid deed of sale, in right of the Courts former graunt vnto them, as alsoe *as alsoe* in right vnto the Courts graunt vnto William Clarke, bought by them, the said Thomas Hinckley and Nathaniel Bacon.

[*187.]

The third day of the fourth month, 1668, according vnto Court order, wee haue layed forth vnto Mr William Brett, Thomas Haward, Senir, Arther

1 6 6 8.

7 July.
Prence,
Govr.

Harris, John Willis, Senr, and John Carey sixty acrees of land, vnto each pson aboue expressed, be it more or lesse, and is bounded as followeth : —

Wee began att the westerly end, next the lands of Henery Andrewes, att a brooke called by the name of South Brooke; the first lott, namly, John Careyes, begins att the abouesaid brooke, and runeth for his westerly line as the brooke runeth vntill it extends vp into the woods for his full length, and from the said brooke for his breadth vpon a northeast line vntill it meets with two white oake trees marked, which two trees rangeth for theire length about nort west and south east, which easterly syde of the first lott must soe range.

The second lott, which is Arther Harrises, rangeth from the abouesaid white oake trees northeast till it meets with a smale liue oake tree marked and standing in a smale swamp.

The third lott, which is Thomas Hawards, Seniers, begins att the abouesaid liue oake tree, and extends for its breadth northeast till it meets with a great white oake tree marked standing neare a run of water haueing alowance in measure as to the breadth for the meanes of it.

The 4th lott, which is Mr William Bretts, begins att the abouesaid great white oake, and rangeth on the same point of compas for its breadth vntill it meets with a red oake tree marked standing on a little knowle neare Trought Brooke, on the easterly syde of the brooke.

The fift and last lott, which is the lott of John Willis, Senr, begins att the abouesaid red oake, and runeth on the same point as the rest doe vntill it meets with a smale white oake tree marked a little aboue the path goeing to Teticutt; all these last four lotts runeth for breadth and length as the easterly syde of the first lott doth; and because wee found that the land was very mean, excepting a little stripp along the riuer, wee haue extended theire lines to run for euery of theire lotts sixty pole on the northerly syde of the riuer, vpon the same point of compas as their lotts run on the southerly syde.

WILLAM BRADFORD,
CONSTANT SOUTHWORTH.

[*188.]

*In reference vnto a controuersy between an Indian called Peter and James Bell, of Taunton, about a dear, the Court haue ordered, that the said Bell shall pay or cause to be payed vnto the said Indian the sume of fifteen shillinges; and for his neglect and contempt in not obserueing of the order of the celect men of the towne of Taunton about that matter, hee was centanced by the Court to pay the sume of ten shillinges to the collonies vse.

In reference vnto an Indian called Mekamoo, allies Steuen, now in durance on suspition for killing of a cow belonging to William Pointing, of

COURT ORDERS. 191

Taunton, the Court haue ordered, that hee shall pay vnto the said Pointing the sume of fifty shillinges; and incase it appeer betwixt this and the next Court that hee did not kill the cow, or that any other killed it, then hee is to haue the said sume returned to him againe; but if it appeer that hee did kill it, that then hee shall pay the full worth of it.

1668.
7 July.
PRENCE,
Gouʳ.

July 9, 1668. Those Indians whose names are vnderwritten stand engaged that the said sume shalbe payed forthwith on theire returne home.

  Witnes,

    The mark **F** of FRANCIS, the Sachem of Nausett.
    The mark **S** of SAM: HARRY.
    The marke **V** of PYANT.
    The marke of POMPECANCHE.
    The marke of JOSEPH, allies TATAWASHAW.

Thomas Perrey acknowlidgeth to owe vnto our soū lord the Kinge the sume of . . . . } 10 : 00 : 00

Richard Dwelley the sume of . . . . 10 : 00 : 00

The condition, that if the said Thomas Perrey doe appeer att the Court of his maᵗⁱᵉ to be holden att Plymouth the last Tusday in October next, to answare his p̄sentment, and not depart the said Court without lycence; that then, &c̄.

Richard Dwelley acknowlidgeth to owe vnto our soū lord the Kinge the sume of forty pounds, to be leuied on his lands, goods, and chattles.

The condition, that if the said Richard Dwelley be of good behauior towards our soū lord the Kinge and all his leich people, and appeer att the Court of his maᵗⁱᵉ to be holden att Plymouth the last Tusday in October next, and not depart the said Court without lycence; that then, &c̄.

Richard Dwelley, for being drunke the third time, was centanced, according to order, to be bound to his good behauior.

In reference vnto the other p̄sentments of Richard Dwelley, wherby hee is convicted of fighting, and abusiue words, and other misdemenors, the Court haue centanced him to pay a fine of twenty shillings to the vse of the collonie.

John Williams engaged to pay towards his wifes maintainances a barrell of beife and a barrell of porke, to be deliuered good and marchantable somtime in Nouember next vnto Mʳ Thomas Clarke att Boston, and a good cow not exceeding eight yeare old, and as much corn as will made the beife, porke, and cow ten pounds, to be deliuered att the now dwelling house of John Williams, in Scittuate, the second Tusday in May next, to the said Elizabeth Williams or her assignes.

Wheras, att the Court held att Plymouth the seauenth of June, 1665, a

1668.

7 July.
PRENCE,
Gouʳ.

The conditions of this graunt see in the records of the Court, June, 1665; and by the old path heer is ment the old path that goeth from Plymouth to Namassakett.

[*189.]

smale gussett of land was then graunted vnto Sacaryah Eedey, it is layed out to him, and the bounds of it are as followeth : it, lying betwixt his land and a brooke, is bounded with a blacke oake tree on the south syde of the old path and a maple tree aboue his house att a bridge; this was done according to order of Court by

HENERY WOOD, and
Sarjeant EPHRAIM TINKHAM, his E T marke.

Hugh Cole and Samuell Bacon, refusing to stand exequitors of the last will and testament of Richard Foxwell, deceased, are ordered by the Court to adminnester on the said estate.

*Wheras Marcye, the wife of William Tubbs, being a woman of ill fame and light behauior apparently manifest, hath for the space of four yeares and vpwards absented and withdrawne herselfe from her husband into another collonie, pretending shee is att libertie, and that, notwithstanding all the meanes and waies her husband can vse with safety, shee will not be reclaimed nor pswaded to returne and abide with him as shee ought to doe ; and that, alsoe, by letters to the goﬃment of Road Iland from this goﬃment, due course hath bin taken to giue her certaine intelligence, that incase shee would not returne vnto and apply herselfe to her husband to liue with him as shee ought to doe betwixt the date of the said letters and this ꝑsent Court, that then hee should be diuorced from her ; and that shee hath since, before competent witnes, professed and affeirmed that shee will neuer returne againe vnto him while her eyes are open ; hee, the said Tubbs, appeering att this Court, and earnestly againe sollissiteing the Court for a diuorce from her, —

This Court, therfore, sees cause and doe heerby declare, that the said William Tubbs is legally cleare from his couenant of marriage formerly made with Marcye, his late wife, and free him from those dutyes relateing therto ; and that the said Marcye hath cutt of herselfe from any right henceforth to the ꝑson or estate of the said William Tubbs, her late husband, and heerby alowing him libertie further to dispose of himselfe in marriage, if hee see fitt soe to doe.

*Wee, whose names are vnderwritten, being ordered by the Court to lay out highwaies and appoint such roads as might be most suitable to the inhabitants of the towne of Bridgwater, being sworne as a jury theron, did as followeth : —

Impʳ. From the meeting house to Arther Harris his range vnto the comon, and thence throw a swamp vnto the sandy hill, and then to John Haward, Juniʳ, his range, and then crosse his lott to Daniell Bacon his house,

COURT ORDERS.

and then into the old way to widdow Bassetts lott to a place called the Woolfe Trapp, and then ouer the same lott to Thomas Haward, Juni^r, his lott, vnto Goodman Tomkins, of Salem, his lott, and soe through it to the peece of land left for a highway betwixt him and Thomas Snell, and then ouer a corner of Thomas Snells lott joyning neare the riuer to the bridge, and then throwgh Nicholas Byrams land to his house, and soe ouer a little riuer, and soe ouer the plaine to a narrow place in the swamp, and soe to Arther Harris his fifty acree lot, and then by the swamp syde on the hard grownd vnto his son Samuell his house, and from thence straight to a bridge on Satuckett Riuer as the rockes will pmitt, from thence straight away to an oake in the middest of the highway neare to Robert Lathams barne, and then to the vsuall way or road to Plymouth as farr as the bounds of our township doth extend, onely in the way wee fech a little compas to avoid a steip hill a little way from Robert Lathams lott.

1668.
7 July.
PRENCE, Govr.

Secondly. Wee haue agreed on a way or road to Boston, and is as followeth : from the meeting house on the same road aboue mensioned vnto John Hawards range, and then into the vsuall roads which reacheth into the bay as farr as our bounds doe extend.

Thirdly. It is further agreed on by vs, the way to Taunton is from the meeting house to John Haward, Seni^r, and then followeth ouer the riuer, and soe between the lotts that were Mr Brewsters and Edward Vobes theire lotts, and soe in the vsuall way that leads to Taunton.

Fourthly. It is agreed alsoe by vs, that the way to the great meddow shall come out of Taunton way att the head of Edward Vobes his six acree lott, and soe att the head of Samuell Edsons six acree lot, to William Snowes, and then between the said Edsons and Snowes lands vnto the comon, and then to the riuer. These waies were laied out by vs att seuerall times as in the yeare 1667, 1668.

        NICHOLAS BYRAM,
        SAMUELL EDSON,
        NATHANIEL WILLIS,
        ROBERT LATHAM,
        MARKE LAYTHORP,
        ARTHER HARRIS,
        JOHN CARY,
        THOMAS HAWARD, Seni^r,
        THOMAS HAWARD, Juni^r,
        JOHN HAWARD, Seni^r,
        SAMUELL PACKER, Seni^r,
        JOSEPH ALDIN.

1668.

7 July.
PRENCE,
Gov.

[*191.]

*This indenture, made the 24th day of September, 1667, in the 19th yeare of the raigne of our soū lord Charles the Second, Kinge of Great Brittaine, et cetī, witnesseth, that Richard Handy, of the towne of Sandwich, in the collonie of New Plymouth, woolcomber, hath couenanted, agreed, and put himselfe an apprentice to and with James Skiffe, Juni^r, of the same towne, cooper, to liue with the said James from the 25th of October next ensueing vntill that hee judge in himselfe that hee hath fully attained the skill and craft of a cooper. The conditions on Richards p̄te are, first, that vpon the sealing heerof, hee deliuer vp to James his whole cropp of Indian corne, beanes, and pumpianes, which hee hath now growing in Ensigne Dexters land, and that hee p̄forme halfe the worke with James in gathering and conveying home the said cropp. 2^{condly}. That hee worke dilligently and faithfully with and for the said James in the occupation of a cooper, according to the vsuall costoms of prentises, not absenting himselfe needlesly and att his pleasure from his worke either day or night, but att lawfull houres, during his abode with James; likewise, that hee shall not sett vp for himselfe, or instruct any other in the craft of a cooper, in the lymetts of Sandwich, without lycence from James, but vpon the forfeiture of ten pounds sterling to be payed to the said James vpon euery such acte. In consideration wherof, James doth agree with and engage to deliuer to the said Richard seauen bushells of marchantable corne and his diett, good, wholsome, and sufficient, during the said tearme; and, further, hee doth engage to instruct the said Richard faithfully in the whole craft of a cooper soe farr as James himselfe vnderstands, with what expedition the said Richard shall from time to time be capable to receiue it; and likewise that hee will not hinder the said Richard by busying about worke which doth not tend to his obtaining insight into the abouesaid trade; and that when that Richard shall judge, that by his owne dilligence and instruction of James hee hath sufficient skill in coopering, then James shall giue him full leaue to depart, without any disturbance. For confeirmation wherof wee haue enterchangably sett to our hands and seales, this 24th day of September, 1667.

RICHARD HANDY, and a (Seale.)

Read, signed, sealed, and deliuered in the
p̄sence of vs, witnesses,
  Ichabod Wiswall,
  Remember Wiswall.

GENERAL INDEX.

GENERAL INDEX.

Abell, Joanna, ... 46, 54
   Robert, ... 13
      estate of, ... 46, 54
Accord Pond, ... 23, 31, 110
   lands, ... 46, 99, 174
Acomont, an Indian sachem, ... 189
Acushenah, Acushena, rates, ... 40
   town officers, ... 15, 38
   and Ponagausett, and Coaksett made a town-
      ship by the name of Dartmouth, . . . 65
Adams, John, one of the first born children, land
   granted to, ... 19
Aimes, John, ... 155
Alarm, how given, ... 144
Alcarmus, Alkarmus, Field, ... 80, 173
Alden, Aldin, John, 4, 8, 11, 17, 25—27, 30, 35, 41,
   44, 45, 47, 48, 49, 56, 59, 69, 70, 74, 79, 87,
   89, 105, 111, 113, 119, 132, 134, 135, 140,
   145, 157, 160, 167, 173, 186, 188.
   one of the council of war, ... 142
   deputy governor, ... 81
   an Assistant, . . 13, 36, 60, 90, 122, 147, 179
   land granted to, ... 95, 109
   Joseph, ... 123, 155, 193
   Rebekah, ... 7
   Mr., ... 40
   one of the first born children, land granted
      to, ... 19
Aldredge, William, ... 170
   See Eldredge.
Alewives, passage kept open for, in Taunton River, 57,
      66
Allen, Allin, Anna, ... 89
   Francis, ... 85
   George, way laid out for, . . . 46, 48, 117, 183
      complaint against Richard Chadwell, . . 82

Allen. Gideon, ... 164
   James, ... 91
   John, . 13, 17, 61, 105, 150, 164, 167, 176, 184
      complaint against Indians, ... 17, 53
      settlement of his estate, . 28, 35, 39, 81, 89
      deputy to General Court, ... 180
      complaint againt Ralph Smith, ... 175
   Joseph, ... 88
   Robert, inquest upon, ... 9, 13
   Samuel, ... 155
   Sarah, ... 88
   Captain, ... 175
      cast away on Cape Cod, ... 179
      Goodman, ... 89
Allerton, Isaac, ... 81
Ammadown, see Annadown.
Ammunition, ... 23, 144
   brought into the government, invoice of, to be
      taken, ... 23
   account of, ... 52
Ancient freemen, lands of, ... 18
   servants, land granted to, ... 189
Andrew, Andrews, Andrewes, John, ... 79
   Henry, ... 70, 123, 160, 170, 189
      ancient freeman, land granted to, ... 20
   John, ... 79
      bond to Nathaniel Warren, ... 77, 78
      fined for several offences, ... 139
   Joseph, ... 12, 39, 61
      fined for absence as juror, ... 45
   Sarah, her portion paid her, ... 70
   Thomas, ... 188
Annable, Anible, Anthony, ... 19, 41
   prosecuted for removing landmarks, . . . 50
Annadown, Annadowne, Roger, ... 13, 83, 84
   land granted to, ... 18, 96

(197)

GENERAL INDEX.

Apportionment of rates, see Rates.
Aquetaquesh, ... 26
Archer, John, ... 186
Arms to be secured, ... 145
Arnold, Samuel. vs. William Thomas, . . . 112
Arther, John, prosecuted, ... 104
   complaint of, against Indians, ... 168, 183
Assistants chosen, . . 13, 36, 60, 90, 122, 147, 179
Assonett River, ... 45
Assoot, an Indian, ... 167
Atwood, Adwood, John, ... 40
Auntaenta, ... 4
Austin, Austine, Jonah, ... 71
   Jonah, Jun., ... 171
Bacon, Daniel, ... 123, 192
   Nathaniel, 21, 23, 31, 39, 64, 82. 93, 97, 112, 124,
   140, 146, 157, 158, 167, 173, 175, 183, 188,
   189.
     officer of excise, ... 67
     one of the council of war, ... 142
     deputy from Barnstable, . 14, 37, 60, 90, 122
     an Assistant, ... 147, 179
     land granted to, ... 96, 102, 160
   Samuel, ... 192
   Mr., ... 64, 128, 153, 184
Baddow, Francis, fined for breach of Sabbath, . . 50
Baiting Brook, ... 45
Baker, Francis, fined for breach of peace, . . . 116
Bangs, Banges, Edward, ... 100, 169
   John, ... 149
   Jonathan, ... 181
   Joshua, ... 176
Barker, Isaac, ... 130
   way through land of, ... 129
   John, his guardian appointed, ... 108
   Robert, ... 129, 187
     fined for exchanging gun with an Indian, 11, 17
     his lands, ... 141, 174
     wife and son of, fine remitted, ... 17
Barlow, George, ... 7, 17, 37, 66
   and wife, reproved, ... 10
   bound for his good behavior, ... 88, 117
   fined, ... 117
   his children punished, ... 10
Barnabey, James, ... 112, 113
Barnes, John, ... 12, 36, 70, 133, 149, 152
   controversy with Jone Tilson, ... 9
   vs. Thomas Pope, ... 79, 89
   fined, ... 106
   vs. Thomas Dotey, ... 158
   Jonathan, ... 152, 153
   fined, ... 115
   Thomas, a servant to John Barnes, . . . 133
   Mr., ... 61
Barnstable, ... 6, 23, 41, 52, 118, 146
   rates, ... 5, 29, 47, 63, 72, 77

Barnstable, excise officers, ... 67, 151, 183
   town officers, 15, 38, 61, 91, 112, 123, 124, 148,
     150, 181, 182
   bounds, ... 21
   ordinary, ... 40
   controversy with Indians, ... 70
   lands, ... 20, 82
Barrow, John, fined for contempt of Court, . . . 116
Barstow, Berstow, William, 46, 50, 63, 74, 99, 123,
     137, 138, 149, 187
   to repair North River bridge, ... 41
   William, Sen., contracts to keep in repair
     North River bridge, ... 68, 69
     complaint against, as innholder, ... 129
   land granted to, ... 160, 188
Bartlett, Benjamin, ... 14, 23, 124, 149, 182
   officer of excise, ... 67
   his complaint against servant, ... 154
   land granted to, ... 173
   claims land formerly William Brewster's, . . 80
   Joseph, ... 177
     fined for breach of peace, ... 139, 176
     paid for loss of horse, ... 161
Bassett, William, 21, 64, 68, 70, 85, 97, 109, 128, 145,
     160
   one of the first born children, land granted
     to, ... 19
   deputy from Sandwich, ... 14
   surrenders his license as retailer, ... 9
   William, Sen., administration of his estate, . 155
   William, Jun., ... 37, 155
   ———, widow, ... 193
Bates, John, fined for breach of peace, ... 137
   Elder, ... 68
Bayley, John, fined for breach of peace, ... 50
Bearce, Austine, ... 14
Beare, Richard, land granted to, ... 18, 128
Bedle, Beedle, Joseph, ... 50, 75, 76, 79, 181
   land granted to, ... 18
Bell, Esther, ... 170
   James, ... 8, 71, 170
   fined, ... 77
   his suit against an Indian, ... 190
Berry, Berrey, Richard, ... 183
   and others, fined for playing cards, . . . 47
Bessey, Anna, ... 7, 10
   Anthony, ... 17, 70
   Dorcas, ... 7, 10
   Jane, her claim against George Barlow, . . 17
   Mary, ... 7, 10
   Nehemiah, punished for smoking in meeting
     on Lord's day, ... 47
   put in possession of his estate, ... 70
Billington, Francis, ... 136
   one of the first born children, land grant-
     ed to, ... 19

GENERAL INDEX.

Billington, Joseph, ... 69
   fined for breach of peace, ... 137, 140
   Mary, presented, ... 69
   Thomas, administration of his estate, . . . 16
Bird, Thomas, punished for adultery, ... 22
Bisbee, Besbey, Elisha, ... 130
Bishop, Biship, Richard, lands granted to, . . 18, 136
Black Sachem's Field, ... 171
Blacke, Miles, ... 50, 138
   to purchase lands of Indians, ... 45
Blackstone, Mr., ... 64
Blackwell, Michael, ... 148
   Myles, ... 181
Blisse, Jonathan, ... 180
Blush, Abraham, ... 37, 148
Boardman, Thomas, ... 9
———, ... 152
Bobbitt, Edward, ... 180
Bonny, Thomas, prosecuted, ... 7
Bonum, George, ... 53, 55, 80, 104, 173, 181
   one of the first born children, land granted
     to, ... 20, 94
Both, John, ... 139
Bound Brook, ... 97
Bourne, Henry, ... 61, 181
   Job, ... 123
   John, ... 91, 104, 113, 120, 121, 124, 150
     deputy from Marshfield, ... 122, 148
     officer of excise, ... 67
     Richard, 28, 48, 68, 85, 97, 109, 119, 128, 131,
       145, 155, 161, 189
     to purchase lands of Indians, ... 45
     deputy from Sandwich, . . . 60, 90, 122, 148
     his lands, ... 3, 4, 161, 174
     his petition in behalf of Indians, ... 80
   Thomas, claims a stray horse, ... 43
   Mr., ... 128, 131
Bowin, Richard, ... 124
Bradford, John, land of, ... 27
   Joseph, ensign of Plymouth company, . . . 65
   his lands, ... 27, 94
   William, 4, 8, 11, 19, 21, 23, 26, 30, 35, 39, 40,
     44, 45, 48, 49, 69, 74, 79, 81, 87, 89, 103,
     105, 111—113, 119, 132, 134, 140, 145, 157,
     160, 167, 173, 188, 190.
   one of the council of war, ... 142
   an Assistant, . 13, 36, 60, 90, 122, 147, 179
   paid for services, ... 63
   his lands, ... 26, 41, 94
   William, Sen., ... 40
   Ensign, ... 149
   Mr., one of the first born children, land grant-
     ed to, ... 19
Brewster, Jonathan, ... 173
   William, ... 174
   his land, ... 80

Brewster, Mr., ... 193
   one of the first born children, land granted to, 19
Bridge at Dartmouth, ... 129
   at Eel River, ... 108, 109, 159
   at Jones River, ... 23, 41, 109, 123
   at North River, ... 41, 68, 69
   over Taunton River, ... 159
Bridgewater, ... 23, 146
   rates, ... 6, 30, 40, 48, 63, 77
   excise officers, ... 67, 151, 183
   town officers, 15, 38, 61, 91, 123, 124, 149, 150,
     181, 182
   land granted to, ... 18
   petition for enlargement granted, . . 160, 188
   ways at, laid out, ... 154, 192
   military officers, ... 73
Briggs, Clement, ... 127, 128
   and sons, land of, ... 74
   children of, land granted to, ... 68
   David, ... 68
   one of the first born children, land granted
     to, ... 20
   John, ... 181
     takes oath of fidelity, ... 185
   John, Sen., fined for breach of Sabbath, . . 50
   Jonathan, ... 28
   one of the first born children, land granted
     to, ... 20
   Remember, ... 68
   Richard, ... 171
   Walter, ... 30, 91, 139
   ordered to collect rates, ... 136
Brett, Britt, William, ... 21, 23
   land of, ... 96, 189, 190
   deputy, ... 14, 37, 60, 90
Brooks, Brookes, Gilbert, ... 123, 125, 146
   William, ... 114, 139, 148
Browne, Broune, James, ... 13, 37, 150, 180
   an Assistant, ... 90, 122
   deputy, ... 122
   Peter, one of the first born children, land
     granted to, ... 19
   William, ... 36
   will of, ... 28
   vs. Henry Saunders, ... 57
   land granted to, ... 161
   Mr., ... 175
   land of, laid out, ... 64
   fined for setting up meeting at Rehoboth, . 162
Bryant, John, 14, 29, 37, 46, 76, 99, 130, 148, 153,
   187
   Stephen, ... 37, 55, 187
   and others, bounds settled, ... 35
Buck, Bucke, Isaac, ... 145, 182
   deputy from Scituate, ... 37, 60, 90
Bullocke, Richard, ... 13, 23

200 GENERAL INDEX.

Bullocke, Richard, officer of excise, ... 67
   to keep ferry at Rehoboth, ... 54
Bump, alias Sampson, an Indian, ... 136, 137
Bumpas, Edward, one of the first born children,
   land granted to, ... 19
   Edward, Jun., ... 75
   Hannah, punished for fornication, ... 22
Bundey, John, ... 110
   one of the first born children, land granted to, 20
Burcher, Thomas, ... 27
Burden, William, fined for breach of peace, . . . 137
Burge, John, ... 170
   Joseph, fined for misdemeanor, ... 155
   land granted to, ... 160, 161
   Thomas, Sen., ... 3, 50
Burgis, Jacob, ... 14
   John, ... 61
   Joseph, ... 123
   Thomas, ... 15, 149
   deputy from Sandwich, ... 14, 180
   Thomas, Sen., ... 61
   Goodman, ... 85
Burman, Hannah, one of the first born children,
   land granted to, ... 19
   Thomas, estate of, ... 41
Burt, Richard, ... 148, 151
Butler, Daniel, vs. William Browne, ... 36
   Thomas, ... 36, 124
   lands of, ... 97, 109, 152
Butterworth, John, ... 13, 84, 176
Byram, Biram, Nicholas, 61, 124, 146, 150, 155, 181,
                                    182, 193
Cape Cod, Captain Allen cast away at, . . . 179
Cape Head, ... 185
Captain, commission of, ... 142
Carey, Carrey, John, . . 14, 150, 155, 182, 190, 193
   land of, ... 96, 190
Carpenter, Joseph, ... 13
   Samuel, ... 123
   William, admitted a freeman, ... 38
Carver, John, ... 61
Casley, John, fined for breach of peace, ... 116
Castle Rock, ... 139
Caswell, Thomas, ... 14, 171
Causumsette, ... 62
Chacapaquin, ... 58
Chadwell, Richard, ... 15, 91
   controversy with George Allin, ... 82
   complaint about a way, ... 48, 117, 183
Chandler, Chandeler, Roger, land granted to chil-
   dren of, ... 110, 112
   Samuel, ... 123
   his bounds settled, ... 48, 120
   land of, ... 18, 104
Chapell, Robert, inquest upon, ... 176
Charles, alias Pampmumitt, an Indian, ... 152

Charles II., ... 194
Chettenden, Isaac, 30, 50, 61, 76, 124, 126, 145, 149,
                                  160, 183
   deputy from Scituate, ... 90, 122, 148
   land of, ... 110
   licensed to keep an ordinary, ... 117
Child, Richard, ... 105
Chipman, John, 98, 112, 124, 133, 146, 150, 182, 184
   deputy from Barnstable, . 37, 60, 90, 122, 180
   land of, ... 131
Church, Nathaniel, punished for fornication, . . . 34
   Richard, deposition of, ... 85
   land of, ... 159
Church government, ... 86
Churchill, Hannah, her petition for land granted, . 58
   widow, ... 173
Clarke, Faith, ... 8
   estate of, ... 39
   Henry, ... 39
   James, ... 103
   Thomas, ... 43, 191
   Thurston, ... 39
   estate of, ... 8
   Thurston, Sen., inquest upon, ... 12
   William, ... 14, 128, 149, 173, 180, 189
   lands of, ... 95, 160, 161
Coahassett, ... 62
Coaksett, ... 30
   and Cushenett, rates, ... 48
   and Acushena, and Ponagausett made a town-
   ship by the name of Dartmouth, . . . 65
Cobb, Henry, deputy from Barnstable, ... 14
   deposition of, ... 20, 21
   officer of excise, ... 67
   James, ... 148, 187
   John, ... 71, 124, 168, 171
Cobleigh, John, ... 164
Cockshall, Joshua, ... 12
Coggen, Bathsheba, ... 5, 10
   Henry, land of, to be sold, ... 64
   John, ... 64
   discharge of, to his guardians, ... 77
   Thomas, ... 5
   land of, sold, ... 10
Cole, Daniel, ... 23, 61, 169, 182, 184
   deputy from Eastham, ... 122, 148, 180
   lands of, ... 160
   Hugh, ... 123, 149, 160, 168, 185, 192
   lands of, ... 159
   James, Sen., ... 184
   suits against several persons, . 11, 57, 69, 112
   lands of, ... 18, 94
   fined for keeping disorderly house, . . . 107
   James, Jun., ... 187
   lands of, ... 160, 161
   prosecuted for breach of peace, ... 88

GENERAL INDEX.

Cole, John, ... 176, 187
Collier, Colyare, Collyare, William, 4, 8, 11, 26, 30, 35, 41, 44, 45, 43, 103, 105, 111, 122, 135
   an Assistant, ... 13, 36, 60, 90
   lands of, ... 17, 27, 39, 40
   lands granted to, for his grandchild, ... 159
Collymore, Peter, land granted to, ... 18
Colony, freemen of, declare that they will maintain their rights, ... 62
   bounds settled, ... 92, 133
Colony House, bought of Edward Gray, . . . 21, 44
   at Plain Dealing, ... 184
Combe, Comb, Francis, ... 148
   lands of, ... 127, 171, 172
Commissioners of the United Colonies chosen, 14, 46, 60, 90, 122, 147, 180
   paid for services, ... 72
   instructions of, ... 156
Commissioners from England, reception of, . . 62, 72
   proceedings of, . . . 85, 86, 92, 101, 102, 110
Commissions of military officers, ... 142
Confederation of the United Colonies, letter to be sent to Massachusetts concerning, . . . 92
Conihassett lands, trespasses on, ... 75
Constables, . . . 14, 37, 61, 91, 123, 148, 180
Cooke, Francis, ... 54
   one of the first born children, land granted to, ... 19
   Jacob, ... 14, 61, 123, 148
   John, ... 109, 146, 173, 185, 186
     deputy from Dartmouth, . . 122, 148, 180
     magistrate at Dartmouth, ... 153, 163
     land granted to, ... 67, 114
   Josiah, ... 124, 131, 146
     magistrate at Eastham, ... 65, 74
     lands of, ... 18, 67, 110
     deputy from Eastham, . . . 14, 37, 60, 122
Cooper, John, ... 154
   fined for misdemeanor, ... 133
   Thomas, ... 84, 146
   Thomas, Jun., ... 83
Copp, John, licensed to distil liquors, ... 132
Coteticutt River, ... 161
Council, standing, proposition concerning, . . . 103
   of war, their orders and names of members, 142—147
Covell, Nathaniel, . . . 52, 134, 154, 155, 168, 183
   prosecuted for defaming government, . . . 157
Cowine, John, ... 105
Craggs, Edward, ... 84, 85
Crimes : adultery, ... 22
   abusing officers, ... 115, 137, 183
   blasphemy, ... 168
   breach of peace, 5, 34, 43, 49, 50, 76, 83, 88, 115, 116, 137, 139, 140, 155, 177, 187, 191
   breach of Sabbath, ... 5, 28, 29, 42, 50

Crimes : buying land of Indians, . . . 44, 49, 58, 59
   drunkenness, 29, 33, 42, 43, 51, 83, 106, 107, 117, 132, 162, 168, 187
   fornication, 22, 34, 42, 47, 77, 83, 106, 141, 162, 168, 182
   lewdness, ... 47, 50, 116
   lying, . 9, 29, 34, 43, 89, 101, 106, 129, 139. 187
   neglecting public worship, ... 42, 43
   offering marriage without parents' consent, 140, 141, 158, 159
   playing cards, ... 42, 47
   pound breach, ... 51, 117
   selling liquor to Indians, ... 32, 162
   sedition, ... 131
   slander, . . . 11, 29, 44, 51, 140, 158, 187
   smoking in meeting on the Sabbath, . . . 47
   stealing, ... 22, 33, 51, 106
   swearing, ... 43, 52, 76, 77
   threatening words, ... 34
   trespass on Indians, ... 66, 177, 178
   vagrancy, ... 154
Crippen, Frances, ... 116
   Thomas, ... 116
   to give bonds for his appearance, . . 116, 117
Crispe, George, ... 100, 177
   fined for keeping disorderly house, ... 29
   wife of, presented for lying, ... 29
Crooker, Ann, ... 103
   Francis, ... 61
   John, Sen., ... 181
   Moses, ... 103
     apprentice to Thomas Hiland, Jun., . . . 93
     punished for stealing, ... 33
   William, ... 41, 133, 148, 150, 182
Crosbey, Thomas, propounded as freeman, . . . 61
   Mr., ... 100
Crow, John, ... 170, 183
   fined for breach of peace, ... 117
   William, ... 35, 91, 130, 149, 174, 182
   land granted to, ... 40
   Yelverton, ... 117, 150
     deputy from Yarmouth, ... 37, 122, 148
     land of, ... 128
Cudworth, James, ... 75—77, 82, 130, 153
   bond of, to the Court, ... 114
   lands of, divided, ... 138
   James, Jun., fined for fornication, ... 106
   Mary, fine of, remitted, ... 9
   Captain, ... 27, 126
Curtis, William, ... 61
Cushing, Cushen, John, ... 123, 151
Cushenag, rates, ... 6
Cushenah and Coaksett, rates, ... 30
Cushman, Thomas, ... 43, 81
   Thomas, Jun., land granted to, ... 27
   fined for fornication, ... 83

Cushman, Elder, land granted to children of, . . 94
Daman, Damman, John, 14, 23, 30, 139, 141, 145, 180
   officer of excise, ... 67
   to train Scituate company, ... 127
Daniel, alias Paquaho, an Indian, ... 92
   alias Pumpanaho, ... 138
   alias Tumpasscom, an Indian, ... 132
Darbey, John, vs. John Chipman, ... 98
   Richard, evidence of his will, ... 98
Dartmouth, ... 118
   excise officer, ... 183
   rates, ... 63, 72, 77, 98
   town officers, . 61, 91, 123, 124, 149—151, 181
   bridge at, ... 129
   inhabitants to be exercised in arms, . . 146, 153
   See Acushena, Ponagausett, and Coaksett.
   made a township, ... 65
   magistrate, ... 153, 163
   dispute about bounds, ... 168, 185
Davenport, Rachel, ... 113
   vs. Thomas Little, ... 119
Davis, Nicholas, ... 17, 53, 54
Deane, Dean, Alice, ... 16, 160
   Isaac, legacy paid to, ... 16
   John, ... 61, 71, 160, 171
   one of the first born children, land granted to, ... 20
   Stephen, one of the first born children, land granted to, ... 19
   Thomas, ... 71
   Walter, ... 5, 10, 71, 124, 150, 160, 182
   one of the first born children, land granted to, ... 20
Delano, Delanoy, Hester, ... 7
   Mary, ... 53
   Philip, ... 48, 58, 91, 148
   one of the first born children, land granted to, ... 19
   Thomas, fined, ... 168
Dennis, Denis, Robert, . . . 9, 23, 32, 52, 91, 116
   excise officer, ... 105, 110
Deputies to the General Court, 14, 37, 60, 90, 122, 148, 180
   fined for absence, ... 107
   sent home, ... 37
Deputy Governor, John Alden, ... 81
Devell, Joseph, takes oath of fidelity, ... 130
Dexter, Thomas, ... 15, 85
   Thomas, Sen., vs. inhabitants of Sandwich, . 70
   vs. Lieutenant Fuller and others, ... 21
   lands of, measured, ... 133
   Thomas, Jun., lands of, ... 132, 155, 161
   Ensign, to train Sandwich military company, . 39
   Mr., ... 68
   Mr., Sen., ... 40
   Mr., Jun., ... 70

Dillingham, Edward, estate of, ... 155
   Henry, ... 123, 155
   John, ... 155
Dingley, John, ... 37, 91, 124, 125, 148
Distillery at Scituate, ... 132
Doane, Done, Daniel, ... 100, 176
   child of, drowned, ... 169
Ephraim, fined for supplying Indians with liquor, ... 32, 33
   complaint of, against Indians, ... 46
   John, ... 100, 125
   magistrate at Eastham, ... 43
   lands of, ... 27, 131
   John, Jun., ... 31, 180
   officer of excise, ... 67
Doggett, Doged, John, fined for lying, ... 43
   suit against Martin's Vinyards, ... 27
   Thomas, ... 75, 123
Dotey, Desire, ... 164
   Edward, land granted to, ... 27
   lands of, ... 94, 160, 161
   Faith, ... 39, 164
   marriage contract of, ... 163
   John, land of, ... 160, 161
   Samuel, ... 177
   Thomas, ... 158
Doughtey, James, ... 15
   punished for misdemeanor, ... 168
Dudson, Dodson, Anthony, ... 175
   Mary, ... 175
Dunham, Benajah, ... 169, 176
   admitted a freeman, ... 61
   John, Sen., deputy from Plymouth, . . . 14, 60
   John, Jun., lands granted to, ... 67, 94
   prosecuted for abusing his wife, ... 104
   one of the first born children, land granted to, ... 20
   John, the younger, ... 103, 104
   Jonathan, ... 104
   lands granted to, ... 95
   Joseph, lands granted to, ... 95
   Samuel, ... 49, 61, 115
   deputy, ... 180
   lands granted to, ... 94
Dutch war, ... 144
Duxbury, ... 23, 145
   rates, ... 5, 29, 47, 63, 72, 77, 118, 123
   excise officers, ... 67, 150, 183
   town officers, 14, 15, 37, 38, 61, 91, 123, 124, 148, 149, 180—182
   bounds, ... 8
   controversy with Robert Barker, ... 174
Dwelley, Dwelly, Richard, ... 107, 123, 177
   fined for drunkenness, ... 162, 191
Eames, Anthony, ... 30
   John, ... 15, 183

GENERAL INDEX. 203

Eames, Mark, ... 113, 182
   deputy from Marshfield, 14, 37, 60, 90, 122, 148, 180
   land granted to, ... 67, 110, 160
   one of the first born children, land granted to, ... 20
   Ensign, ... 76, 150, 124
   Mr., Sen., ... 103
Earle, Ralph, punished for abusing wife, ... 47
   takes oath of fidelity, ... 185
Eastham, ... 5, 6, 23. 100, 118, 146, 185
   rates, ... 6, 29, 48, 63, 72, 77
   excise officers, ... 151, 183
   town officers, 15, 33, 61, 91, 123, 124, 149, 181, 182
   magistrates, ... 43, 65, 74
   military officers, ... 41, 64
   Mannamoiett and Paomett annexed to, . . 185
Eaton, Benjamin, lands of, ... 95
   Samuel, ... 136
   admitted a freeman, ... 38
Eddy, Eedy, Eedey, John, ... 77
   Samuel, one of the first born children, land granted to, ... 19
   Obadiah, ... 85
   Zachary, lands of, ... 95, 123, 192
Edson, Samuel, ... 141, 146, 155, 193
   juryman, fined for non-appearance, ... 107
Eel River, inhabitants, bounds settled, ... 173
   bridge, ... 108, 109, 159
Eldredge, Eldred, John, ... 170
   Robert, ... 52, 134, 154, 155, 168
     prosecuted for defaming government, . . 157
   William, ... 15
Ellis, John, ... 99, 111
   Lieutenant, lands of, ... 131
Elmes, Rodulphus, ... 139
England, an agent proposed to be sent to, . . . 92
English commissioners, . . 62, 72, 85, 86, 92, 110
Ensign, commission, ... 143
Ensigne, John, ... 55, 139, 149
   Sarah, punished for fornication, ... 106
   Thomas, estate of, ... 55
Ewell, Henry, ... 130
Ewen, John, ... 84
Ewer, Thomas, estate of, settled, ... 151, 153
Excise, persons prosecuted for not paying, . . . 107
   See Liquors.
   receivers, ... 67, 110, 150, 183
Falland, Thomas, Sen., land of, ... 96, 102
Fallowell, Gabriel, complaint of, against Indians, ... 82
   land of, ... 94
   ancient freeman, land granted to, ... 20
Farms, against Rhode Island, rates of, . . . 6, 30
Ferry at Pocassett, ... 185

Ferry at Rehoboth, ... 54, 175
Finney, John, ... 77
   lands of, ... 128
   John, Sen., ... 181
   lands of, ... 189
   Robert, ... 39, 64, 123, 124
   deputy from Plymouth, ... 14, 37, 60
   ancient freeman, land granted to, 20, 67, 128, 160
First born children, lands granted to, and their names, ... 18, 19
Fish, John, estate of, ... 58
   Nathaniel, ... 23
   deposition of, ... 85
   Syselia, ... 58
   Thomas, inquest upon, ... 84, 85
Fitch, John, ... 83, 84
Fitzrandall, Mary, ... 83
   Nathaniel, ... 88
   fined for fornication, ... 42
Forbes, Vobes, Edward, ... 193
   John, land granted to, ... 18
Ford, Foard, Edmund, ... 177
   William, Sen., ... 124, 143
   fined for breach of Sabbath, ... 29
   William, Jun., ... 15, 123
Foster, Timothy, ... 139
Fowler, Christopher, a runaway servant, ... 39
Foxwell, Richard, estate of, ... 192
Francis, sachem of Nausett, ... 26, 179, 191
Freeman, Edmund, ... 37, 152
   land of, ... 97
   Edmund, Sen., ... 82, 118
   land of, ... 40, 45
   Edmund, Jun., . . 46, 82, 159, 131, 148, 182
   land of, ... 128
   John, 21, 22, 64, 100, 157, 167, 170, 173, 183, 188
   an Assistant, ... 122, 147, 179
   deputy from Eastham, . . . 14, 37, 60, 90
   land of, ... 96, 162
   Samuel, ... 181
   Lieutenant, ... 96, 124, 131, 146, 152, 167
   Mr., ... 48, 68
Freemen meet to consider propositions of the commissioners of Charles II., ... 92
   propositions submitted to by the Court, . . 102
   admitted, ... 33, 86
   propounded and admitted, ... 61
   declaration of, to maintain their rights, . . 62
   ancient, lands of, ... 18
   of Taunton, lands of, see Taunton.
French war, preparations for, ... 144
Fuller, Robert, ... 78, 84, 181
   Samuel, ... 50, 123
   lands of, ... 27

GENERAL INDEX.

Fuller, Samuel, Sen., ... 162
  Samuel, Jun., fined for selling liquor to Indians, ... 162
  one of the first born children, land granted to, ... 19
  Lieutenant, ... 21
  one of the first born children, land granted to, ... 19
Gage, Gadge, Thomas, ... 124, 149, 170, 181
Gannett, Ganett, Matthew, ... 30, 139, 180
Garrett, Lydia, licensed as retailer, ... 44
General training, ... 38, 39, 64, 161
Gibbs, John, ... 85
  Thomas, ... 143
Gifford, John, ... 85
Gilbert, Giles, prosecuted for several offences, . 56, 66
  John, one of the first born children, land granted to, ... 20
Godfrey, John, receipt of, to Ormsbey's administrator, ... 164
Goggen, see Coggen.
Gorham, Gorum, John, ... 82
  land of, ... 41
  Mr., ... 93
Governor elected, . . 13, 36, 60, 90, 122, 147, 179
  house of, enlarged, ... 44
  salary of, ... 62, 97, 108
  allowance to, for extraordinary charges, . . 44
Governors, proposition concerning salary of, . . 102
Grand inquest, . . . 14, 37, 61, 91, 123, 148, 180
Gray, Edward, ... 21, 101, 123
  vs. Joseph Billington, ... 137
  fined for slander, ... 187
  lands of, ... 19, 36, 94, 173
  Joseph, and others, complaint against Taunton, 57
  bound to good behavior, and fined, . . 56, 66
  Mr., ... 28
Great Creek, ... 139
Great Neck, ... 138
Green, Henry, fined for breach of peace, . . . 50
Greenfield, Thomas, vs. Henry Saunders, . . . 54
Griffin, Griffen, William, ... 28
  and wife, fined, ... 47
Gulf Island, ... 138
Gurney, Isaac, punished for pilfering, ... 51
Hacke, Mary, ... 153
  petitions for leave to marry, ... 156
  William, ... 156
  estate of, settled, ... 151, 155
Hailstone, William, ... 171
Hall, George, ... 124, 150, 160, 171, 182
  one of the first born children, land granted to, ... 20
  John, ... 61, 71, 123, 170, 180
  Joseph, ... 170
  Nathaniel, ... 170

Hall, Samuel, ... 61, 170
Hallett, Hallott, Hollet, Andrew, ... 148, 167
  Elizabeth, ... 141
  John, ... 30, 61, 139, 153
  Joseph, and wife, fined, ... 141, 162
  Josias, punished for abusing John Doane, Jun., 31
Halloway, Halloway, Grace, portion of, paid her, . 136
  Jane, ... 187
  Timothy, fined for several offences, . . 29, 42, 50
  William, ... 136
Handy, Richard, deposition of, ... 95
  apprentice to James Skiffe, Jun., ... 149
Hammore, John, ... 189
  land granted to, ... 18
  lands of, ... 75, 131
Harding, Joseph, ... 91, 100
Harlow, William, ... 23, 61, 115
  officer of excise, ... 67, 182
  one of the first born children, land granted to, ... 20
  land granted to, ... 67, 94
Harper, Robert, punished for several offences, . . 51
Harris, Arthur, ... 151, 155, 190, 192, 193
  land of, ... 96, 189, 190
Harry, Sam, an Indian, ... 191
  Samuel, an Indian, ... 82
  an Indian, ... 82
Harvey, William, 15, 70, 71, 112, 124, 145, 150, 171,
                                      182, 183
  deputy from Taunton, . . 60, 90, 122, 148, 180
Hatch, Jeremiah, ... 30, 83, 139
  guardian of Nathaniel Man, ... 105
  Jonathan, ... 31
  punished for misdemeanor, ... 117
  Thomas, estate of, ... 31
  Walter, ... 76, 110
Hatherley, Timothy, ... 16, 22, 28, 31, 75
  magistrate at Scituate, ... 22, 43
  land of, laid out, ... 30, 46, 99, 104
  estate of, settled, ... 138, 155
  Wampatuck's release to, ... 185
  Mr. 44, 68, 75, 95, 142, 174
Hatheway, Hathawey, Hathewey, Haddawey, Arthur, ... 14, 27, 61, 150, 180
  to exercise the men in arms in Dartmouth, . 153
  John, fined for breach of peace, &c., . . 43, 187
  complaint of, against Indians, ... 92, 93
Haukes, Lodowick, ... 85
Haward, Howard, John, ... 138, 155, 180
  land granted to, ... 18
  John, Sen., ensign of Bridgewater company, . 73
  John, Jun., ... 192
  Sarah, land granted to, ... 159
  Thomas, ... 91, 155
  Thomas, Sen., ... 155, 193
  land of, ... 96, 189, 190

GENERAL INDEX. 205

Haward, Thomas, Jun., ... 155, 159, 193
   lieutenant of Bridgewater company, . . . 73
   Lieutenant, ... 124
Hawes, Edmund, ... 117, 124, 146, 150, 182
   deputy from Yarmouth, ... 90
   land of, ... 96, 102
   John, ... 183
      punished for slander, ... 11
   Mr., officer of excise, ... 67, 105
Hazard, Robert, ... 168
Hedge, Abraham, ... 115, 152, 153, 183
   fined for pound breach, ... 51
   Elisha, ... 28, 52, 116, 152
      punished for misdemeanor, . . 31, 32, 41, 42
      liquors of, forfeited, ... 82
   Eliza, ... 183
   William, ... 135
      captain of Yarmouth company, ... 15
   Mr., ... 28, 52
Hedges, Trustrum, ... 134, 154
Hicke, Daniel, ... 76
Hicks, Hickes, Margaret, estate of, ... 117
   Robert, lands of, divided, ... 27
   Samuel, ... 27, 91, 146, 150, 151
      wounded by Indians, ... 132, 133
Higgins, Higgens, Benjamin, . . . 169, 176, 177
   Richard, ... 100, 124, 146, 176, 182
      deputy from Eastham, ... 90
      petition of, for land, ... 96
High, Pine, ... 49
Hiland, Thomas, ... 30
   Thomas, Jun., ... 93
Hinckley, Hinckly, Samuel, will of, proved, . . . 36
   Thomas, 4, 8, 26, 30, 31, 34, 35, 45, 48, 49, 51, 59,
      69, 70, 74, 79, 81, 82, 87, 89, 93, 96, 97, 105,
      113, 119, 128, 129, 132—135, 140, 146, 153,
      157, 158, 162, 167, 173, 183, 184, 188, 189
      one of the council of war, ... 142
      an Assistant, . 13, 36, 60, 90, 122, 147, 179
      commissioner of United Colonies, . . 60, 147
      lands of, ... 96, 102, 135, 160
   Mr., ... 40, 55, 64
Hinde, Ann, deposition of, ... 93
Hingham, inhabitants petition for land, ... 67
Hoare, Hore, Hezekiah, ... 37, 55, 71, 91, 131
   Rebekah, land of, ... 131
Hodgis, alias Miller, Nicholas, estate of, ... 113
Holbrooke, Lieutenant, land of, ... 119
Holley, Holly, Experience, ... 88
   Joseph, ... 61, 141
   Joseph, Sen., heirs of, their release to William
      Newland, ... 88
   Joseph, Jun., ... 88
Holmes, John, ... 158, 179
   N. Soule's acknowledgment to, ... 178

Holmes, William, ... 15, 119
   lands of, ... 132
   Goodman, ... 75
Homicide, accidental, ... 49, 50
Honywell, William, ... 136
Hopewell, the ship, ... 171
Hopkins, Giles, ... 15, 177
   land granted to, ... 129, 152
   Stephen, ... 100
Horses, Indians allowed to buy, ... 93
Hoskins, Anne, ... 111
   fined for lewdness, ... 50
   William, ... 50, 98, 113
      one of the first born children, land grant-
      ed to, ... 19
   vs. Robert Ransom, ... 111
House, Elizabeth, ... 5
   Samuel, estate of, ... 45
   Samuel, Sen., estate of, ... 5
   Samuel, Jun., ... 5
Howes, Jeremiah, ... 180
   admitted a freeman, ... 38
   Joseph, ... 91, 96, 102, 117, 124, 135
      vs. Thomas Starr, ... 115
   Mary, ... 117
   Thomas, ... 21, 146, 148, 167, 182
      deputy from Yarmouth, ... 14, 180
      vs. William Nickarson, ... 183
      estate of, settled, ... 117
   Thomas, Sen., lands of, ... 96, 102
   Thomas, Jun., ... 37
   Mr., excise officer, ... 105, 110
   Mrs., vs. Edward Sturgis, ... 115
Howland, Arthur, Jun., prosecuted for misde-
      meanor, ... 140, 141, 158
   Henry, ... 181
   Jabez, fined for breach of peace, . . . 137, 140
   John, ... 91, 124, 125
      deputy from Plymouth, ... 37, 122, 148
   Joseph, ... 181
   Samuel, indicted for murder, and acquitted, 49, 50
      fined for breach of Sabbath, ... 28
   Zoeth, fined for breach of Sabbath, ... 5
   Mr., ... 173
      way to be laid out for, ... 114
      lands of, ... 95, 131
      one of the first born children, land grant-
      ed to, ... 19
Howse, William, killed by accident, ... 49
Hubbert, Josiah, ... 100
Huckens, Thomas, 15, 52, 107, 123, 151, 153, 182,
                                183
   to keep an ordinary at Barnstable, ... 40
   lands of, ... 160, 161
Hull, Joseph, guardians of, ... 175

GENERAL INDEX.

Hull, Trustrum, 31, 53, 91, 100, 112, 124, 125, 135, 175
   estate of, settled, ... 141
Hunt, Peter, ... 13, 21, 23, 83, 84
   officer of excise, ... 67
   deputy from Rehoboth, 14, 37, 60, 90, 148, 180
   Samuel, ... 148
      admitted a freeman, ... 61
   Lieutenant, ... 115, 151, 165
   deputy, fined for non-appearance, ... 107
Hyde, Nicholas, ... 15
   paid for services, ... 151
Indian affairs: Squa Sachem protected in her
   rights, ... 8
   complaint against Wamsitta for selling lands
      to strangers, ... 8
   Indians' complaints against Wamsitta, . . 16, 17
   controversy between Philip and other Indians, 24, 25
   Philip renews his league, ... 25, 26
   Philip's complaint against inhabitants of Rehoboth, ... 54
   Philip granted leave to buy a horse, . . . 93
   committee to buy land of Philip, ... 109
   Philip charged with aiding our enemies, . . 151
      summoned to answer the charge, ... 151
      appears and makes an explanation, . 164, 165
   Quachattasett vs. Josias, an Indian, ... 8
   Quachattasett acknowledges other Indians' interest in Mannomet lands, ... 115
   Mattaquason and son vs. William Nicarson, Sen., ... 64, 162, 163
   Keencomsett allowed to buy a horse, . . . 93
   Indian Josias, a sachem, killed, ... 33
   Ninnegret charged with plotting, ... 165
   Powa's complaint against Peter Pitts, . . . 183
   Wampatuck's release to Mr. Hatherley, . . 185
   Namumpam defrauded of her lands, . . . 186
   Indian Peter vs. James Bell, ... 190
   Indians punished for stealing, . . 22, 92, 112, 167
   Indians prosecuted for trespasses, 17, 51, 57, 82,
         132, 137, 138, 168, 179, 190, 191
   persons prosecuted for trespasses upon Indians, ... 66, 68, 109
   trespasses on their lands prevented, ... 31
   persons punished for selling liquor to, . . 32, 162
   liquor taken from Indians, ... 32
   Nantucket Indians charged with murder, search for, ... 80, 81
   Indians under care of Richard Bourne, privileges granted to, ... 80
   persons to make satisfaction for buying Indian lands, and these lands seized by government, ... 44, 49, 58, 59, 96
   lands purchased of Indians for ancient freemen, ... 5, 18, 20

Indian affairs: lands at Satucket purchased of Indians, ... 20
   lands purchased for Mr. Freeman and Mr. Paddy, 45
   lands purchased for Barnstable, ... 70, 82
   lands purchased for Yarmouth, ... 97
   lands purchased for Thomas Butler, ... 109
   lands purchased by Captain Willet, ... 109
   lands purchased for the country, ... 171
   lands purchased for Henry Wood, ... 167
   controversy with Indians about Dartmouth line, ... 168
   Indians' aid requested in war, ... 144
   bounty to them for killing wolves, ... 6
Indian names: Aquetaquesh, ... 26
   Acushena, ... 65
   Assoot, ... 167
   Chacapaquin, ... 58
   Coaksett, ... 65
   Kanoonus, ... 80
   Keencousett, ... 80
   Mckamoo, ... 190
   Monchase, ... 167
   Mattaquason, ... 162
   Mocrust, ... 80
   Metacom, alias Philip, sachem, ... 26
   Nanumatt, ... 115
   Nakatay, ... 114
   Nocroft, ... 115
   Namumpam, ... 17, 186
   Namumpum, ... 183
   Napoietan, ... 20
   Nantuckett, ... 80
   Napames, ... 92
   Ninnegrett, ... 151
   Nanquidnumacke, ... 80
   Pompecanche, ... 191
   Pyant, ... 191
   Pampmumitt, ... 152
   Paquaho, ... 92
   Pagenatowin, ... 58
   Ponagansett, ... 65
   Paupmunnucke, ... 80
   Pumpanaho, ... 138
   Pametoopauksett, ... 3
   Pumpasa, ... 26
   Punckquaneck, ... 26
   Powas, ... 183
   Quason, ... 162
   Quiquequanchett, ... 24
   Sasamon, ... 26
   Seketegansett, ... 5
   Sucquatamake, ... 58
   Tacomacus, ... 21
   Tetannett, ... 22
   Tassacausett, ... 152
   Tatacomuncah, ... 16

GENERAL INDEX.

Indian names : Tatawashaw 191
   Tumpasscom, ... 132
   Uncumpowett, ... 26
   Wapoompauksett, ... 3
   Wampatucke, ... 185
   Wawanquin, ... 57
   Watanumatucke, ... 80
   Wannamoisett, ... 169
   Webcowett, ... 119
   Weesunka, ... 58
   Winnatucksett, ... 42
   Woomham, ... 58
Indian Head River, ... 131
Indians, land to be purchased of, ... 82
   not to make contract or bargain about land
     with William Nicarson, ... 163
Ingham, Thomas, fined, ... 47
Inquests, 12, 13, 70, 71, 83, 84, 130, 169, 170, 176,
   177
Irish, John, land granted to, ... 18
Iron, order respecting manufacture of, at Taunton, 98
Iron works at Taunton, ... 46
Irons, John, ... 171
Jackson, Abraham, ... 14, 105, 117
   prosecuted for fraud, &c., ... 111
   vs. Rose Morton, ... 11
   vs. Nathaniel Warren, ... 120
   Samuel, fined for breach of peace, . . . 155
   claim of, against Hugh Cole, ... 168
Jacob, John, ... 68, 119, 127, 187
   vs. John Sutton, ... 53
   and others, petition for division, ... 174
Jacus, Thomas, ... 66
Jenkins, Jenkens, Edward, 23, 30, 50, 91, 114, 115,
   139, 141, 145, 151
   officer of excise, ... 67
   vs. John Williams, Jun., ... 75
Jenney, Jeney, Samuel, ... 15, 27, 80
   Sarah, estate of, ... 43, 80
   John, an Indian, ... 112
Jones, Teague, ... 52, 153
   punished for drunkenness, ... 29
Jones River bridge, . . . 23, 41, 109, 121, 128
Joseph, an Indian, complaint of, against Giles Gilbert, ... 66
   alias Tatawashaw, an Indian, ... 191
Josias, an Indian sachem, ... 8, 33
Jourdaine, John, land of, ... 94
Joyce, Hosea, ... 141
   John, ... 15, 91, 125
   estate of, ... 141
   Walter, fined for drunkenness, ... 187
Judkin, Job, ... 130
Jury summoned to make division of lands, . . . 139
Jyde, Nicholas, ... 84
Kanoonus, ... 80

Keencomsett, ... 53, 54, 80
   allowed to buy a horse, ... 93
Kean, Keine, Josiah, ... 120, 124, 148
   land of, ... 110, 171
Keith, Mr., admitted a freeman, ... 61
   land granted to, ... 188
Kendricke, Kenericke, George, ... 124, 181
Kennebec, sale ratified, ... 17, 33
King, addressed for confirmation of patent, . . 62, 92
King, Kinge, Clement, ... 181
   Thomas, ... 124, 139, 149, 182
   deputy from Scituate, ... 180
   magistrate at Scituate, ... 169
Knap, Aaron, ... 71
Knowles, John, fined for selling liquor to Indians, ... 32, 33
   Richard, ... 169, 177
Land, Edward, fined for misdemeanor, ... 133
Land to be purchased of the Indians, ... 167
Lands at Taunton River, trespasses prevented, . . 8
   of the country to be sold, ... 109, 188
   lying dormant, order concerning, ... 73
   common, suit concerning, ... 75
   on Namasskett River, ... 94
   purchased of Indians for the country, . . . 171
Latham, Robert, ... 155, 193
Lawrence, an Indian, ... 167
Laws of war, ... 146, 147
Leichfield, Josiah, ... 81
   choice of guardian, ... 35, 39
   grant to, from John Allin's estate, ... 39
   settlement with guardians, ... 89
Leonard, Lenard, Leanard, James, ... 16, 71
   vs. James Bell, ... 8
   exempt from training, ... 15
   licence of, recalled, ... 54
   Philip, ... 50
   Thomas, ... 57, 123
   fined for breach of the peace, ... 5
   Thomas, Sen., licensed as retailer, ... 45
   ensign of Taunton company, ... 93
Lettice, Thomas, ... 15, 123
Leverich, Mr., ... 3
Lewis, George, ... 14
   estate of, ... 55
   James, ... 123
   Thomas, ... 15
   widow, ... 55
Lieutenant, commission of, ... 143
Linkorn, Linkorne, Linkhorne, Samuel, . . . 57
   fined for several offences, ... 56, 66
   Thomas, ... 148
   Thomas, Sen., fined for breach of peace, . . 83
Linnell, Robert, estate of, ... 31
Linnitt, Shubael, ... 153
Liquors, committee to take account of, . . . 23, 67

208 GENERAL INDEX.

Liquors, account of, ... 28, 52, 100, 152, 158
   receivers of excise, ... 105
Little, Thomas, ... 15, 61, 79, 113
   fined for disclosing secrets of grand jury, . . 101
   suit against Rachel Davenport, ... 119
   lands of, ... 16, 110
Long Point, ... 12
Long Square, ... 45
Lothrop, Laythorp, Laythorpe, Barnabas, . . . 107
   lands of, ... 160
   Joseph, . . . 23, 31, 53, 61, 106, 150, 151, 175
     deputy from Barnstable, . . 122, 148, 180
     land of, ... 160
   Mark, ... 155, 193
   Thomas, ... 37, 91, 107, 133, 153
     Lieutenant, ... 182, 183
Lovell, James, ... 75
   lands of, ... 74, 82, 97, 99
Lucas, Thomas, punished for swearing, . . . 66, 101
   fined for drunkenness, ... 33, 51, 55, 106
Luce, Henry, ... 139
Lumbert, Lumbard, Lumber, Barnard, 81, 96, 102,
                                                  133, 135
   lands of, ... 128, 189
   Caleb, ... 81
   Jabez, ... 180
   Jedediah, ... 81
     fined, ... 182
   Thomas, estate of, ... 81
Lumpkin, William, ... 170
   fined, ... 140
Maaz, or Maze, William, punished for swearing, 52, 77
Macey, Macye, George, . . . 14, 23, 70, 171, 181
   lieutenant of Taunton company, ... 93
Maconesett Neck, ... 131
Magistrates, Treasurer to provide for table of, . . 44
   rates of, ... 97, 98
   proposition concerning the number and com-
     pensation of, ... 102, 103
Major's Purchase, ... 172
   proprietors' names, ... 95
Man, Nathaniel, guardians of, ... 105
   Richard, punished for stealing, ... 33
Mannomoiett, Mannamoiett, Manamoiett, Mama-
   moite, ... 59, 64, 162
   petition to be made a township, . . . 153, 154
   annexed to Eastham, ... 185
   annexed to Yarmouth, ... 96, 97, 101, 102
Mannamucheoy, ... 4
Mannomett, Manomett, ... 115
   River, ... 4
   Ponds, ... 110
Marchant, John, ensign of Yarmouth company, . 65
Marda, servant of Wamsitta, ... 8
Marriages, by whom solemnized, 10, 22, 43, 65, 73, 74,
                                                  108, 186

Marriho, Mary, presented, ... 69
Marshall, Richard, punished for several offences, . 11
Marshfield, ... 23, 118, 145
   rates, ... 6, 29, 48, 63, 72, 77, 91, 98
   excise officers, ... 67, 151, 183
   town officers, 15, 39, 61, 91, 113, 123, 124, 148,
                                           150, 181, 182
   deputies, ... 37
   controversy with Captain Thomas, ... 173
Martin's Vineyard, ... 166
   John Doged, suit against, ... 27
Martine, widow, estate of, ... 8
Massachusetts line run, ... 24, 63
   letter to, about confederation, ... 92
Mattapoisett River, ... 159
Mattaquason, an Indian, ... 162
   sachem of Mannamoiett, ... 64
Mathewes, Mathews, James, . . 37, 117, 124, 150, 182
   deputy from Yarmouth, ... 60
   John, ... 187
Maycomber, William, ... 14, 23
   William, Sen., ... 151
Mayne, Ezekiel, ... 130
Mayo, Hannah, ... 8
   John, ... 22, 100, 169, 176
   Nathaniel, estate of, ... 8
   widow, land granted to, ... 129, 152
Mecoy, Mocoy, John, land granted to, . . . 159
Mekamoo, an Indian, ... 190
Merrick, Merricke, William, ... 169
   land granted to, ... 18, 136
   lieutenant of Eastham company, ... 41
   Ensign, ... 183
Metacum, see Philip.
Military officers: Bridgewater, ... 73
   Eastham, ... 41, 64
   Plymouth, ... 65
   Rehoboth, ... 65
   Scituate, ... 117, 126, 127
   Taunton, ... 93
   Yarmouth, ... 15, 65
   form of commissions, ... 21, 142, 143
Miller, John, 14, 32, 117, 123, 124, 135, 151, 182, 183
   admitted a freeman, ... 38
   licensed to keep an ordinary, ... 167
   Jone, widow of Obadiah Miller, . . . 4, 5, 10
   Nicholas, ... 113
   Obadiah, land of, sold, ... 4
Mitchell, Michell, Experience, ... 12, 123
   lands of, ... 27, 67, 94, 132, 185
   Richard, ... 52
   and wife, fined, ... 47
Mocoy, see Mecoy.
Mocrust, ... 80
Mokency, Mokaney, John, ... 152, 153
Monchase, an Indian, ... 167

GENERAL INDEX.   209

Monchasacke, an Indian, ... 167, 209
More, Cornelius, administration of estate of, . . 81
    Elizabeth, suit against, ... 141
    George, land of, sold, ... 72
Morey, Jonathan, ... 181
Morton, Ephraim, ... 182
    deputy from Plymouth, 14, 37, 60, 90, 122, 148,
        180
    ancient freeman, land granted to, ... 20
    lieutenant of Plymouth company, ... 65
    lands of, ... 67, 94, 173
    John, ... 21, 23, 37, 91
        officer of excise, ... 67
        deputy from Plymouth, ... 14
        lands of, ... 94, 128
        ancient freeman, land granted to, ... 20
    Nathaniel, 10, 20, 35, 68, 78, 79, 87, 98, 157, 172,
        173
        ancient freeman, land granted to, ... 20
        lands of, ... 67, 94
    Rose, ... 11
    Thomas, ... 14, 61, 79
        bond to Nathaniel Warren, ... 77, 78
    Sergeant, ... 53
    Lieutenant, ... 80, 124, 149, 184
        to sell land for the colony, ... 184
Moses, an Indian, ... 167
Muddy Hole, ... 3
Mullins, William, one of the first born children,
    land granted to, ... 19
Myles, Mr., ... 169
    fined for setting up a meeting at Rehoboth, . 162
Nakatay Island, part of, purchased, ... 114
Namasskett, Namassakett, ... 41, 184
    inhabitants belong to Plymouth, ... 41
    land granted to, for a minister, ... 94
    proprietors, ... 73, 94
    River, ... 160, 172
Namumpam, a squaw sachem, ... 17, 24, 186
Nanquatnumacke, complaint of, against inhabitants
    of Sandwich, ... 68
Nanquatnumucke, bounds of, ... 28
Nanquidnumacke, ... 80
    See Nonquitnumacke.
Nantucket Indian, ordered out of the colony, . . 22
    Indians, suspected of murder, search to be
        made for, ... 80, 81
Nanumett, an Indian, ... 115
Napames, an Indian, ... 92
Napoietan, Indian sagamore, ... 20
Nash, Samuel, marshal, ... 135
    Marshall, ... 96, 102
    complaint of, against constable of Marsh-
        field, ... 121
    Lieutenant, ... 20, 21, 48, 58, 66
Nausett, ... 26

Nelson, William, ... 95
    wife of, one of the first born children, land
        granted to, ... 19
    land of, ... 95
    vs. Abraham Jackson, ... 105
New England's Memorial, appropriations made for
    printing, ... 173, 186, 189
Newland, William, discharged from bond, . . 87, 88
Newman, Samuel, ... 14, 38, 61, 143
    administration of estate of, ... 54
    admitted a freeman, ... 38
    Samuel, Jun., ... 54
    Mrs., ... 54
Nicarson, Nickarson, John, ... 154
    Joseph, ... 154, 184
    Nicholas, ... 153, 154
        prosecuted, ... 153
        child of, choked to death, ... 170
    Robert. 154
    Samuel, ... 154, 183, 184
    William, ... 28, 101, 153
    lands granted to, ... 96, 97, 101, 135
    prosecuted for buying lands of Indians, 44, 49,
        58, 59
    lands sold for the use of the colony, . . . 61
    William, Sen., ... 154
        prosecuted, ... 49
        Thomas Howes against, ... 183
        acknowledgments of, . . . 87, 134, 135, 140
        prosecuted, . . 134, 135, 140, 155, 157, 163
        controversy with Indians, . . . 64, 162, 163
    William, Jun., ... 154, 184
Nicolls, James, inquest upon, ... 176
    Colonel Richard, defamatory letter sent to, by
        William Nickarson, 134, 155, 157, 158, 163
Nimrod, alias Pumpasa, ... 26
Ninnegrett, Narraganset sachem, ... 165, 166
Nonquitnumacke, ... 161
    See Nanquatnumacke.
Nocroft, an Indian, ... 115
Norkett, William, fined for fornication, . . . 47
Norman, Samuel, fined for lying, ... 101
North Hill in Duxbury, ... 17
North River, controversy about lands at, . . . 76
    bridge, ... 41, 69
Norton, Nicholas, ... 27
Nye, Benjamin, ... 46, 82, 85, 180
Ordinaries at Barnstable, ... 40
    at Duxbury, ... 129
    at Rehoboth, ... 158
    at Saconeesett, ... 80
    at Scituate, ... 117
    at Yarmouth, ... 167
Ormsbey, Richard, estate of, ... 105, 164, 167
    Sarah, ... 105
Osamequin, ... 20

GENERAL INDEX.

Otis, Ottis, John, ... 14, 30, 61, 180
Ouldum, Thomas, ... 29
Packer, Samuel, ... 61
    Samuel, Sen., ... 193
    Thomas, Sen., ... 155
Paddy, Samuel, ... 40
    Thomas, ... 40
    William, land granted to children of, . . 40, 45
Paducke, Zachariah, ... 170
Pagenatowin, ... 58
Paine, Nathaniel, ... 15
    Stephen, ... 150
    deputy from Rehoboth, . . . 37, 60, 90, 122
    magistrate at Rehoboth, ... 65, 73
    Stephen, Sen., ... 13, 84
    Thomas, ... 15, 61, 100, 176, 187
    land granted to, ... 152
    Mr., deputy, fined for non-appearance, . . 107
    Mr., Sen., ... 145, 175
Palmer, John, Sen., fined for deceit, ... 5
    John, Jun., ... 137
    fined for slander, ... 29
    William, ... 123
Pametoopauksett, ... 3
Pampmumitt, alias Charles, an Indian, . . . 152
Pampaspised River, ... 3
Paomet, annexed to Eastham, ... 185
Paquaho, alias Daniel, an Indian, ... 92
Parker, Alice, ... 16
    John, ancient freeman, land granted to, . . 20
    William, estate of, ... 16
    ancient freeman, land granted to, ... 20
Partridge, Partrich, George, ... 12, 181
    land granted to, ... 18
    one of the first born children, land granted to, ... 19
    land of, ... 189
Passuntaquanuncke Neck, ... 189
Patent, address to the king for confirmation of, . 62
Patonumatucke, ... 110
Pateckett River, ... 62
Paule, William, fined for drunkenness, &c., . . 43
Paupmunnucke, ... 80
Pausatucke Neck, ... 128
Paybody, William, 21, 42, 48, 58, 104, 120, 155, 161, 174, 182
    deputy from Duxbury, ... 14, 37
    ancient freeman, land granted to, ... 20
    fined for misdemeanor, ... 66
    lands of, ... 67, 119, 131, 159
    to oversee the rebuilding of Jones River bridge, 109
    fine remitted to, ... 129
Peakes, Judith, ... 35
    William, ... 35, 123, 139, 181
Peck, Pecke, John, . . 15, 83, 91, 105, 125, 164, 167
    Joseph, magistrate at Rehoboth, ... 21

Peck, Joseph, estate of, ... 55
    Nathaniel, ... 181
    Nicholas, ... 50, 55, 83, 84, 143
    Samuel, ... 55, 83, 123
Peirce, Peirse, Abraham, Jun., acknowledgment of, ... 7
    prosecuted for abusive speeches to his father, . 47
    Michael, ... 89, 148
    petition of, respecting John Allin's estate, . 81
    Mr., ... 127
Penquine Hole, ... 119
Perram, John, ... 84, 123
Perren, John, Sen., ... 83
Perry, Perrey, Anthony, ... 84, 91
    Edward, ... 181
    vs. Henry Saunders, ... 16
    prosecuted for libel, ... 44
    Ezra, ... 4
    lands of, ... 131, 159
    Thomas, prosecuted, ... 177, 191
Peter, an Indian, ... 190
Phelpes, Thomas, fined for lying, ... 166
Philip, the sagamore, committee to treat with, for purchase of lands, ... 109
    alias Metacum, sachem of Poconakett, 25, 26, 151, 164
    Indian sachem, ... 54
    sachem of Sowams, ... 24
    an Indian, ... 92
    sachem, see Indians.
Phillips, John, ... 136, 163, 164
    marriage contract of, ... 163, 164
    Mary, fined for breach of peace, ... 187
Phinney, see Finney.
Pickles, Jonas, estate of, ... 106
Pidell, William, inquest upon, ... 176
Pincen, Thomas, ... 123
Pinion, Robert, punished as a vagrant, . . . 154
Pitts, Peter, ... 37, 71, 160, 171, 181
    prosecuted by an Indian, ... 183
Plain Dealing, owners of lots at, ... 53
Plymouth, ... 23, 41, 145
    rates, ... 5, 29, 47, 63, 72, 77, 118
    excise officers, ... 67, 150, 183
    town officers, 14, 15, 37, 38, 61, 91, 123, 124, 148, 149, 180—182
    inhabitants at Plain Dealing, lots enlarged, . 53
    military officers, ... 65
    South Meadows, ... 70
    minister's land at Namassaket, ... 94
    and Sandwich, bounds to be settled, . . . 40
    colony, see Colony.
Poconakett, Pacanacutt, Pocanacett, 25, 26, 151, 164
Pochasett, ... 62
    ferry, ... 185
Pointing, William, vs. Indian Stephen, ... 190

GENERAL INDEX.   211

Pompecanche, ... 191
Ponagausett, Acushena, and Coaksett, made a township by the name of Dartmouth, . . . 65
Pontus, William, ... 58
   one of the first born children, land granted to, ... 19
Poole, John, ... 160
   Timothy, inquest on, ... 170
   William, ... 170
   Captain, ancient freeman, land granted to, . 20
Pope, Susannah, ... 80
   Thomas, ... 43, 49, 187
   land granted to, ... 18
   vs. Giles Rickard, ... 79
   complaint of John Barnes against, . . . 79
   prosecuted for breach of peace, ... 48
   wife of, heir to Sarah Jenney, ... 80
   complaint against, ... 89
Pottamumaquate Neck, ... 131
Powas, an Indian, ... 183
Pratt, Prat, Pratte, Abigail, ... 88
   Benajah, ... 37, 104, 115, 150, 183
   land of, ... 132
   Jonathan, ... 11, 88
   Phineas, ... 74
   lands of, ... 68, 97
Prence, Elizabeth, ... 140, 141, 159
   Thomas, Gov., 3, 4, 8, 25, 26, 30, 35, 44, 45, 48, 49, 56, 59, 69, 70, 74, 79, 87, 89, 103, 105, 109, 111—113, 119, 132, 134, 135, 137, 140, 145, 153, 157, 166, 167, 173, 185, 188.
   governor, . . 13, 36, 60, 90, 122, 147, 179
   president of the council of war, . . . 142
   allowance to, for extraordinary charges, . 44
   commissioner of the United Colonies, 14, 36, 90, 122, 180
   privileges granted to, ... 108
   land granted to, ... 128, 184
   proposes to buy house at Plain Dealing, . 184
   Mr., one of the first born children, land granted to, ... 19
Presentments, . . . 28, 29, 33, 34, 42, 43, 50, 51
Pressbury, Dorcas, ... 66
Printing, appropriation for, . . . 173, 186, 189
Prior, Joseph, ... 12
Propositions made by the Court to the several townships for consideration, . . . 102
Protest of John Wing, ... 171
Pumpanaho, alias Daniel, an Indian, ... 138
Pumpasa, alias Nimrod, ... 26
Punckquaneck, ... 26
Pyant, an Indian, ... 191
Quachattasett, Quachatasett, an Indian sachem, 8, 115, 128, 189
Quason, John, an Indian, ... 64, 162
Quenaumett, ... 189

Quequequancett, ... 167
Ramsden, Joseph, goods of, attached, ... 11, 12
Randall, William, ... 47, 153
   fined for several offences, ... 9, 29, 83
   land of, laid out, ... 82, 100
Ransom, Ransome, Robert, ... 111
   prosecuted for inclosing common lands, . . 88
   fined for breach of Sabbath, ... 50
Rates, proposition concerning, ... 102
   ordered and apportioned, 5, 29, 40, 47, 63, 72, 77, 91, 97, 98, 118, 129, 157
Rawlins, Lydia, ... 46
   Nathaniel, estate of, ... 46
Reed, Read, John, ... 13
   admitted a freeman, ... 33
   John, Sen., ... 83, 84
Redley, Redly, Mark, ... 141, 183
Redway, James, ... 83
Rehoboth, ... 23, 41, 54, 72, 77, 118, 145
   rates, ... 6, 29, 48, 63
   excise officers, ... 67, 151, 183
   town officers, 15, 38, 61, 91, 123, 124, 148, 150, 181
   deputies, ... 37
   magistrates, ... 65, 73, 186
   ordinary, ... 158
   military officers, ... 65
   land granted to, ... 185
   meeting set up at, by Miles and Brown, . . 102
   and Sowamsett united, ... 72, 93
Rhode Island, farms against, rates of, ... 6
   claims certain lands here, ... 44
   claims resisted by this colony, ... 62
   ferry, ... 163
Rickard, Ricard, Giles, ... 79
   Giles, Sen., ancient freeman, land granted to, 20
   lands of, ... 94
   fined for keeping disorderly house, . . . 106
   license of, recalled, ... 136
   fined for several offences, . . . 48, 76, 101
   Giles, Jun., ... 115, 117
   vs. Abraham Jackson, ... 111
   vs. Joseph Ramsden, ... 12
   Hester, vs. William Hoskins, ... 111
   fined, ... 50
   John, ... 50, 111
   vs. Elizabeth More, ... 141
Rider, Samuel, Sen., ... 124
   See Ryder.
Ridman, Thomas, fined for selling liquor to Indians, ... 32
   bound to appear, &c., ... 33
Ring, Ringe, Andrew, one of the first born children, land granted to, ... 19
   land of, ... 152
Robbins, John, ... 12

GENERAL INDEX.

Robinson, Isaac, ... 77
    land granted to, ... 128, 189
    licensed to keep an ordinary, ... 80
    John, ... 116
Robinson's Creek, ... 141
Rocke, Mr., ... 133
Rocky Nook, ... 114
Roes, Thomas, administrator of Jonas Pickles, . . 106
Rogers, John, ... 12, 37, 123, 130, 169, 180
    ancient freeman, land granted to, ... 20
    lands of, ... 67, 132
    John, Sen., land granted to, ... 161
    Joseph, Lieutenant, ... 37, 102, 169
        land granted to, ... 67, 96
        punished for several offences, . . . 42, 47
        lieutenant of Eastham company, . . . 64
    Joseph, Jun., estate of, ... 55
    Thomas, ... 55
        propounded as freeman, ... 61
    Lieutenant, freed from office, ... 5
Rollocke, Robert, ... 85
Rootey Brook, ... 128
Rouse, John, ... 15
    land granted to, ... 18
Rowley, Moses, ... 15
Russell, George, ... 53, 91, 174
    John, ... 37, 109, 146, 150
    deputy to General Court, ... 90
    complaint against Indians, ... 57, 58
    bound to appear at Court, ... 101
Ryder, Joseph, ... 152
    Samuel, ... 37
    Zechariah, ... 183
    See Rider.
Saberry, Seaberry, Saberey, Samuel, . . 12, 91, 180
    prosecuted for defamation, ... 140
Sabine, Sabin, Samuel, presented, ... 69
    William, ... 13, 61, 83, 84, 115
    fined for pound breach, ... 117
Saconeesett, annexed to Barnstable, ... 41
    lands at, to be purchased, ... 97
Saconett, Saconet, ... 128
    Wamsitta complained of for selling, . . . 17
    granted to servants, ... 97
    Point, ... 62
Sale, Edward, ... 83
    Rebecca, inquest upon, ... 83
Salt House Beach, ... 49
Samson, Sampson, an Indian, ... 177
    alias Bump, an Indian, ... 136
    Abraham, land granted to, ... 18
    fined, ... 33
    Henry, ... 37, 150, 183
    lands of, ... 27, 67, 94, 160
Sampson's Neck, ... 129
Sandwich, ... 5, 6, 23, 29, 72, 77, 118, 145

Sandwich, land granted to, ... 161, 162
    rates, ... 47, 63
    excise officers, ... 67, 151, 183
    town officers, 15, 37, 38, 61, 91, 123, 124, 148,
                        149, 180—182
    bounds, ... 21, 40
    land granted to, ... 18
    land of inhabitants to be bounded, . . . 113
    to send but one deputy, ... 159
    complained of by Indians, ... 68
    sued by Thomas Dexter, Sen., ... 70
Sanford, John, ... 186
Sargeant, William, lands of, ... 96, 102
    Mr., ... 97
Sasomon, John, ... 26
Satuckett lands, purchased of Indians, . . . 20
    Pond, ... 21, 42, 43
    River, ... 42, 73
Saunders, Henry, ... 7, 16, 54, 57
Savory, Joseph, fined for breach of peace, . . 50
    Thomas, ... 88
    land granted to, for his children, . . . 95
Scituate, . . 23, 65, 72, 77, 117, 118, 126, 135, 145
    allowed to make sale of land, ... 72
    rates, ... 5, 29, 47, 63
    excise officers, ... 67, 151, 183
    town officers, 14, 15, 37, 38, 61, 91, 123, 148, 149,
                        180—182
    distillery at, ... 132
    order of Court to townsmen of, ... 51
    bounds, ... 8, 46
    ordinary, ... 117
    order about Randall's land, ... 100
    military company censured, ... 126
    magistrates, ... 22, 43, 73, 169
Seabury, see Saberry.
Sears, Saers, Saeres, Paul, ... 170, 180
    Richard, deputy from Yarmouth, . . . 14
Secumcke, bounds, ... 31
    cartway, ... 5
    lands to be viewed, ... 39
Seketegansett, ... 5
Selectmen, ... 112, 113, 117, 124, 149, 150, 182
Sepitt, an Indian sachem, ... 128, 189
Servants, ancient, lands of, at Saconett Neck, 18, 97,
                              128
Shaw, James, ... 27, 61
    to exercise the inhabitants of Dartmouth, 146, 153
    complaint of, against an Indian, ... 57
    John, one of the first born children, land
        granted to, ... 19
    Sergeant, ... 183
Shelley, Shilley, John, sentenced for several of-
    fences, ... 42, 106
    Robert, ... 51
Sherman, John, takes oath of fidelity, . . . 185

GENERAL INDEX. 213

Sherman, William, land granted to, ... 18
Shurtleff, Shirtliffe, William, land granted to, . 18, 131
    vs. Thomas Little, ... 79
Silvester, Dinah, ... 141
    fined, ... 162
    John, ... 76
    fined, ... 137
    Joseph, ... 29, 91
    Naomi, relief afforded to, ... 46
Simmons, Simons, Simonson, John, fined for misdemeanor, ... 133
    Moses, ... 15, 48, 69
    one of the first born children, land granted to, ... 19
    land of, ... 104
    bounds settled, ... 120
Simon, an Indian, ... 167
Sisson, Mary, ... 186
    Richard, ... 148, 186
Skiffe, James, ... 28, 68
    officer of excise, ... 67
    deputy from Sandwich, ... 37, 60, 90, 122
    land granted to, ... 131
    James, Sen., ... 145, 149, 182
    James, Jun., ... 194
    Stephen, ... 91
Slocome, Anthony, ... 15
Smalley, Smaley, John, ... 91, 100, 125, 176
    land granted to, ... 18
    land of, ... 27
    John, Sen., child of, perished, ... 177
Smith, Daniel, ... 14, 83, 84, 148, 151, 183
    licensed to keep an ordinary, ... 158
    Francis, ... 23, 61
    officer of excise, ... 67
    Henry, ... 83, 84
    ensign of Rehoboth company, ... 65
    deputy from Rehoboth, ... 14, 148, 180
    magistrate, ... 186
    John, ... 91, 105, 109, 162, 187
    vs. Richard Child, ... 105
    John, Jun., vs. Stephen Tilden, ... 79
    Ralph, ... 32, 100
    punished for several offences, . . 34, 89, 175
    Richard, ... 85
    Samuel, ... 91, 181
    fined for threatening words, ... 34
    takes oath of fidelity, ... 177
    Sarah, ... 141, 162
    Ensign, ... 151, 165
Snell, Thomas, ... 193
Snow, Snowe, Anthony, 8, 14, 23, 75, 104, 113, 120, 123, 124, 150, 182, 183
    deputy, ... 90
    guardian of Robert Waterman, ... 113
    ancient freeman, land granted to, ... 20

Snow, Anthony, deputy from Marshfield, . . 60, 180
    land of, ... 67, 94
    Joseph, ... 176
    Mark, ... 148, 176
    Nicholas, ... 15, 100, 175, 182
    William, ... 193
Soule, Elizabeth, punished, ... 34, 162
    George, one of the first born children, land granted to, ... 19
    George, Sen., ... 179
    John, ... 179
    Nathaniel, ... 178
    prosecuted for several offences, . . 179, 186
South Brook, ... 190
South Meadows of Plymouth, ... 70
South Sea, ... 189
Souther, Nathaniel, ... 74, 82, 99
Southworth, Constant, 6, 7, 23, 40—42, 44, 68, 70, 95, 109, 113, 119, 121, 127—129, 131, 142, 145, 160, 164, 166, 184, 186, 188—190.
    deposition of, ... 20
    deputy from Duxbury, 14, 37, 60, 90, 122, 143, 180
    to give deeds of land to Governor Prence, . 185
    Treasurer, . . . 14, 37, 60, 90, 122, 147, 180
    lands of, ... 58, 95
    paid for services, ... 151
    Thomas, 4, 8, 11, 19, 21, 24, 26, 30, 35, 44, 45, 48, 49, 56, 59, 69, 72, 74, 78, 79, 81, 87, 89, 95, 97, 99, 100, 103, 105, 109, 111—113, 119, 132, 134, 136, 140, 157, 160, 164, 166, 167, 172, 173, 184, 188.
    one of the council of war, ... 142
    an Assistant, . 13, 36, 60, 90, 122, 143, 179
    commissioner of the United Colonies, 14, 37, 60, 90, 122
    ancient freeman, land granted to, ... 20
    paid for services, ... 63, 108, 151
    land granted to, ... 95
    appointed to purchase land of the Indians, . 167
    three pounds granted to, for services as commissioner, ... 72
Sowams, Sowamsett, ... 118
    rates, ... 6, 30, 40, 48, 63, 72, 77
    annexed to Rehoboth, ... 41, 72, 93
Sparrow, Jonathan, ... 23, 123, 169, 176
    admitted a freeman, ... 33
    lands of, ... 27, 129, 131, 152
    deputy from Eastham, ... 180
Spiller, Benjamin, ... 177
Spooner, Hannah, ... 101
    William, ... 101, 123
Sprague, Francis, ... 7
    one of the first born children, land granted to, ... 19
    license recalled, ... 129

214 GENERAL INDEX.

Sprague, John, ... 12, 37, 66
    fine remitted to, ... 99
    allowance to, ... 12
    Ruth, ... 7
    Samuel, ... 181
    Mr., ... 152
Sprout, Robert, ... 76, 174
Stacye, Richard, ... 71
Standish, Alexander, ... 14, 123
    lands of, ... 27, 73
    Josiah, . 18, 21, 61, 124, 131. 145, 148, 149, 174
    deputy, ... 90
    land of, ... 4
    Miles, lands of, ... 21, 42
    Sarah, ... 69
    Captain, ... 20
Standlake, Richard, ... 139
Starr, Thomas, ... 53, 183
    punished for several offences, . . 31, 32, 115, 187
Stetson, see Studson.
Stevens, Peter, ... 120, 133
    Simon, ... 167
Stockbridge, Charles, ... 123
Stony Brook, ... 97
Streame, Sergeant Thomas, ... 119
Studson, Stetson, Benjamin, ... 180
    Robert, 21, 23, 24, 27, 30, 31, 38, 39, 41, 44, 64,
    74, 75, 95, 96, 99, 100, 109, 115, 124, 128,
    145, 149, 159, 171, 181, 188, 189.
    deputy from Scituate, ... 14, 122, 148
    to oversee the rebuilding of Jones River
      bridge, ... 109
    guardian to Josiah Leichfield, ... 89
    paid for services, ... 151
    lands granted to, ... 95, 127, 142
Sturgis, Edward, ... 15, 52, 115, 150, 183
    deputy from Yarmouth, ... 60, 122, 148
    prosecuted, ... 42
    Edward, Sen., license recalled, ... 54
    prosecuted, ... 107
    Edward, Jun., ... 52, 152
    Samuel, ... 52, 150, 152, 183
    punished for misdemeanor, ... 31, 32
Sturtivant, Samuel, ... 61, 123
Suckquatamake, ... 58
Summers, Sumers, Thomas, ... 108
    fined for drunkenness, ... 83
Surveyors of highways, . . 15, 38, 61, 123, 149, 181
Sutliffe, Abraham, ... 168
Sutton, Sutten, John, ... 37, 45, 53, 112, 182
    a colt given up to, ... 27
    William, ... 129, 177
Swansey, made a township, ... 169
    privileges of, ... 176
    town officers, ... 181
Swift, Joane, will of, proved, ... 55

Swift, William, ... 50, 180
Tacomacus, ... 21
Talbut, Jared, ... 70
    Jehud, ... 170
Talmon, Peter, ... 186
————, ... 104
Talmud, ... 8
Tanner, Mr., ... 162
Tassacausett, ... 152
Tassacust, ... 128
Tatacomuncah, ... 16
Tatawashaw, alias Joseph, an Indian, ... 191
Taunton, ... 23, 118, 145
    rates, ... 5, 29, 47, 63, 72, 77
    excise officers, ... 67, 151, 183
    town officers, 15, 37, 38, 61, 91, 123, 124, 148.
                    150, 181, 182
    general training appointed at, ... 161
    deputies, ... 37
    grants to the ancient freemen of, . . 5, 19, 160
    magistrate, ... 10
    lands granted to, ... 28, 45
    bounds, ... 31
    complaint against intruders, ... 34
    military officers, ... 93
    iron works, ... 98
Taunton River, passage kept open for alewives, 57, 66
    Taunton River bridge, ... 159
Taxes, see Rates.
Taylor, Tayler, Henry, ... 31
    John, ... 117
    Lydia, ... 31
    Richard, ... 9, 181
    officer of excise, ... 67
    vs. Thomas Starr, ... 53
Ten Mile River, ... 96
Tetacutt, Tetiquott, ... 45, 131
Tetannett, alias Ned, a Nantucket Indian, whipped
    for stealing, ... 22
Teticutt River, ... 188
Thacher, Anthony, 9, 14, 23, 28, 52, 117, 124, 146,
                          151
    one of the council of war, ... 142
    deputy from Yarmouth, ... 37, 90
    land granted to, ... 96, 102
    magistrate at Yarmouth, ... 108
    suit against Thomas Starr, ... 115
    estate of, settled, ... 168, 175
    Elizabeth, ... 175
    John, ... 123, 167, 168, 174, 182
    deputy from Yarmouth, ... 180
    Judah, ... 149, 181
    Mr., ... 52, 152
    excise officer, ... 105, 110
Thomas, John, ... 61
    Nathaniel, ... 15, 91, 180, 187

GENERAL INDEX. 215

Thomas, William, ... 112
 Captain, *vs.* Town of Marshfield, ... 173
Thornton, Thomas, ... 158
Thresher, Christopher, ... 71
Ticknor, Tickner, William, ... 36, 181
Tiffeney, Humphrey, ... 51, 54
Tilden, Tildin, Joseph, 14, 27, 30, 31, 82, 91, 110, 114,
  138, 148, 153, 155
 guardian of Nathaniel Man, ... 105
 vs. Edward Bumpas, Jun., ... 75
 and another, *vs.* John Palmer, ... 137
 Stephen, ... 79
 Thomas, ... 37
 Mr., ... 44, 45
Tillson, Tilson, Ephraim, prosecuted for breach of
 peace, ... 88
 Joane, *vs.* John Barnes, ... 9
Tinkham, Ephraim, ... 35, 103, 125, 192
 land of, ... 130
 Sergeant, ... 128, 187
Tisdall, John, ... 50
Titus, John, ... 148
Tobey, an Indian, ... 92
 Thomas, ... 23, 46, 82, 151, 183
 officer of excise, ... 67
Tompkins, Samuel, ... 148
 Goodman, ... 193
Tomson, Tompson, Thompson, John, 29, 61, 112, 124,
  125, 150, 182
 lands of, ... 160, 161
 fined for absence as juror, ... 29
 suit of, against Richard Wright, ... 54
Torrey, Ann, ... 110
 James, Lieutenant, 21, 27, 30, 31, 39, 46, 65, 74
  —76, 89, 95, 96, 99
 deputy from Scituate, . . . 14, 37, 60, 90
 magistrate, ... 73
 estate of, ... 106, 110
 land granted to sons of, . . . 110, 119, 127
 William, ... 110
 Captain, ... 119
 Lieutenant, ... 171
Totman, Mary, inquest upon, ... 130
 Thomas, punished for fornication, ... 83
 inquest upon wife of, ... 130
Toute, Hercules, ... 171
Towns, relief afforded to, when attacked, . . . 144
 to provide places of security for women and
  children, ... 145
Tracye, John, ... 12, 61
Treasurer chosen, . . 14, 37, 60, 90, 122, 147, 180
 to provide for the magistrates' table, . . . 44
 allowance to, ... 99
 accounts of, examined by a committee from
  each town, ... 21
Trespasses on colony lands prosecuted, ... 62

Trinity, doctrine of the, vindicated, ... 112
Tripp, Peleg, ... 149
Troopers, duty and pay of, ... 144, 151
Trout Brook, ... 199
Trowbridge, Thomas, ... 16
Truant, Trewant, Joseph, fined for drunkenness, . 187
 Morris, ... 105
Tubbs, Bethiah, ... 7
 Mercy, ... 42, 46, 47, 66, 187, 192
 William, ... 42, 46, 66, 174
 land granted to, ... 18
 complaint against John Arthur for enter-
  taining the wife of, ... 104
 refuses to pay wife's debts, ... 66
 divorced, ... 187, 192
Tumpasscom, alias Daniel, an Indian, ... 132
Tupper, Thomas, ... 14
 Thomas, Sen., ... 85, 149, 182
 lands granted to, ... 159
 deputy from Sandwich, ... 37, 148
 Thomas, Jun., ... 85, 151, 183
Turner, George, ... 12
 Humphrey, ... 100, 130
 John, ... 11, 30, 31, 115, 130
 estate of, ... 151, 153
 John, Sen., ... 37, 180
 John, Jun., ... 75
 Joseph, prosecuted for misdemeanors, 11, 177, 187
 vs. Hester Wormall, ... 178
 Nathaniel, ... 177
 Ruhamah, punished for fornication, . . . 77, 84
 part of fine remitted to, ... 99, 101
Tussukes, ... 41
Twiney, William, ... 14
Twining, William, ... 177
Uncumpowett, ... 26
United Colonies, dissolution of the, proposed, . . 92
 instructions to commissioners of the, . . 156, 157
Utley, widow, ... 22
 administratrix of her husband's estate, . . . 16
Vaughan, Vaugham, Elizabeth, and another's com-
 plaint against Indians, ... 136
 George, ... 136
 fined for neglect of public worship, . . . 43
Vicory, Vicorey, George, lands of, ... 18, 189
Vinall, Ann, estate of, ... 81
 John, ... 81
 Stephen, ... 15, 81
Vincent, Henry, ... 123
 John, fine of, remitted, ... 23
 Mr., ... 48
Vixon, Robert, ... 123, 125, 169, 177
Vobes, see Forbes.
Wade, Nicholas, land granted to, ... 18
Wadlen, Crispen, ... 175
Wadsworth, Christopher, 7, 12, 15, 115, 124, 149, 182

GENERAL INDEX.

Wadsworth, Christopher, deputy from Duxbury, 122, 148
   John, ... 180
   Joseph, ... 12, 123, 180
Walker, Elizabeth, found dead, inquest upon, . . 83
   James, . 28, 50, 57, 66, 124, 145, 150, 160, 182
   officer of excise, ... 67
   land granted to, ... 5
   licensed to marry persons, ... 10
   deputy from Taunton, . . . 14, 122, 148, 180
   ancient freeman, land granted to, ... 20
   complaint of, against Witherell and Gilbert, . 56
   complaint against, for stopping alewives, . . 66
   Peter, ... 28
   Philip, ... 83, 84, 180, 187
   William, ... 101, 151, 181
   officer of excise, ... 67
Walley, Thomas, admitted a freeman, ... 61
   Thomas, Jun., licensed as retailer, ... 55
   Mr., ... 51
Wamant, an Indian, ... 167
Wampatucke, Josiah, ... 119, 185
Wamsitta, Wamsutta, ... 8, 16, 17, 186
Wannamoirett, made a township, and land granted to, ... 169, 175
Wanton, Edward, ... 130
Wapoompauksett, ... 3
War, preparations made, ... 142—147
Warren, Joseph, ... 15, 91, 115, 148
   ancient freeman, land granted to, ... 20
   lands of, ... 67, 94, 156
   Nathaniel, 64, 77—79, 103, 109, 113, 120, 128, 149
   one of the first born children, land granted to, ... 19
   deputy from Plymouth, ... 37, 60, 90
   bond from Morton and Andrews, ... 78
   suit against James Barnabey, ... 112
   suit against Peter Stevens, ... 133
   land granted to, ... 156
   estate of, settled, ... 168
   Sarah, ... 168
Washburn, Washburne, Washbourne, John, . . 125
   John, Jun., ... 91
   land granted to, ... 18
   John, Sen., land granted to, ... 18
Watanamatucke, ... 80
Watch to be kept, ... 144, 145
Waterman, Joseph, guardians of, ... 113
   Robert, guardians of, ... 113
Watson, George, ... 55—57, 117, 124
Way, to the harbor, suit concerning, ... 75
   to be laid out for Mr. Howland, ... 114
   for George Allen, ... 46, 48, 117, 183
   through Isaac Barker's land, ... 129
   in Bridgewater, ... 154, 192, 193

Way at Rocky Nook, ... 173
   at Conihassett, ... 75
   at Yarmouth, ... 98
Webcowett, ... 119
Weekes, William, ... 27
Weesunka, ... 58
Wequasett, ... 189
West, Francis, ... 14
Weymouth, town of, ... 128
Whales, brought on shore, country's part of oil, 6, 9, 99
Wheaton, Wheaten, Robert, ... 13, 37
Wheston, see Whiston.
Whetcombe, Robert, fine of, remitted, ... 9
Whetstone's Vineyard Brook, ... 130
Whiston, John, ... 129, 139
   land of, ... 27
   estate of, ... 75, 76, 114
   John, Jun., choice of guardian, ... 139
   Joseph, ... 75, 114, 139
   land of, ... 129
   Susannah, ... 76
White, Elias, ... 177
   Gowen, estate of, ... 81
   Joseph, ... 81, 139
   Nicholas, ... 171
   Peregrine, ... 21, 113, 182
   deputy from Marshfield, ... 14
   land granted to, as the first born child in the colony, ... 110
   one of the first born children, land granted to, ... 19
   Resolved, ... 181
   one of the first born children, land granted to, ... 19
   Timothy, ... 81
   Lieutenant, ... 75, 124
Whitmarsh, John, ... 68, 119, 127
Whittacus, Robert, ... 13
Wilbore, Joseph, ... 91, 148, 171
Wilcockes, Daniel, ... 91, 185
   takes oath of fidelity, ... 175
Willett, Willitt, Thomas, 8, 9, 13, 18, 27, 28, 30, 31, 43, 46, 49, 51, 54, 55, 59, 69, 96, 131, 145, 175
   an Assistant, ... 13, 36, 60
   authority of, as magistrate, ... 8
   lands of, ... 109, 113, 114, 169, 176
Williams, Edward, ... 33, 34
   settlement with Ann Croocker, ... 103
   Elizabeth, ... 153
   reputation of, vindicated, ... 107
   divorced, ... 125, 126
   claim against husband for alimony, 153, 167, 191
   John, ... 37, 106, 153
   discharged from office of ensign, ... 117

GENERAL INDEX. 217

Williams, John, fined for breach of peace, . . . 50
   land of, divided, ... 30
  John, Sen., ... 34
    land of, divided, ... 27, 30
    administration of estate of, ... 175
  John, Jun., ... 123, 167
    prosecuted for abusing his wife, 93, 107, 121,
                                      125, 191
    suit of Edward Jenkens vs. 75
    guardian to John Barker, ... 108
    land of, ... 138, 139
  Joseph, ... 171
  Nathaniel, ... 170
  Richard, . . . 5, 10, 124, 145, 150, 160, 182
    ancient freeman, land granted to, . . . 20
    deputy from Taunton, ... 60, 90
    order to, about Coggen's estate, . . . 10
    land granted to, ... 96
  Roger, ... 165
  Samuel, ... 61, 71, 124
  Thomas, ... 169
    land granted to, ... 18
Williamson, Timothy, ... 141
Willis, John, ... 23, 37, 124, 146, 150, 182
  officer of excise, ... 67
  deputy from Bridgewater, . . 60, 122, 148, 180
  land granted to, ... 96
  John, Sen., land granted to, ... 190
  John, Jun., ... 141
  Nathaniel, ... 91, 155, 193
  Richard, punished for several offences, . . 50, 51
  suit against Peter Stevens, ... 120
Wilson, John, fined for selling liquor to In-
      dians, ... 32
  bound to appear, &c., ... 33
Winge, John, ... 148
  protest of, ... 171
  Stephen, ... 61, 124
Winnatucksett River, ... 42
Winslow, Edward, ... 98
  Gilbert, heirs of, land granted to, . . . 40
  John, ... 53
    one of the first born children, land grant-
      ed to, ... 19
  Jonathan, ... 123
  Josiah, 4, 8, 17, 19, 21, 24—27, 30, 35, 40, 41,
    44, 45, 47—49, 56, 59, 63, 68—70, 74, 79,
    84, 87, 89, 95, 97, 103—105, 109, 112, 113,
    119, 120, 127, 128, 132, 134—136, 139,
    140, 142, 157, 164, 166, 167, 171, 173,
    184, 188.
    one of the council of war, ... 142
    an Assistant, . 13, 36, 60, 90, 122, 147, 179
    commissioner of the United Colonies, 14, 36, 60,
                                 90, 122, 147, 180

Winslow, Josiah, one of the first born children,
    land granted to, ... 19
  three pounds granted to, for services as com-
    missioner, ... 72
  land granted to, ... 95
  suit of, against Ephraim Tinkham, . . . 103
  paid for services, ... 151
  guardian of Robert Waterman, ... 113
  Josiah, Sen., ... 50, 115, 145
  Kanelme, Jun., fined for breach of Sabbath, . 29
  Nathaniel, ... 148
  Penelope, ... 69
  Mr., ... 20
Winter, Christopher, fined for neglect of public
    worship, ... 42
  bound to answer, &c., ... 76
Wiswall, Wiswell, Ichabod, ... 194
  Remember, ... 194
  Mr., ... 51
Witherell, William, ... 15, 56, 130
  prosecuted and fined, ... 55, 68
Wixam, see Vixon.
Wolf trap, ... 193
Wolves, bounty for killing, ... 6
Wood, Henry, ... 80, 128, 180, 192
  ancient freeman, land granted to, . . . 20
  lands of, ... 94, 159, 167
  wife of, heir to Sarah Jenney, ... 80
  John, ... 180
    ancient freeman, land granted to, . . . 20
  lands of, ... 94
  Sarah, ... 80
  Thomas, ... 164
Woodcocke, John, ... 91, 105, 164, 167
Woodward, Walter, ... 30, 100, 129
  land of, ... 75
Woodworth, Walter, land granted to, . . . 18
Woomham, ... 58
Worden, Hopestill, ... 88
  Peter, fined for misdemeanor, ... 141
  Samuel, ... 88
Wormall, Esther, ... 75, 178
  Joseph, estate of, ... 16, 75
  Josias, ... 16
  Miriam, ... 16, 75
Wright, Edward, ... 130
  Richard, ... 54
    ancient freeman, land granted to, . . . 20
  land of, ... 67
  Mr., licensed as retailer, ... 55
Wyate, Wyat, Wyatt, James, ... 16, 21, 39
  ancient freeman, land granted to, . . . 20
  deputy from Taunton, ... 14, 37, 60
  found dead, inquest upon, ... 70, 71
Yarmouth, . . 6, 23, 52, 82, 99, 108, 118, 146, 152

Yarmouth, general training to be at, . . . 39, 64
    rates, ... 6, 29, 47, 63, 72, 77, 98
    excise officers, ... 67, 105, 110, 151, 183
    town officers, 15, 37, 38, 61, 91, 117, 123, 124,
        148—150, 181, 182
    military officers, ... 15, 65

Yarmouth, Mannamoiett annexed to, ... 97
    Indians, lands purchased for, ... 97
    committee to dispose of lands, ... 167
    complaint about duty on whales, ... 9
    ordinary, ... 167
Young, John, ... 177

www.ingramcontent.com/pod-product-compliance
Lightning Source LLC
Chambersburg PA
CBHW071436150426
43191CB00008B/1141